VERGIL

THE AENEID

Translated, with an introduction, by

JAMES H. MANTINBAND

Assistant Professor of Classical Languages
Brooklyn College of the City University of New York

FREDERICK UNGAR PUBLISHING CO.
NEW YORK

Printed in the United States of America

ISBN 0-8044-6952-0

Library of Congress Catalog Card No. 64-15700

INTRODUCTION

Mantua me genuit, Calabri rapuere, tenet nunc
Parthenope. Cecini pascua, rura, duces.[1]

This epitaph sums up the life and works of Publius Vergilius
Maro, Rome's greatest poet. Vergil (the spelling "Virgil" is common, but without ancient authority) was born near Mantua in
70 B.C. His early works, the *Eclogues* and *Georgics*, gained for
him immediate and widespread fame (as well as membership in
the literary circle of Maecenas). The former are pastoral poems,
in imitation of the *Idylls* of Theocritus, and the latter is a didactic
poem on agriculture, in four books, which has been called the
most perfect poetry in the Latin language.

Vergil was thus at the height of his powers when, in 30 B.C., he
began to write the *Aeneid*, his great epic on the founding of Rome.
It was at least partly at the instigation and encouragement of
Augustus that the poet undertook the task, which he had been
contemplating for some time. The last eleven years of his life were
occupied with the composition of the *Aeneid*. On his deathbed,
Vergil, who considered that he had not finished the poem, gave
instructions to his literary executors to destroy the manuscript.
Augustus rescinded these instructions, however, and the *Aeneid*
was issued with no additions and very few deletions. Instantly
it was recognized as the great Roman epic—the worthy successor
to the works of Homer. Its influence on subsequent literature
has been enormous. All during the Dark Ages, the poem was
known, read, quoted, and loved. It was even used as a means of
divination, called the "Sortes Vergilianae," in which the book
was opened at a random page, and a prophetic message was read
from the first passage seen. Whole new poems, some of them

---

[1]Mantua gave me birth, Calabria slew me, Parthenope now holds me.
I sang of pastures (*Eclogues*), farms (*Georgics*), and heroes (*Aeneid*).

iii

quite obscene, called "centones" or crazy-quilts, were made by combining lines and half-lines from the *Aeneid*.[2]

The first six books of the *Aeneid* roughly parallel the story of Homer's *Odyssey*, and the last six, the *Iliad*. Aeneas, a prince of Troy, is sailing from Sicily, in his attempt to find a new home for himself and his followers, when a storm sent by the jealous and vindictive Juno scatters his fleet. He makes his way to the coast of Africa, where he is hospitably received by the beautiful Dido, queen of Carthage. In Book II, which bridges the gap between the *Iliad* and the *Odyssey*, he tells her of the sack of Troy, from whose ruins he has escaped with his aged father, his young son, his companions, and the Trojan household gods. The third book tells the story of his wanderings. Monsters, portents, plagues, and other natural and supernatural phenomena beset the weary Trojans. The book ends with the death of Anchises in Sicily. Book IV, the tragedy of Dido, is perhaps the most moving and romantic episode of the entire work; certainly Dido is the most sympathetically drawn character: the reader is compelled to feel sympathy with her, even at the expense of the hero. In Book V the funeral games in honor of Anchises are vividly described, and Book VI shows the descent of the hero to the Lower World to see the ghost of his father Anchises, and to learn of the future glories of his people.

The second half of the *Aeneid*, though perhaps somewhat inferior in construction and execution, nevertheless contains many beautiful, moving and vivid episodes. In Book VII, the Trojans arrive at the Tiber, where they "eat their tables," fulfilling the prophecy of the Harpy Celaeno. Juno sends the Fury Allecto to stir the Latins to war: the actual *casus belli* is the wounding of a pet stag by Ascanius. In Book VIII Aeneas goes to King Evander for aid. Here is told the story of Hercules and Cacus; the book ends with a description of the Shield of Aeneas.[3] Book

---

[2] E.g. the *Cento Nuptialis* of Ausonius and the *Medea* of Hosidius Geta.

[3] An obvious borrowing from Homer, like so many episodes in the *Aeneid*, with this important difference: the scenes depicted on the shield of Achilles (*Iliad* xviii) show life in general; but those in the *Aeneid* deal solely with the future kings, wars and heroes of Rome.

IX tells of a fierce battle and many deeds of derring-do, chiefly by the Italian hero Turnus, but is especially noteworthy for the beautiful episode of the exploits and death of Nisus and Euryalus. Book X continues the battle: in it the young Pallas is slain, and Aeneas himself enters the fight for the first time. Turnus is induced by Juno to pursue a phantom Aeneas. In the eleventh book the war continues with the funeral of Pallas; the introduction of Drances, a rather unpleasant character, possibly modelled on Homer's Thersites; and the deeds and death of the warrior-maiden Camilla. The last book brings the war to an end. Juno is finally mollified and consents to the union of the Trojans and Latins, provided that the Trojans do not retain their hated name. Turnus is slain by Aeneas, who wavers at the last moment, but the sight of Pallas' sword-belt on the shoulder of Turnus re-awakens his grief and rage. The parallel to the *Iliad* is an obvious one: Achilles slays Hector in revenge for the death of Patroclus.

The echoes of Homer, in fact, are present on nearly every page and in nearly every line: in the story itself, the verse with its similes and stock-epithets; the plunging *in medias res;* in the flashback account of the hero's wanderings; his descent to the Underworld (and many incidents in the lower world, e.g., the meetings with Palinurus, Deiphobus and Dido, which immediately recall the similar meetings of Odysseus with Elpenor, Agamemnon, and Ajax, even to the angry silence of the latter). Sometimes we can see almost verbatim translations from Homer (e.g., the attempts of Aeneas to embrace the ghosts of Creusa and Anchises; a simile in which Turnus is compared to a horse galloping across the fields; Mercury putting on his golden sandals, etc.). Other parallels are the funeral games, the armor of Aeneas, the burning of the ships, the broken truce, the rescue of a hero from the battlefield by a divine agency, the council of the gods, the final duel, and many, many others. The similes, too, are reminiscent of Homer's. Here, too, they are long and vivid, drawn most frequently from nature (lions, wolves, bulls, wild boars, eagles, swans, flowers, trees, snakes, winds, the sea, fire, etc.), as well as from daily life, politics, the theater, children's games, art, and mythology.

Nor is Homer the only Greek author whose influence is seen in the pages of the *Aeneid*. Book IV has many echoes of Euripides and Apollonius of Rhodes, and Book VI suggests Plato's *Republic*. Roman influences, such as Lucretius and Catullus, as well as earlier poets (e.g., Ennius and Naevius) can also be seen. The astonishing fact about the *Aeneid* is that, despite all the indebtedness to earlier works, it remains a highly original poem. The reasons for this are not far to seek.

First, there is the miracle of Vergil's language: the choice and order of words, the felicitous juxtapositions, the use of metaphor and simile, of alliteration, assonance and onomatopoeia—in short, all the poetic devices of the master-craftsman, which are all but impossible to recapture in translation. Vergil was a completely self-conscious literary artist: there is little of the formulaic writing that is found in Homer.

Secondly, the *Aeneid* is a good story, well told. It is full of vivid and unforgettable incidents, related in language that is simple and direct. The story of the fall of Troy is one that can never be forgotten by anyone who has read it. The Funeral Games in Book V are not only vivid and dramatic, but contain fine characterizations, and even flashes of humor, a quality not usually present in the *Aeneid*. The battle scenes in the second half are vigorous, bloody, and brutal, like war itself. Many characters, such as Dido and Turnus, Latinus and Anchises, Camilla and Juturna, are extremely well drawn. Only the figure of Aeneas himself (together with his equally shadowy "trusty Achates") is lacking in three-dimensional qualities. There is a reason for this (see below, page vii).

Thirdly, there is the earnest moral tone of the *Aeneid*. By linking the present race of Romans to the gods, Vergil is trying to instill in them the ancient Roman virtues of piety, courage and dignity. This was a new age, an age of peace after more than a century of civil strife, and it is this peace, the *Pax Augusta*, which the *Aeneid* celebrates. Vergil's attitude toward war is never the almost primitive "battle-glee" of Homer; the entire poem is filled with tenderness and compassion for human suffer-

ing: "Sunt lacrimae rerum et mentem mortalia tangunt."[4] As has
been mentioned before, humor has little place in Vergil: his
humor is mostly a grim, savage sort.[5] But pathos, tenderness, devotion, love, in short the "lacrimae rerum"—these are to be found
on every page. Of particular beauty and interest are the many
examples of filial and paternal devotion: Pallas and Evander,
Mezentius and Lausus, Aeneas himself and Anchises on the one
hand, Ascanius on the other. When the hero leaves the burning
Troy, he carries his father on his back and leads his son by the
hand. His wife, Creusa, is following behind, and so she is lost.
The picture of the fierce Metabus tying the infant Camilla to a
spear and throwing her across a swift river is a most touching
one. The devotion of friends, such as Nisus and Euryalus, brother
and sister (Turnus and Juturna) and even for animals (Silvia and
the pet stag)—all these are beautifully rendered. Conjugal love
seems of less importance.

The *Aeneid* is the supreme achievement of Latin poetry. Just
as Homer had been the model and example for all epic poets to
follow, so Vergil became the inspiration for all succeeding generations. The poem is the perfect reflection of the spirit of the
Age of Augustus. It is, first and last, a Roman poem. We are
never permitted to lose sight of this fact for long. And this is
surely why the hero is almost never described in physical terms,
but as Father Aeneas, and Aeneas the Good: he is only important
insofar as he typifies the Roman virtues. There are several of the
so-called "Roman passages" in the *Aeneid*: one in the first book,
where Jupiter describes the future of the race to the anxious
Venus; one in Book VIII, where the shield of Aeneas shows
Romulus and Remus, Horatius, and other heroes, culminating
in the Battle of Actium and the triumph of Augustus himself;
and, most important, perhaps, in Book VI, where Anchises shows
his son a vision of what the future holds in store for his descendants. This is both literally and figuratively the center of the

---

[4]"Here are tears for misfortune, and here men's hearts are touched by
human plight." *Aeneid.* I 462-3.

[5]Cf. V 175 ff; 330 ff.

Aeneid. It ends with a deeply moving tribute to the young Marcellus, nephew and designated successor of Augustus, whose
death in 23 B.C. had been an occasion for national mourning.

Every age has paid its tribute to the *Aeneid* and its author.
In the Middle Ages, Vergil was thought to have prophesied the
birth of Christ.[6] Dante, whose reverence for the Roman poet
amounted almost to worship, calls him:

> *"O anima cortese Mantovana*
> *di cui la fama ancor nel mondo dura*
> *e durerà quanto il moto lontana."*[7]

Tennyson ends his fine poem to Vergil with the words:

> *"I salute thee, Mantovano,*
> *I that loved thee since my day began,*
> *Wielder of the stateliest measure*
> *ever moulded by the lips of man."*

The translator has aimed throughout at clarity and faithful-
ness to the Latin. The meter is a line of six beats, predominantly
iambic but not exclusively so: the number of syllables ranges from
eleven to seventeen, to suggest the flexibility of Vergil's hexa-
meter. The translation corresponds, as far as possible, line for
line to the original. Repeated lines have been rendered in the
same words, where this is at all possible. Even the surprising
changes in tense have been left, for the most part, as Vergil wrote
them, except where a change is necessary for reasons of meter
or sense. The "pathetic half-lines" have been left incomplete.
Clichés, such as "he bit the dust" and "fear lent wings to his feet,"
have been left as clichés deliberately, because in most cases, the
clichés come from Vergil. The aim throughout has been to in-
terpose as thin a veil as possible between Vergil's Latin and the
reader of today. If any of the "chosen coin of fancy, flashing
out from many a golden phrase"; any "charm of all the Muses

---

[6]The Fourth Eclogue describes a Golden Age which will soon be ushered
in with the birth of a child.

[7]"O courteous Mantuan spirit, whose fame still lasts in the world, and
will last as long as time."

often flowering in a lonely word"—have survived, the translator counts himself fortunate.

Finally, I must express my deep gratitude to my colleagues in the Department of Classical Languages and Comparative Literature in Brooklyn College, for their interest, encouragement, and many suggestions for corrections and improvements; and to my wife for her help in reading proofs, suggesting elusive words and phrases, and for listening.

THE AENEID

Contents

Book I
Aeneas Lands at Carthage   3

Book II
The Sack of Troy   25

Book III
The Wanderings of Aeneas   48

Book IV
The Tragedy of Dido   69

Book V
The Funeral Games   89

Book VI
The Lower World   114

Book VII
The War in Latium   140

Book VIII
The Embassy to Evander   163

Book IX
The Siege of the Trojan Camp 185

Book X
The Battle on the Shore   209

Book XI
The Council of the Latins   235

Book XII
The Death of Turnus   261

Glossary of Names   289

BOOK I

AENEAS LANDS AT CARTHAGE

I sing of arms and the hero who, from Trojan shores,
a fated exile, first set foot on Italian soil
and the Lavinian coast; driven on land and sea
by force of Heaven's gods and the unremitting anger
of cruel Juno; he suffered also much in war   5
to found his city and to bring his gods to Latium,
whence Latins, and Alban Fathers, and walls of mighty Rome.
Tell me the reasons, Muse, what slight to her will divine,
suffering what hurt did Heaven's Queen drive on a man
so righteous, to endure so many woes and afflictions?   10
Can gods harbor such resentment in their immortal breasts?

There once was a city, colonized by Tyrians,
Carthage by name, across the sea from Italy,
a town of wealth untold, well-versed in the arts of war,
preferred by Juno to any other land on earth   15
including even Samos; here she kept her arms,
and here her chariot. This town, if the Fates permitted,
the goddess wished to hold dominion over the earth;
But she had heard it said that now, from Trojan blood,
a race was issuing forth which one day would destroy   20
her Tyrian citadel, a race to rule the world,
proud warriors, Libya's ruin: thus the Fates had decreed.
So, fearing this, still mindful of the ancient war
that she had waged at Troy for her beloved Argives—
for not yet had the bitter cause of hate and anger   25
and savage pain departed from the goddess' breast:
she still remembered Paris' judgment, and the slight
to her insulted beauty, still recalled the race

she hated, and the honors of ravished Ganymede—
incensed by these, for years she drove the remaining Trojans   30
left by the Danaans and pitiless Achilles
over all the seas, and kept them far from Latium.
So mighty a task it was to found the Roman race!

 Scarce out of sight of Sicily, they were setting their sails
most joyously to sea, and ploughing the salty spray   35
with brazen prow, when Juno, nursing her deep wound,
said to herself, "Am I to renounce my dearest wish,
be vanquished, and not keep the Trojans from Italy
because the Fates forbid it? But Pallas burned the fleet
of Argos and engulfed them in the raging sea,   40
only for Oelian Ajax's foolish fault and crime;
she hurled from the clouds the speedy thunderbolt of Jove,
dispersed the ships and overturned the seas with storms,
and Ajax, breathing fire from his transfixed breast,
she caught in a cyclone and impaled him on a crag.   45
But I, the queen of the gods, the sister and spouse of Jove,
have waged a war for years with just one puny people.
Who then will deign to worship Juno's will divine?
Who will do sacrifice to her, or offer prayers?"
 These thoughts revolving in her flaming heart and mind,   50
the goddess comes to Aeolia, the storm-clouds' home,
raging with furious gales, and here in a lofty cavern
King Aeolus rules the wrestling winds and shrieking storms
and keeps them all in chains, while they with mighty murmur
rage round the gate in anger; Aeolus meanwhile sits   55
enthroned on high, holding his scepter, and soothes their wrath
and mollifies their rage, for otherwise the winds
would sweep across the land and sea and Heaven's arch,
confound the elements, and whip over all the world.
But fearing this, the almighty Father hid the gales   60
in gloomy caverns, under a mass of mighty mountains,
having a king with limited powers fixed by treaty
who knows exactly when to pull or slacken the reins.
 To him now suppliant Juno went and spoke these words:

"O Aeolus, for to you the Father of gods and men   65
has given the right to soothe and stir the windy waves,
a race despised by me now sails the Tyrrhene main,
transporting Troy and her conquered gods to Italy.
Whip up your whirling winds, overwhelm and sink their ships!
Drive them apart and scatter their corpses in the sea!   70
Twice seven nymphs I have of wondrous loveliness:
of these Deiopea is by far the fairest.
Her will I give to you, to have and hold forever
in wedlock, as reward for this one trifling favor,
to make you father of a race of beautiful children."   75
And Aeolus answered her: " 'Tis yours, O Queen, to command,
and mine the task to execute your every wish.
All that I have I owe to you: my sovereignty,
my scepter and Jove's grace, and thanks to you alone
I feast on the gods' ambrosia and I rule the winds."   80

   So saying, he upturned his spear and struck the side
of the hollow mountain, and the winds, in serried ranks,
rush out through the breach, and hurricanes attack the earth:
the East and South Winds join the squally Southwestern wind
and fall upon the sea and stir it up from its depths   85
and roll the weighty waves and breakers back to the shore.
The shrieks of men are mingled with the creaking shrouds;
a sudden inky cloud blots out the day and sky
from the Trojans' eyes, and murky night lies on the ocean.
The poles of Heaven crash with thunder, lightning flashes   90
illumine the sky, and all things threaten instant death.
Straightway Aeneas' limbs dissolve in an icy chill,
and stretching both his hands to Heaven he cries aloud:
"O thrice and four times blessed are they who died at Troy
beneath the eyes of their fathers, by the lofty walls.   95
O Diomedes, bravest of all the Achaean race,
why was it not my fate to fall to your mighty hand,
where valiant Hector and the great Sarpedon lie,
beneath the spear of Achilles on the Trojan plain;
where Simois caught up and churned beneath his waves   100

so many helmets and shields and bodies of brave men!"
And even as he spoke, a blast from the shrill North Wind
strikes his vessel head-on, and lifts the waves to the sky;
the oars are shattered to pieces, the prow swung round, and the side
is offered to the waves; a mountain of water descends.   105
Some hang on the billow's summit, while others see the ground
between the lofty waves—the seething tide and sand.
The South Wind seizes three ships and hurls them on the rocks
amid the waves the Italians are wont to call the Altars:
a mighty reef in the sea. Three more the East Wind brings   110
from deep seas to the shallows, piteous to behold!
and runs them aground and girdles them with sandy walls.
On one, which carried Lycian troops and faithful Orontes,
in front of his very eyes, a mighty sea descends
astern, the pilot is thrown down and rolls headlong,   115
the ship is caught by the wave and spun three times around
before the hungry maelstrom engulfs her once and for all.
And swimming men appear here and there in the midst of the
                                                    whirlpool,
armor and men and planks, and the wealth of Troy in the waves.
Now the strong ships of Ilioneus and the brave Achates,   120
and those that carried Abas and the aged Aletes
are vanquished by the stormy blast, their hulls are weakened,
and they admit the hated waves through gaping cracks.
    But meanwhile Neptune was disturbed to hear the din
of raging seas and howling winds released from their prison,   125
and stagnant water churned and boiled from the gloomy depths.
He peered around, lifting his placid brow from the waves,
and saw Aeneas' ships strewn all about the ocean,
the Trojans overwhelmed by the sea and furious gales.
Straightway he recognized the anger and tricks of Juno.   130
He called the East and West Winds to him, and spoke as follows:
"Does such presumption come from your pride of birth, O winds?
Dare you, without my order, confound the sea and sky
and raise such a turbulent mass of stormy ocean waves?
Whom I—but better first to calm the raging billows;   135
a second time you'll not escape so easily.

Now go and take this message to your royal master:
dominion over the rolling seas, and the savage trident
were given not to him, but me. Let him hold his court
on the massive rocks, his home and yours, East Wind, and there   140
let Aeolus play the king in the prison of the winds."

   He spoke, and swifter than words he calms the swollen waters
and, scattering the collected clouds, brings back the sun.
Cymothoë and Triton together push the ships
off the rugged rocks; the god gives aid with his trident,   145
and opens the vast Syrtes and soothes the ruffled waters,
skimming along the crest of the waves with his light wheels.
Just as when in a crowd of people, a riot begins,
the common multitude are raging in their minds,
and stones and firebrands fly (their madness supplies the weapons), 150
if suddenly they see a man they all respect,
the mob falls silent: they listen with attentive ears;
he calms their spirits and soothes their angry hearts with words—
just so the tumult of the waves is quelled, as Neptune
looking ahead beneath a sunny, cloudless sky,   155
guides his steeds, and his chariot flies with loosened reins.
   The weary men of Aeneas now head for the shore
where it is nearest: they make for the coast of Libya,
and soon they come upon a lonely, landlocked harbor
formed by a little island thrusting forth its flanks.   160
The wavelets break there, then they separate in the bay.
On either side enormous crags threaten the heavens.
Beneath their crests the sheltered waters gently run,
silent and calm. Above is a backdrop of rustling forest
and overhanging woods with black and bristling shadows.   165
And opposite the island is a rocky cavern
with sweet fresh springs, and seats cut out of the living rock:
the home of woodland nymphs. And here the weary ships
need neither chains to hold them nor anchors' crooked teeth.
Hither with seven ships (for they were all that remained)   170
Aeneas sailed, and overcome with love of land,
the Trojans climb from battered vessels to the shore

and fling their dripping, salty limbs upon the beach.
Achates strikes a spark from a piece of flinty rock,
gives fodder to the newborn flames in a bed of leaves,   175
and lays dry kindling round to feed the hungry fire.
The weary men now bring utensils from the ships
and start to parch and dry the waterloggèd grain
which they have rescued, and they grind it on the rocks.

   Aeneas meanwhile climbs a rock and looks about.   180
He scans the ocean wide to see if now perchance
Antheus' storm-tossed ships, or Capys or Caïcus
are anywhere in sight with their lofty Phrygian biremes.
No ship is to be seen, but three enormous stags
he sees a-wandering on the shore; a herd then follows   185
grazing in close formation across the rolling valley.
He stops and seizes his curvèd bow and deadly arrows
(the weapons carried by his trusty friend Achates).
First he shoots the leaders with their branching antlers
and stately heads held high, then he attacks the others,   190
and drives them headlong through the forest with his shafts,
nor does he stay his weary hand from slaughter until
seven stags, as many as his ships, are slain.
Then he returns to the harbor and shares the food with his men.
The vintage wine that good Acestes had given them,   195
a gift to speed the guests departing from Sicily,
he shares and soothes their sorrowing hearts with hopeful words:
   "O my comrades, not heretofore unschooled in grief,
to these misfortunes too the god will make an end.
You all have seen the raging rocks and torrents of Scylla,   200
and likewise known the cliffs of the savage Cyclopes.
Recall your courage, put away your fear and sorrow:
some day, perhaps, we may remember even this
with gladness. Now, through many perils and disasters,
we steer our course for Latium where Fate has promised us   205
a new abode, where a new Troy will rise again.
So persevere, and save yourselves for happier days."
Thus speaks Aeneas, and though sick with weighty cares,

he simulates a hopeful mien and hides his sorrow.
The Trojans now prepare the venison for the feast: 210
they skin the deer, lay bare the flesh and ribs and entrails;
some cut the meat in strips and put it quivering still
on spits, while others place the cauldrons and feed the flame.
Then they restore their strength with food, and lie on the grass,
partaking of vintage wine and rich fat venison.   215
After hunger is banished and the tables cleared,
they talk regretfully and long of their absent comrades,
caught between hope and fear, not knowing if they live
or move among the shadows, and hear their names no more.
Especially Aeneas mourns his friend Orontes   220
the valiant, and laments the sad fate of Amycus,
and Lycus' doom, and brave Gyas, and strong Cloanthus.

    And now they made an end of tears, and Jupiter
looked down upon the sail-winged seas and outstretched lands
and seacoasts and broad countries; standing at Heaven's peak   225
he fixed his lordly gaze on the land of Libya,
and as he stood there, troubled in heart, there came to him
his daughter Venus—her eyes were overflowing with tears.
She sadly said: "O ruler over all the world
of men and gods forever, lord of the thunderbolt,   230
what has my Aeneas done to make you so angry?
What have the Trojans done? So many now are dead;
the rest find doors barred everywhere for Italy's sake.
Yet it was from these, in the course of time, the Romans should
                                                             come,
the rulers of the world, renewing Teucer's race,   235
holding all lands and seas beneath their mighty dominion:
this was your promise, father: what has changed your mind?
With this at least I consoled myself amid the ruins
of fallen Troy, opposing fate to adverse fate.
But now the same misfortunes relentlessly pursue them.   240
What end, great King, do you intend to make of their labors?
Antenor was able to escape the Achaeans' midst,
and penetrate the Illyrian bays and inmost kingdoms
of the Liburnians, and scale Timavus' fount,

from which, through nine mouths, and amid the mountain's
murmur 245
a headlong tide comes, covering fields with resounding waters.
Yet here he set the city of Patavium:
a home for Trojans, gave his own name to the people,
and hung up Trojan arms; and now he is at peace.
But we, your children, promised by you a heavenly home, 250
have lost an entire fleet, and for one goddess' anger
we are betrayed and thrown far away from Italy's shores.
What price piety then? Is it thus you restore our scepter?"

Smiling down on her, the Father of gods and men,
with the glance that calms the overcast sky and raging tempests, 255
gently kissed his daughter's lips, and made this answer:
"Fear not, Cytherea, your people's fate remains unchanged,
and you shall see your city and the Lavinian stronghold,
and lift on high, up to the starry poles of Heaven,
your great Aeneas; and I have not changed my mind. 260
But since your soul is tortured by such grievous cares,
I shall unroll the secret record of Destiny:
he shall wage a mighty war, subdue fierce nations,
give laws unto his people, yes, and build them walls,
until the third summer shall see him ruling Latium, 265
and three winters shall have passed for the conquered Rutulians.
But the boy Ascanius (henceforth to be called Iülus—[1]
he was known as Ilus, while Ilium remained)—
for three times ten long years with their revolving months
the boy shall reign. He shall transfer the Trojan kingdom 270
from Lavinium, to make a fortress of Alba Longa.
And here, for three hundred years, the stock of Trojan Hector
shall rule the land, till Ilia, the royal priestess,
shall bear twin offspring, heavy from the embrace of Mars,
and Romulus, rejoicing in the tawny pelt 275
of the she-wolf, his foster-mother, will rule the race,

---

[1]Thus, by implication, Aeneas is the ancestor of Julius Caesar, and of
Augustus, his adopted son.

and build them walls, and call them Romans, from his own name.
For them I ordain no boundary of time or space,
but everlasting dominion. And even the cruel Juno,
who now stirs up with fear the earth and sea and sky, 280
shall change to milder counsels; shall cherish, even as I,
the toga-bearing Romans, lords of all the earth.
Thus it is destined. There will even come a day
when Assaracus' house will rule the fertile Phthia,
conquer famous Mycenae and defeat the Argives. 285
From Trojan stock will come a Caesar, whose dominion
will be bounded by the ocean, his glory by the stars:
Julius, who will inherit great Iülus' name.
One day you shall receive him safely into Heaven,
laden with Eastern spoils, and men will pray to him. 290
Then wars shall cease, and the harsh centuries grow soft,
and white-haired Faith, and Vesta, Remus and Quirinus
shall make the laws. The hideous iron gates of War
shall close forever. Sacrilegious Fury, within,
his hands behind him bound with a hundred brazen shackles, 295
sitting on weapons, shall rage in vain with bloody mouth."

He spoke, and sent the son of Maia[2] from on high,
so that the lands and towers of the new town, Carthage,
would open for the Teucrians, and Dido, the queen,
all ignorant of Destiny, not repulse them. The god 300
plies the air with his wings, and soon arrives in Libya.
He does as he is told: the Carthaginians
put down their savage temper at the god's command;
the queen has charity and pity for the Trojans.

But good Aeneas, thinking many thoughts at night, 305
as soon as day breaks, is resolved to explore the land
and see what sort of place the winds have blown him to—
what people (it seems to be deserted) or savage beasts;
to make a search and bring the tidings to his comrades.

---

[2]i.e. Mercury

He hides the ships in a secluded inlet, beneath   310
a rocky cliff, with bristling woodlands all around,
while he goes forth, accompanied by trusty Achates
who clutches two broad-headed javelins in his hand.
And as he walks in the forest, Venus his mother meets him,
with face and arms and garments of a Spartan maiden,   315
or such as Thracian Harpalyce, when she tires
her horses and outstrips the wingèd Hebrus in flight.
For like a huntress, she wears a curvèd bow on her shoulders,
her hair is flying freely and her knees are bare,
her garments' flowing folds collected in a knot.   320
She speaks to them: "Young men, have you by chance beheld
one of my sisters wandering through the leafy forest,
with quiver on her shoulder, clad in a spotted lynx-hide,
or shouting as she pressed on the track of a foaming boar?"
So Venus spoke, and Venus' son made answer thus: 325
"I've neither seen nor heard of any of your sisters,
O, how shall I address you, maiden, clearly not mortal,
either in face or form—you must be a goddess, surely,
perhaps the sister of Apollo, or one of the Nymphs.
Be good to us, whoever you are, and lighten our burden,   330
and tell us beneath what sky, at length, and on what shores
we have been thrown. We are utterly lost and know not where
we wander, driven on our way by wind and wave.
We shall sacrifice full many a victim at your altar."

Venus replied: "I am not worthy of such an honor;   335
for young Carthaginian maidens always wear a quiver,
and always bind high purple sandals on their feet.
This is the Punic kingdom, the Tyrians' town and Agenor's;
the land is the land of Libya, race of hardened warriors.
Our queen is Dido, who fled away from Phoenician Tyre,   340
escaping her brother. Long the tale of woe, and many
are her disasters, but I will merely tell you the outline:
Sychaeus was her husband, and he was richest in land
among the Phoenicians, loved by her, poor lady, with passion
(her father had given her untouched, with virgin rites);   345

but alas! her brother Pygmalion ruled the land of Tyre,
the most abominable man that ever lived!
A furious hatred came between the two: the brother,
blinded by love of gold, without pity for his sister,
murdered Sychaeus by stealth at the altar, wicked man!   350
For a long time the wretch concealed his evil deed,
deluding his sister with crafty ruse and empty hope,
but she beheld one night, in her dreams, the unburied corpse
of her husband, lifting up his face that was wondrous pale.
He showed her the pitiless altar, his body pierced by the sword,   355
and he unwove the whole dark crime of the wretched house.
He advised her to flee in haste, to leave the country,
disclosing to her long-buried treasures, to aid her escape:
an untold mass of ruddy gold and shining silver.
And Dido, moved by this, prepared her people for flight.   360
All those who hated the wicked tyrant, and all who feared him,
all came together, seized the ships that chanced to be ready,
and loaded them with gold—Pygmalion's hoarded riches
they trusted to the sea, and a woman was their leader.
At last they reached the land where you will soon behold   365
the massive walls and rising citadel of New Carthage.
They purchased land, as much as they could encircle with
the hide of a bull, and called the land, accordingly, Byrsa.
But tell me, who are you, and from what land do you come?
and where are you going?" The good Aeneas thus replied,   370
sighing deeply, and drawing the words from deep in his chest:
    "O goddess, if I began to tell you of all our troubles
(and if you had time enough to listen to them all)
the evening star would close day's eye before I had finished.
We are from ancient Troy—if perchance that wretched name   375
has come to your ears—and as we sailed across the sea,
capricious tempests drove us to the Libyan coast.
I am Aeneas the Good, and I carry in my vessels
Penates snatched from the foe: my fame is known in Heaven.
I seek my country, Italy, the cradle of my race.   380
With twenty ships I embarked upon the Phrygian sea.
My mother, a goddess, and oracles pointed out the way.

But now, alas, scarce seven survived the tempest's blast.
Myself, unknown and destitute, I wander over
the Libyan wilderness, driven from Europe and Asia."   385
But Venus his mother broke in on Aeneas' half-told plaints:
"Whoever you are, you must be dear to the Immortals,
I think, since you already have reached the Tyrian town.
Only go on from here, till you come to the Queen's abode.
For I declare to you: your ships and men have been rescued,   390
and driven safely into port by the shifting North Wind,
unless my parents taught me the arts of augury fasely.
For look you, twelve white swans were flying in happy array;
the eagle, bird of Jove, had scattered them through the sky.
Already they have either reached the ground in safety,   395
or, in orderly ranks, they now are coming to earth.
And just as they are playing joyfully, flapping their wings
and screaming raucously as they circle through the air,
even so, your ships and friends are either safe in port,
or else just now are gliding under full sail to harbor.   400
So go on, direct your feet wherever the pathway leads you."

She spoke and turned away, and a light shone from her head,
the ambrosial locks of her hair were fragrant with heavenly odor,
her robe became unbound, and fell flowing down to her feet,
and by her walk she revealed herself as immortal goddess.   405
He recognized his mother and followed her steps with words:
"O cruel mother, why do you always mock your son
with these disguises? Why may I never touch your hand?
Why may we never speak to each other without pretense?"
With such reproaches Aeneas directs his steps to the city.   410
But Venus surrounds them as they go with a heavy cloud
and wraps them both, with her magic art, in a mantle of mist,
so that no man may behold them, nor anybody touch them,
or delay them as they go, or ask wherefore they have come.
Venus herself floats through the air to beloved Paphus,   415
joyfully she revisits her home and temples and altars,
fragrant with Sabaean incense and garlands of flowers.

The two men meanwhile hasten along the path where it leads
                                                          them,
and now are climbing a lofty hill overlooking the city,
whence they can see from above the mighty towers rising.   420
Aeneas marvels at the buildings—recently huts—
he marvels at the gates and bustle and new-paved streets.
The Tyrians work eagerly: some extend the walls,
construct the citadel, roll massive blocks of stone,
some choose a site for a building, surrounding it with a furrow. 425
They elect their judges and magistrates and august Senate.
Here they dig out harbors, others lay deep foundations
for a great theater, and hew out massive columns
from the cliff: the high proscenium for a future stage.
Just so, in early summer, through the flowery meadows,   430
the bees all labor in the sun, leading forth the grown ones,
or pressing the liquid honey and straining the cells to bursting
with their sweet nectar, or they receive the incoming burdens,
or, forming their battalions, they drive away from the hive
the idle throng of drones, and keep them far from the fold.   435
The work is all aflame, and the honey is fragrant with thyme.
"O fortunate ones, who see their city rising already!"
Aeneas cries as he looks down at the lofty rooftops.
Wrapped in his cloud he passes among them (wonder of
                                                    wonders!)
and mingles with the people, but he is seen by no one.   440

There was a grove in the city's center, deep and shady,
where first the Phoenicians, battered long by wind and wave,
unearthed the sign that royal Juno had told them of:
a stallion's head, a sign that the people would always be
renowned in war, abundant in peace, for ever and ever.   445
And here Sidonian Dido was building a temple to Juno,
vast and rich with costly gifts, and the goddess' presence.
For brazen steps led to the threshold, and brazen beams
held it in place, and brazen doors creaked on their hinges.
And in this grove a wonderful, reassuring sight   450
met Aeneas' eyes: here he dared to hope for safety;

here in his misery first he hoped for a better future.
For as he looked at the massive temple towering o'er him,
awaiting the Queen, as he marveled at the city's fortune,
and at the consummate craftsmanship and toil of her artists,   455
he suddenly beheld the battles of Troy, in order:
the war whose fame had already spread throughout the world,
the sons of Atreus and Priam, and, cruel to both, Achilles.
He stopped and, weeping, cried: "What land remains, Achates,
what place is there on earth that is not full of our sorrows?   460
For here is Priam, here too the rewards of glory.
Here are tears for misfortune, and here men's hearts are touched
by human plight. Fear not, this fame will bring us safety."
   He speaks, and feeds his spirit on the empty pictures,
and sighing deeply, wets his face with floods of tears.   465
He sees before his eyes the battle around fair Troy-land,
and here the Greeks are fleeing, pursued by the Trojan youth;
and there the Phrygians in flight before the plumed Achilles.
Nearby, weeping, he beholds the tents of Rhesus,
all white and snowy, which were betrayed in the early evening   470
and laid waste by Diomedes with bloody slaughter;
the fiery steeds were turned away to the camp, before
they tasted the Trojan pasture, or drank the water of Xanthus.
In another picture, Troilus has lost his armor and flees—
unhappy youth, he was no match for the mighty Achilles!   475
and borne by his horses, tangled with the empty chariot,
he holds the reins, his hair and neck drag on the ground,
his spear, reversed, makes little furrows in the dust.
And here the Trojan women go to Minerva's temple,
unfriendly Minerva, holding the peplos suppliant-fashion,   480
with streaming hair, beating their breasts with open palms,
but the goddess turns away her head and looks at the ground.
Three times around the walls of Troy Achilles had dragged
the luckless Hector, and now was selling his corpse for gold.
Aeneas draws a heavy sigh from deep in his breast   485
as he sees the spoils and chariot and body of Hector,
and aged Priam stretching out his helpless hands.
He sees himself as well, in combat with the Acheans;

the Oriental troops, the armor of black Memnon;
and furious Penthesilea leads her Amazons,   490
the crescent-shielded maidens, amid the swarming warriors,
clasping a golden girdle beneath her naked bosom,
a soldier-maiden, not afraid to battle with men!

While Aeneas gazed at all these wondrous pictures
as he remained enraptured, absorbed in contemplation,   495
Queen Dido came to the temple, radiant in her beauty,
a youthful band of followers thronging in her train.
And as on Eurotas' banks, or on the Cynthian ridges
Diana leads her thousand Oreads in the dance—
the goddess carries her quiver on her stately shoulder,   500
and as she moves, surpasses all the nymphs in height;
Latona's heart is thrilled as she watches with silent joy—
just so Queen Dido gladly advanced amid the throng,
encouraging the tasks and work of her growing empire.
Before the sanctuary's portal she takes her seat,   505
enthroned on high beneath the vault, surrounded by soldiers.
And she was giving justice and laws to the Carthaginians,
assigning or alloting tasks in fair proportion;
when suddenly Aeneas saw in the thronging crowd
Antheus advancing, and Sergestus, and brave Cloanthus,   510
and all the rest of the Trojans whom the raging tempest
had separated and carried away to other shores.
He was thunderstruck: both he and Achates felt joy and fear.
They eagerly burned to grasp the hands of their rescued comrades,
but the uncertainty of their state disturbs their minds.   515
They contain themselves, remaining hidden in their cloud,
to learn what fortune befell the men, and where they have left
the fleet, and why they have come (for they, being chosen
by the others to pray for mercy, now came to the temple).

When they had entered and received permission to speak,   520
the aged Ilioneus began with placid mien:
"O Queen, whom Jove has given the right to found this city
and put the bridle of justice on the haughty nations,

hearken to the prayer of the wretched Trojans,
driven over all the seas: do not burn our ships,   525
but spare a pious people and look at our sad plight.
We have not come here to lay waste the Libyan homes,
nor yet to plunder and bring booty to the shores,
for conquered peoples do not show such insolence.
There is a land—the Greeks call it Hesperia—   530
an ancient land, mighty in arms and rich in soil.
Oenotrians inhabit it, but now men say
that their descendants call it Italy, after their king;
hither we set our course . . . .
But suddenly the stormy Orion with raging billows   535
carried us off to the shoals and scattered us afar.
Through salty seas and trackless ways we were dispersed,
and only a few of us have floated to your shores.
What race are you? What savage land permits such a custom?
For, seeking refuge, we are driven from the shore.   540
Your people threaten us: we cannot set foot on your beaches.
If you have scorn for the human race and mortal weapons,
at least remember, the gods have knowledge of good and evil.
Aeneas was our king, the best man that ever lived
both for his righteousness and military prowess.   545
If Destiny preserves him, if he breathes the air
and has not gone to rest amid the pitiless shades,
fear not, you never shall regret a generous action.
In the land of Sicily we have towns and arms.
Acestes himself is there, of royal Trojan blood.   550
But let us bring ashore our tempest-battered vessels,
and cut down timber from your forests for planks and oars,
so that, if we ever find our friends and king again,
we may steer our course for Latium and Italy.
But if all hope is gone, if the Libyan sea engulfs you,   555
father and lord of the Trojans, if little Iülus has perished,
at least we shall seek the straits of Sicily, the homes
that wait for us, from which we sailed, and King Acestes."
Thus spoke Ilioneus, and all the nearby Trojans
assented with a murmur . . .   560

Then Dido with downcast eyes speaks to the Teucrians:
"Be reassured, O Trojans, banish your alarm.
Harsh circumstances and the newness of our kingdom
compel us to guard our borders in such unfriendly manner.
Who has not heard of Troy, or the race of Aeneas' children,   565
the heroes and the deeds, and the war's great conflagration?
We Carthaginians are not so gross of spirit;
the sun does not yoke his steeds so far from the Tyrian town.
Whether you choose to go to broad Hesperia
or to Eryx's borders, the country of King Acestes,   570
I shall speed you safely and look to your every need.
Or do you wish to remain in Carthage and share my kingdom?
The city I am building is yours: draw up your ships.
Between your people and mine I will make no distinction.
O would that Aeneas your king were driven here by the tempest   575
to this same land! I shall send my trusted messengers
to search along the Libyan coast for news of him,
and see if perhaps he wanders in nearby towns or forests."

Comforted by these words Aeneas and brave Achates
have long been burning to escape from the opaque cloud.   580
And so the trusty Achates first speaks to Aeneas:
"Son of Venus, what do you now intend to do?
You see that all is safe, your vessels and your comrades;
only one ship is missing—we saw it sink in the waves—
in all the rest your mother's words have been fulfilled."   585
Hardly had he said these words when the cloud burst asunder,
it melted and dispersed into transparent air.
Aeneas stood revealed in a glow of brilliant light,
resembling an immortal god in his face and shoulders,
for Venus had breathed a radiant beauty on his head,   590
the ruddy glow of youth, and a hero's shining eyes;
as when an artist adds perfection to ivory,
or when the whiteness of Parian marble is chased with gold.
Then breaking in on them with unexpected speech
he says to Dido: "Behold, I whom you seek am here: 595
Trojan Aeneas, safely snatched from the Libyan waves.

O Queen who alone had pity for Troy's unspeakable anguish,
and promised to share your city and your homes with us,
the remnants of the Grecian slaughter, on land and sea
exhausted, lacking all, how can we ever repay you,   600
Dido, with fitting thanks, for we are destitute:
the Trojan survivors are scattered now over all the world.
The immortal gods, if they have any regard for goodness,
if there is any justice and consciousness of right,
will reward you, Queen. What happy times have given you birth?   605
What admirable parents have produced such a daughter?
As long as rivers run to the sea, as long as shadows
cross the mountain slopes, and the stars feed in Heaven's pastures,
so long shall your glory, Dido, your name and praises endure,
whatever lands may call me." With these words he advances   610
and gives his right hand to Ilioneus, his left to Serestus,
then to his other friends, brave Gyas and strong Cloanthus.

   Sidonian Dido was stupefied, first at the sight,
then at Aeneas' great misfortunes; and thus she spoke:
"What fate, O goddess-born, follows you through such perils,   615
what violence has thrown you on this savage coast?
Are you in truth Aeneas, whom gracious Venus bore
to Trojan Anchises by Phrygian Simois' waters?
For my part, I remember how Teucer came to Sidon,
expelled from his native land, and seeking a new kingdom,   620
with Belus' aid—for Belus, my father, had even then
despoiled rich Cyprus and held it in victorious sway.
And since that time the fall of Troy has been known to me,
and your name, noble Aeneas, and all the kings of Greece.
For even Teucer, your enemy, had only praise for the Trojans,   625
and claimed his own descent from ancient Teucrian stock.
So come in, noble youths, and enter my abode.
I too have known disasters, and many similar troubles,
before the Fates permitted me to settle here,
and not unschooled in woe, I have learned to help the afflicted."   630
   She spoke, and led Aeneas into the royal palace,
and ordered her men to make sacrifice in the gods' temples.

And she sent twenty bulls to Aeneas' men on the shore;
a hundred swine she also sent, with bristling backs,
and an equal number of rich fat lambs, along with their mothers,   635
all presents for the festive day . . .
The palace within was all bedecked with regal splendor;
a royal banquet was prepared within the halls,
with table cloths all richly embroidered in Tyrian purple,
and massive utensils of silver, and deeds of ancestral glory   640
wrought in gold, the whole great series of events,
through generations of heroes, back to the nation's beginning.

Aeneas, for a father's care gave him no peace,
despatched the loyal Achates forthwith to the ships,
to bring Ascanius the news, and lead him to Carthage,   645
for in the child resided all his love and care.
He bade him bring presents snatched from the flames of Troy:
a cloak that was all stiff with gold-embroidered figures;
a veil with woven border of saffron-colored acanthus,
once worn by Argive Helen, a gift from her mother Leda,   650
when she departed from her home in fair Mycenae
and set out for Troy and her forbidden, lawless marriage;
the scepter, too, which had belonged to Ilione,
Priam's oldest daughter; and a necklace of rich pearls;
and also a double diadem of jewelled gold.   655
Achates hastened with this message to the ships.

But Cytherean Venus was planning new tricks in her mind:
to change the form and face of Cupid and make him resemble
and take the place of gentle Ascanius; with his gifts
set fire to the Queen and inflame her bones with passion.   660
Indeed she feared the palace and duplicity
of the Tyrians; Juno's anger caused her great distress.
So she addresses these words to the wingèd Love:
"My son, my strength, my greatest power, who alone
fear not the Father's thunderbolts that conquered Typho,   665
I come to you, a suppliant to your divinity.
Well do you know how cruel Juno's bitter hatred
has buffeted your brother Aeneas from shore to shore,

for you have often been afflicted by my sorrow.
Now Phoenician Dido holds him with honeyed words;   670
and I mistrust the hospitality of Juno,
for she will not be idle at such a decisive time.
This is why my purpose now is to outwit her:
inflame the Queen with love, that no other god may change her,
but I will hold her enchained by passion for Aeneas.   675
Listen and I will tell you how to accomplish this:
At his father's request, Ascanius (my chiefest concern)
is now preparing to go to the Sidonian city,
bringing the gifts his father saved from burning Troy.
Now I shall put the lad to sleep in my holy temple   680
on Mount Cytherea's ridges or on Idalium
lest he discover my wiles and counteract my plans;
for this one night you will put on his face and form,
and you, a boy, pretend to be that other boy,
so that when Dido, amid the banquets and libations,   685
shall take you, in her festal cheer, upon her knees,
and hold you close and cover you with sweet embraces,
you will infect her with your secret fires and poisons."
   And Cupid obeys the words of his beloved mother:
he doffs his wings and merrily mimics Iülus' walk.   690
But Venus pours a gentle sleep on Ascanius' limbs
and takes him, pressed to her bosom, to Idalium's heights,
in the sacred groves, where soft amaracus folds him round
into its gentle shadows and its fragrant blossoms.
And Cupid, obedient to her words, went with Achates   695
right joyfully, bearing royal gifts for the Tyrians.
When he arrived, the Queen was already on her throne
beneath the splendid tapestries, in the midst of the banquet.
Now Father Aeneas and the other Trojan men
enter and take their places on the purple couches.   700
The slaves pour water on their hands and distribute bread
from baskets, and bring them napkins of the finest cloth.
Within the palace, fifty slave-girls have the task
of keeping the dishes in order and feeding the sacred flames.
A hundred more, and another hundred male attendants   705

are loading the tables with food and bringing in the wine.
The Tyrians all gather at the festal threshold,
and take their appointed places on embroidered cushions.
They marvel at Aeneas' gifts and at Iülus:
the blazing eyes of the god, the simulated speech,   710
and at the cloak, and the veil embroidered with yellow acanthus.
Unhappy Dido, doomed to imminent destruction,
cannot satiate her spirit, but gazes, all afire,
moved alike by the boy and by the royal gifts.
The god embraces Aeneas and hangs upon his neck,   715
and having satisfied with love the deluded father,
he goes to the Queen. She clings to him with eyes and soul,
and fondles him time and again on her lap. Unfortunate Dido,
she knows not what a mighty god she holds to her bosom!
But he, remembering his mother's words, begins   720
little by little to erase Sychaeus' image,
and sow new love in her heart long unaccustomed to loving.
Now when the banquet was finished and the tables cleared,
great mixing-bowls with garlands crowned were set before them.
The hall is filled with the resounding din of voices,   725
and blazing chandeliers hang down from golden chains:
the light of flaming torches puts the gloom to flight.
And Dido called for a heavy cup of jewelled gold:
she filled it with undiluted wine—the cup of Belus
and all of Belus' people—then the din was silenced.   730
   "O Jupiter," she said, "God of Hospitality,
grant joy to Tyrian host and Trojan guest alike.
May our descendants remember this day with happiness.
Be with us, Bacchus, giver of joy, and gracious Juno.
And you, my Tyrians, do honor to this banquet."   735
She spoke, and poured a liquid offering on the table,
and first of all she lightly touched the cup to her lips,
then handed it, challenging, to Bitias, and he
drank deep from the golden cup, and bathed his face in the wine.
The others followed in turn. And then long-haired Iopas   740
sang to the golden lyre the songs he had learned from Atlas.
He sang of the wandering moon, the labors of the sun,

the origins of men and beasts and rain and lightning;
Arcturus, the rainy Hyades, the twin Triones,
and why the winter suns fall so swiftly into the ocean,   745
and why the lingering nights are so slow to appear.
The Carthaginians and Trojans applaud him loudly.
Unhappy Dido, too, prolonged the night with talk
and feasted her enamored eyes on Trojan Aeneas.
She asked him many questions about Priam and Hector,   750
and of the armor that the son of Aurora wore,
and Diomedes' horses, and the mighty Achilles.
"But better still," she said, "tell us the entire story:
the stratagems of the wicked Greeks, your people's woes,
and all your wanderings, for this is the seventh summer   755
that you have been a wanderer on land and sea."

End of Book I.

BOOK II

THE SACK OF TROY

They all grew silent, and every eye was fixed on Aeneas,
and from his elevated couch, the hero began:
"Unspeakable, O Queen, is the grief you bid me recall:
how the Danaans overthrew the mighty city of Troy,
the pitiable kingdom. I saw these terrible things,   5
and took great part in them. Which of the Myrmidons,
or Dolopians, what soldier of the cruel Ulysses
could restrain his tears at the tale? Damp night has long since
                                                    fallen:
already the setting stars are counseling us to slumber,
but still, if such desire to know our calamities moves you,   10
if you want to learn the final agonies of Troy,
although my mind and spirit recoil from the painful remembrance,
I shall begin:
                    "Broken by war, repulsed by Fate,
the Grecian leaders, after many years had passed,
constructed, with Minerva's aid, an enormous horse,   15
high as a mountain; its sides were made from planks of fir.
A feigned offering for safe return: so the rumor spread.
And chosen heroes were selected one by one,
and secretly shut up in the horse's wooden belly:
the whole interior was filled with armed soldiers.   20

"In sight of Troy there is an island, Tenedos,
famous it was, and rich, while Priam's kingdom endured.
Now it is only a bay and an unreliable harbor.
Here the Greeks concealed themselves on the barren shore.
We thought that they had gone and sailed away to Mycenae.   25
So all the Trojans put aside their long-lived grief;
the gates were opened: what joy to see the Dorian camp,

25

the deserted battle-stations, the abandoned shore!
Here were the Dolopian tents, here the cruel Achilles,
here they beached their ships, and here was their battle-line.　30
And some were astonished to see the deadly gift to Minerva:
they marveled at the massive horse, and first Thymoetes
began to urge us to bring it within the city's walls
(whether by treachery, or because the Fates were against us).
But Capys and the others who were of wiser counsel　35
bade us throw the dangerous gift into the sea,
or build a fire beneath it and utterly destroy it,
or pierce its flanks with spears and explore the cavity.
The uncertain crowd is torn by their divergent opinions.

　　"And now appears, in front of a loud and noisy throng,　40
Laöcoon, who comes running down from the citadel.
He cries from afar: 'What madness, wretched men, is this?
Do you believe the Greeks are gone? Do you really think
a Grecian gift lacks treachery? Is it thus you know
Ulysses? I tell you: either there are Greeks inside,　45
or else it is some engine designed to breach our walls,
or spy upon our houses, or come down into the city,
or some sort of deception. Trojans, trust not the horse!
Whatever it be, I fear the Greeks, even bearing gifts!'
As he spoke he hurled a spear with all his might　50
into the horse's wooden flank and curvèd belly.
It stood there quivering, and beneath the javelin's blow
the hollow cavern echoed with resounding groan.
And had we not been blinded by adverse Destiny,
we would have probed the Argive hiding-place,　55
and Troy would still be standing, and Priam's citadel.

　　"And meanwhile, clamoring Trojan shepherds drag to the king
a youth whose hands are bound together behind his back:
an unknown man, who surrendered of his own free will,
to open the mighty gates of Troy for the Achaeans,　60
relying on his courage, prepared for either fate:
to deceive the Trojan people, or die a certain death.
On all sides the Trojan youth flock round the captive,

eager to see him, jeering in friendly competition.
Now, listen to the Danaan's duplicity,   65
and from one crime, learn all . . .
For as he stood in our midst, confounded and unarmed,
and scanned the Phrygian assembly with his eyes,
'Alas!' he cried, 'what land, what sea will receive me now?
What final doom remains for me, wretch that I am?   70
There is no place for me among my fellow-Greeks,
and all the angry Trojans are clamoring for my blood.'
At this lament we changed our mood and stayed our hands.
and we encouraged him to speak, and tell us his race,
and what he brings; on what does he, a captive, rely.   75
[He puts aside his terror and he makes this answer:]¹
    " 'Come what may, O King, I'll tell the truth to you.
I'll not deny,' he said, 'that I am of Grecian blood:
this first. For even if Fortune has made Sinon a wretch,
she will not also make of him a liar and cheat.   80
Perhaps the name of Palamedes has come to your ears,
the glorious and renowned descendant of Belus' race,
whom, just because he wanted peace instead of war,
the Greeks condemned to death on perjured evidence,
(innocent man!) and now, too late, they all bewail him.   85
To him my father sent me as companion in arms,
since he was kin to us, and we were very poor.
Whilst his prestige was great in the council of the kings,
I, too, was held in some esteem and even honor.
But when, because of treacherous Ulysses' malice   90
(which you have known as well), Palamedes was dead,
my life became a gloomy, sad existence, too,
for I, too, suffered from my innocent friend's dishonor,
and like a fool, I could not keep silent. If Fate allowed,
if ever I returned victorious to Argos,   95
I vowed to be his avenger. My words aroused deep hatred.
This was the beginning of my downfall, for Ulysses
ceased not to threaten me with renewed accusations.

---

¹Omitted in some MSS. Taken from III 612.

spread rumors among the Greeks and stirred them up against me.
Nor did he rest until, with Calchas as accomplice— 100
but why should I bore you with this uninteresting story,
and why should I waste your time? If all Greeks are alike to you,
enough that I am a Greek: come, slay me and be done.
Ulysses and Agamemnon will pay you well for it!'

"But we kept pressing him to continue and tell us more 105
(all ignorant as we were of Grecian perfidy!)
and he continued, the hypocrite, with trembling words:
" 'Time and again the Greeks have wished to abandon Troy,
to escape, at last to be finished with this odious war,
(would God that they had done so!) but the stormy seas 110
and raging tempest deterred them every time they tried.
Especially when they made the horse, with maple planks,
the lightning flashed and thunder grumbled in the sky.
Perplexed, we sent Eurypylus to consult Apollo,
and he brought back from Phoebus these foreboding words: 115
"With a butchered maiden's blood you pacified the winds
when you first came, O Greeks, to the shores of Ilium.
Your return must be bought with blood, and an Argive life be
forfeit."

" 'When this ominous response came to the Grecian ears,
our hearts stood still: cold shudders ran through all our bones. 120
Whose doom do the Fates prepare? Whom does Apollo demand?
Ulysses with a mighty shout drags Calchas amidst them
and asks the seer to tell the folk what the gods require.
And now full many warned me of the rascal's designs,
and silently they saw the terrible things to come. 125
For ten days Calchas remained in his tent without a word,
unwilling to condemn anyone to a terible doom,
but finally, compelled by loud cries from Ulysses,
he answers, as arranged, and consigns *me* to the altar.
They all agree: the doom that each one feared for himself, 130
he saw without a qualm descend on my poor head.
" 'And now the dreadful day was at hand, the rites prepared,

the salt, the flour, the fillets to bind around my temples.
I fled—I'll not deny it—I burst my bonds and fled
and hid all night in the salty marshes of a lake,   135
waiting for them to sail, if thus by chance they decided.
Nor had I any hope of seeing my native land,
my dearest children or my much-lamented father.
Perhaps the Greeks would make them pay for my craven flight,
and wash away my crime with the death of innocent people.   140
Therefore, by Heaven's gods, who know the right from the wrong,
and by whatever justice still remains on earth,
have pity, Trojans, on my lamentable woes,
have pity on one who suffers wrongs he does not deserve!'
     "And at these tears we grant him compassion, and his life.   145
Priam himself commands the chains to be removed,
and speaks to the prisoner with friendly words as follows:
" 'Whoever you are, henceforth you must forget the Greeks.
You shall be one of us. But come and answer me truly:
Why have they made this monstrous horse? Who counselled it?   150
What do they seek? Is it a vow or machine of war?'
Thus Priam, and the other, instructed by Grecian wiles,
lifted up to the sky his newly unchained hands.
     " 'O eternal fires,' he said, 'inviolable forces,
bear witness for me, and you too, accursed swords and altars,   155
from which I fled, and the sacrificial fillets I wore:
it is not wrong that I break my oath of Greek allegiance,
nor that I hate the Greeks, and reveal all their secrets,
nor am I bound by any oaths to my former homeland.
But you, O Troy, keep faith, and save the man who saves you,   160
if I tell you the truth and grant you great rewards.
     " 'All the hope of the Greeks, and all the confidence
with which they began the war—all rested on Minerva.
But since the wicked Diomede and rascal Ulysses
dared to steal the Palladium from out of her temple,   165
and killed the sentries on the topmost citadel,
and snatched the sacred effigy with bloody hands
and thus defiled the sacred fillets of the goddess,
since then the Argive hopes went tumbling ever backwards:

their strength was broken and the goddess' mind estranged.   170
And there was no mistaking Minerva's meaning then:
for scarcely was the statue set down in the camp,
when fire flashed from its open eyes, and salty sweat
ran down its limbs and (wonderful to relate!) three times
it leaped from the ground, its spear and buckler all a-quiver.   175
And Calchas straightway says that we must put to sea,
that Troy can never be defeated by Argive arms,
until they first return to Argos, seek new omens,
bring back the auspices which they carried in their ships.
And now, in fact, the wind has carried them to Mycenae   180
to gather arms and friendly gods. They will return
when least you expect them. Thus did Calchas explain the omens.
This horse they built at his warning, for the Palladium,
the goddess' injured will, to atone for sacrilege.
But Calchas bade them make the horse a mighty mass,   185
with oaken beams to elevate it to the sky,
so that it might not enter your gates or come in your city,
nor guard the Trojan people beneath the ancient cult.
For if your hands should violate Minerva's gift,
then great destruction (on Calchas rather fall the blow!)   190
will come to Priam's kingdom and the Trojan people.
But if, with your own hands, you take it into Troy,
Asia will bring a mighty war to Pelops' walls:
this the Fates now hold in store for our descendants.'
And so, by treachery and Sinon's perjured art,   195
it was believed. We were caught by tricks and crocodile tears,
whom neither Diomed could conquer, nor savage Achilles,
nor ten long years of siege, nor a thousand Argive ships.

"And now another portent, far more terrible
comes to our gaze and strikes chill terror into our hearts: 200
Laöcoon, the priest of Neptune chosen by lot
was duly sacrificing a bull before the altars,
when lo! across the tranquil bay from Tenedos
(I shudder to recall it!) came two enormous serpents;
through the sea they advanced together to the shore.   205

Their breasts cut through the water, with their bloody crests
riding atop the waves; the rest of them came after,
curving in massive arcs above the water's surface.
The sea gurgles and spits—and now they have reached the shore,
their bloodshot eyes are all ablaze with flashing fire,   210
their sibilant tongues are darting in their hissing mouths.
We flee in consternation at the sight, but they
make straightway for Laöcoon, and first of all
they wrap themselves around the bodies of his two sons,
and feed with savage bite upon the wretched limbs.   215
Then, as Laöcoon runs to the children's aid,
the huge coils of the serpents seize him and fasten themselves
twice around his waist and twice around his neck
with scaly bodies; they tower above him with their heads.
The wretched man keeps trying to pull the coils apart;   220
his chaplets are bedewed with blackened blood and venom.
He raises loud and horrifying screams to Heaven,
as when a wounded bull has just escaped from the altar
and bellows as he tries to shake the axe from his neck.
And now the serpents glide away to the citadel   225
and seek the sanctuary of Tritonia.
They hide themselves at her feet beneath her circling shield.

"Then fear insinuated itself into our hearts,
and nameless terror. We are convinced that Laöcoon
who pierced the holy wood with desecrating spear   230
has rightly paid the penalty for sacrilege,
and everyone clamors aloud to bring the statue in
and beg Minerva's forgiveness . . .
"We make a breach in the walls and open up the ramparts.
All bend to the task, and rollers are put beneath the feet,   235
and bands of rope are fixed about the horse's neck.
The fatal engine climbs our walls, pregnant with arms.
The boys and the unwedded maidens throng about it,
singing hymns of rejoicing, happy to touch the rope.
The horse advances, menacing, into the city.   240
O Troy my fatherland! Home of the gods! Dardanian walls

famous in war! Four times it stuck on our very threshold!
Four times there came the clang of weapons from its womb!
But we kept pushing and prodding it on: in our blind folly
we plant the ill-omened monster in our citadel.   245
And even then Cassandra raised her warning voice—
a voice we Trojans were fated never to believe—
whilst we, poor wretches, for whom this was the final day
bedecked the shrines with garlands all throughout the city.

"Meanwhile the heavens turn and night comes out of the ocean,   250
enveloping in her dusky shade the earth and sky
and Myrmidon tricks. The Trojans all about the city
are stretched out silently: sleep presses on their limbs.
And now the Argive fleet has sailed from Tenedos
beneath the friendly silence of the quiet moon,   255
seeking the well-known shore. A signal flashed from the flagship,
and Sinon, shielded by the malignity of Heaven,
stealthily unlocked the imprisoned Danaans
from the horse's wooden womb. They joyfully emerge,
disgorged by the monster's hollow cavern into the air: 260
Thessandrus and Sthenelus the leaders, and cruel Ulysses,
and Acamas and Thoas, sliding down the rope,
and Peleus' grandson Neoptolemus, and Machaon,
and Menelaus and Epeus, inventor of the machine.
They rush upon the city buried in slumber and wine.   265
They kill the sentinels and open wide the gates,
receive their friends, join forces with their confederates.

"It was the hour of night when slumber, gift of the gods,
begins for care-worn mortals, stealing into their bodies,
when in my dreams I saw before my eyes sad Hector,   270
with grieving countenance, and shedding many tears.
He looked the same as on the day the chariot dragged him—
bloody and dusty, his feet all swollen from the thongs.
Alas! how wretched he looked—how different from that Hector
who once returned from battle with the spoils of Achilles,   275
or carried Phrygian fire to burn the Grecian ships.

His beard was dirty and his hair matted with blood,
and he had all the wounds he had received in battle
around his country's walls. On seeing him, I, too, wept
and I addressed him first of all with mournful words: 280
   " 'O Light of Dardania! O greatest hope of all the Trojans,
what has delayed you so long? From what place do you come?
O long-awaited Hector, how wearily we behold you!
So many of your kinsmen now are dead, and Troy
has suffered for so long! But what indignities   285
have marred your countenance? Why do I see these wounds?'
   "He did not answer or pay heed to my idle questions,
but drawing a long sigh from deep in his breast he said:
'Fly, son of a goddess, and save yourself from the flames.
The enemy holds the walls and lofty Troy is falling.   290
Enough for Priam and country—if Troy could have been defended
by any mortal hand, be sure that mine would have done so.
She now entrusts to you her gods and holy things:
make them your companions now and seek new walls for them,
which you will build one day in a land beyond the sea.'   295
Thus Hector spoke, and carried in his hands, from the shrine,
powerful Vesta, her fillets and her eternal fire.

   "Meanwhile the town is stirred with cries of agony;
and more and more, although my father Anchises' house
lay deep recessed and sheltered by protecting trees,   300
the sounds grew clearer and the battle's horror increased.
I woke up with a start and climbed the sloping roof
and stood at the top, listening with pricked-up ears;
as when a field of grain catches fire in the wind,
or when a mountain torrent sweeps across the land,   305
ravaging the harvest and the oxen's labors,
dragging trees along in its path, and the shepherd, amazed,
hears the din from a far-off rock without knowing its cause.
Then all was clear: the Argive treachery manifest.
Already Deiphobus' house has crashed in utter ruin,   310
and now the next one—Ucalegon's—is on fire.
The flames are reflected in the broad Sigean bay.

The shouts of men are mingled with the blare of trumpets.
Madly, I seize my weapons; I could not tell you why,
but yet I burn to gather a band of fighting men   315
and reach the citadel with my friends; fury and passion
drive me on: I think it noble to die in battle.

"And now comes Panthus, who has escaped the Achaean arms,
Panthus, son of Othrys, priest of Apollo's temple;
bearing the sacred objects and the conquered gods,   320
and dragging his little grandson, he madly runs to the gates.
'How fares the city, Panthus, and what of the citadel?'
Hardly had I uttered these words when he groaned aloud:
" 'Our final day has come, the inescapable day
for Ilium. No more are we Trojans, no more is Troy   325
and all her glory. Pitiless Jupiter has transported
all to Argos. The Greeks now rule the burning city.
The monstrous horse, standing within our very walls,
is spewing armèd men; victorious Sinon exults
and scatters fire around. Soldiers pour through the gates,   330
as many thousands as ever came from great Mycenae,
while others occupy the narrow streets with arms.
A barrier stands of gleaming weapons drawn from their sheaths,
prepared to deal out death. The sentinels at the gates
are scarcely daring to offer resistance in the shadows.'   335
"At these words from the son of Othrys, by Heaven's will
I am borne into the flaming fray, where the savage Furies
and battle's tumult call me, and clamor arising skyward.
Rhipeus joins me in the fight, and mighty Epytus,
Hypanis and Dymas too, made visible by moonlight,   340
join themselves to us, and also young Coroebus,
the son of Mygdon, who had come by chance to Troy
quite recently, inflamed with love for poor Cassandra,
and bringing aid to Priam and the Phrygians—
unhappy youth, who could not hear the prophetic words   345
of his beloved . . .
"When I saw them joining ranks and ready for battle
I spoke to them: 'My friends, warriors so brave in vain,

if you wish to follow me into certain death,
you see the state to which we have been reduced by Fortune: 350
our temples and altars have been deserted by the gods
on whom we had relied for help. You come to the aid
of a city already in flames. Let us die in the midst of battle.
The only safety for conquered men is to hope for none!'
Thus fighting fury is added to their noble hearts.   355
Then, like ravenous wolves in the darkness, when the rage
of hunger drives them forth, leaving their thirsty cubs,
we march against the ranks and weapons of the foe,
and hold our path to the center of town and certain death.
The black night flits around us, enveloping us in shadows.   360

   "Who could relate the death and destruction of that sad night?
What tears can ever be found to equal our misfortunes?
A city fell whose empire had lasted for many years:
the heaps of lifeless bodies filled the narrow streets,
the houses, and the sacred temples of the gods.   365
But Trojans are not the only ones to forfeit their lives,
for courage also returned to the hearts of those who were
                                             conquered,
and victorious Greeks were slain. Cruel grief is everywhere;
everywhere is fear, and the many faces of death.

   And now there comes Androgeos with a band of Greeks   370
around him. In his ignorance he takes us for friends,
and speaks to us as though we too were Achaean soldiers:
'Make haste, you men! Wherefore this laziness and sloth?
The others are already looting the burning city
while you are only now debarking from your ships.'   375
He finished, and straightway, from our equivocal answer,
he realized that he had fallen among his foes.
His tongue and feet both failed him from the terrible shock,
as when a man on a bushy path, all unawares,
steps suddenly on a snake, and then recoils and flees   380
before the swollen neck and head prepared to strike.
So Androgeos trembled, seeeing us, and fled.
We rushed upon the Greeks, surrounding them with weapons,

and since they did not know the ground, and were afraid,
we slaughtered them. Thus Fortune smiled on our first attempt.   385
    "And then Coroebus, taking heart from this success,
cried out: 'My friends, when Fortune reveals to us the path
of safety, let us follow her, wherever she leads.
Let us exchange our armor and our shields with the Greeks.
Tricks or courage—what does it matter against the foe?   390
The Greeks will give us arms!' So speaking, Coroebus dons
Androgeos' crested helmet and emblazoned shield,
and binds the Argive captain's sword to his own side.
Then Rhipeus does the same, and Dymas and the others,
all gaily arm themselves with the fresh Grecian spoils.   395
We mingle, under alien auspices, with the foe.
Many the battles we fought beneath the sheltering darkness,
many the Greeks we sent to dwell in the House of Hades.
Some flee to their ships and the safety of the shore,
while others, in the clutches of a craven terror,   400
conceal themselves in the monstrous horse's familiar belly.

    "Alas! with gods unwilling, man may count on nothing!
For lo! Cassandra, Priam's daughter, with streaming hair,
was being dragged from Minerva's sanctuary and temple.
Vainly she raised her burning eyes for aid to Heaven;   405
her tender hands were manacled with iron fetters.
Coroebus, drunk with rage, could not bear to behold this,
but flung himself into their midst, to certain death.
We follow him, and rush into the forest of weapons.
But from the summits of the Trojan temples now   410
our fellow-Trojans overwhelm us with their missiles.
A wretched slaughter ensues, from our deceptive armor
and Grecian plumes. The Greeks, enraged at Cassandra's rescue,
fall upon us from every side: the violent Ajax,
the twin Atreidae, and the whole Achaean army.   415
Thus often, when their turbulent cyclones are unchained,
the West and South winds clash with the exultant East wind,
rejoicing in the steeds of Dawn; the forests shriek,
and Nereus with his trident stirs the sea from its depths.

The other Greeks, whom we had already put to flight.   420
by means of our stratagem, and under cover of darkness,
now reappear: at once they recognize the shields,
the lying weapons, and the unfamiliar accents.
They overwhelm us with their numbers—first Coroebus
is felled by Peneleus' hand at Minerva's sacred altar,   425
then Rhipeus falls, the man most righteous of all the Trojans,
the most exact in holding to the path of virtue
(the gods willed otherwise!); Hypanis and Dymas perish,
slain by their comrades' hands, nor did your piety, Panthus,
nor even Apollo's fillets shield you from mortal blow!   430
I call the ashes of Troy and my people's funeral pyres
to witness: I avoided no encounter, no chance of death.
If it had been my destiny, I would have fallen
beneath the Argive weapons. We tore ourselves away,
Iphitus and Pelias and myself; and Iphitus   435
weighed down by years, and Pelias by a wound from Ulysses—
called forth by all the clamor to the house of Priam.
"So fierce was the battle here, it seemed as if no battles
were waged elsewhere, and that no one else in Troy was dying.
Mars, indomitable, rages: the Greeks attack   440
the palace door by rushing with their covered phalanx.
They scale the walls with ladders, even before the doors,
and as they climb they hold their shields in their left hands
to ward off weapons; with their right hands they grasp the
                                                             building.
The Trojans meanwhile tear down towers and pinnacles   445
from house and palace; using these as their only missiles
they now prepare to defend themselves in their final hour.
They rip off gilded beams, ancestral decorations,
while other beset the doors below with their drawn swords,
defending them with close-set ranks of fighting men.   450
We restore our courage to bring aid to Priam's palace
and reinforce the defenders, adding strength to the conquered.

     "Behind the royal palace was a secret doorway
linking Priam's houses, a solitary passage,

where in the happier bygone days, Andromache   455
was wont to go alone to visit her father-in-law,
or bring Astyanax to see his grandfather Priam.
I reached the sloping summit of the roof, from which
the wretched Trojans were hurling down their vain projectiles.
There was a tower here, ascending to the sky,   460
from which there was a splendid view of Ilium,
the Grecian vessels and the whole Achaean camp.
Surrounding it, we attack it with iron, where the joints
may be wrenched loose: we pull it free from its high foundations.
It wavers, then gives way and collapses with a crash   465
and falls upon the Argive ranks in mighty ruin.
But others take their places: neither stones nor weapons
cease to pour from all sides . . .
    "Before the vestibule and on the threshold, Pyrrhus
rejoices in his armor of resplendent bronze,   470
as when a serpent, having fed on poisonous herbs,
kept hidden, swollen, underground by winter's chill,
now fresh and shining, casting his old skin aside,
winds his slippery body and raises it to the sun,
with his triple-forked tongue darting to and fro in his mouth.   475
With him, enormous Periphas and Automedon,
the armor-bearing charioteer of great Achilles,
and Scyrians climb on the roof and throw flames on the housetops.
And Pyrrhus, among the leaders, seizes a battle-axe,
bursts through the door and wrenches it from its brazen hinges,   480
and now he cuts a plank from the solid oaken door
and makes in it a huge and gaping aperture.
The house is seen within; the long halls are discovered,
the secret chambers of Priam and the ancient kings.
And armed soldiers can be seen on the outer threshold.   485
    "The house within is a mass of groans and screams and
                                                            confusion,
from all the courtyards there resounds the wailing of women;
the battle's tumult rises up to the golden stars.
And frightened women wander here and there in the halls,
clinging fast to the doors and kissing them with their lips.   490

But Pyrrhus presses on, as mighty as his father:
neither guards nor bolts are able to withstand him.
The doors, knocked down by battering-rams, fall from their
                                                          hinges.
A way is made by force: the Greeks come pouring in.
They slaughter the first defenders, and fill the place with soldiers.   495
And when a foaming stream bursts its banks in a torrent
and conquers the opposing dykes with gurgling whirlpool,
it sweeps less furiously across the fields and flocks,
as it carries the stables and herds along. I saw in the doorway
the raging Neoptolemus and the sons of Atreus;   500
Hecuba I saw with her hundred daughters, and Priam
profaning with his blood the altar fires he had kindled;
the fifty marriage chambers, so great a hope of offspring,
their doors made glorious by barbarian spoils of gold,
are gutted. Where the fire fails, the Greeks hold sway.   505

    "Perhaps you will inquire what was the fate of Priam.
When he beheld his city captured and in ruins,
his gateway broken open, the enemy in his house,
the old man fastened around his shoulders trembling with age
his armor, long unworn, and girded his useless sword   510
upon his side, and rushed to die amid the foe.
Within the palace, underneath the open sky,
there was a massive altar near an ancient laurel
whose branches guarded in their shadows the household gods.
Here Hecuba and her daughters vainly thronged about;   515
like doves driven together by the tempest's blast
they huddled against each other, clasping the images.
When Hecuba saw old Priam in his youthful armor,
she cried: 'What madness, my poor husband, possesses you
to don your sword and armor? Where are you running to?   520
We have no need of such defenders and weapons now.
No one can save us, not even my Hector, were he alive.
Come here to us: this altar will potect us all,
or we shall die together!' So speaking she drew him toward her,
and set the aged man upon the holy seat.   525

"And now Polites, one of Priam's sons, escaping
from Pyrrhus and his slaughter, through the Argive missiles,
flees, wounded, beneath the colonnades in the empty halls.
Pyrrhus pursues him furiously with deadly intent—
almost upon him, he follows with his threatening spear.   530
And just as Polites is escaping to his parents
he falls and sheds his life in a weltering pool of blood.
Priam, seeing this, although he was in death's clutches,
could not refrain from crying out with angry voice:
'Ah! for this crime,' he said, 'and for this insolence,   535
if there be any power in Heaven that sees such things,
may the immortal gods give you your due reward
for making me a witness to Polites' murder,
staining the eyes of a father with the sight of death.
You lie in claiming to be the son of great Achilles: 540
it was not thus that he dealt with his enemy Priam,
but he respected the rights and trust of a suppliant
and gave me Hector's body and sent me safely home.'
Thus spoke the old man, and threw a weak, unwarlike spear
which was deflected easily by the raucous bronze,   545
and dangled idly, hanging from the buckler's boss.
But Pyrrhus said: 'Then tell him yourself, and take this message
to my father Achilles: remember to report
the bad deeds of degenerate Neoptolemus.
Now die!' So saying, he pulled him to the altar   550
all trembling, and sliding in a pool of Polites' blood;
he seized him by the hair with his left hand, drew his sword,
and buried the blade right to the hilt in the old man's side.
Such was the end of Priam: he died, as he was fated,
seeing Troy in flaming ruins before his eyes,   555
the once proud ruler of many lands and many peoples
of Asia. Now he lies, a great corpse on the shore,
a head severed from the shoulders, a body without a name.

"But then I first was surrounded by a savage terror.
For as I stood there I seemed to see my beloved father   560
(a man of the same age as the king who now lay dying

of Pyrrhus' frightful wound), I saw Creusa deserted,
my house in ruins, the danger of my little Iülus.
I looked about to see who was left of my companions.
They all had given up, exhausted, and leaped to the ground   565
or thrown themselves, poor wretches, into the raging flames.
Now I remained alone, when suddenly I saw,
silently crouching on the threshold of Vesta's temple,
Helen, Tyndareus' daughter. The light of the fire
illuminated the scene as I wandered, looking about.   570
For she, afraid of Trojan anger for Ilium's downfall,
afraid likewise of the Greeks and her abandoned husband—
this evil genius of Troy and her native land alike
had taken refuge and crouched unseen at the sacred altar.
My spirit burned with rage, and a sudden desire for vengeance   575
possessed me: vengeance for her crimes and burning Troy.
'What, will she live, foorsooth? Will she behold Mycenae?
And rule again in Sparta as triumphant queen?
And see her husband, her ancestral home, and her children,
attended by a throng of Trojan women to serve her?   580
And Priam dead, and Troy devoured by hungry flames?
And the Dardanian shore so often drenched in blood?
It shall not be! For even if there is no honor
or victory to him who punishes a woman,
yet I will be praised for destroying such a monster,   585
and it will be a joy for me to assuage my soul
with fires of vengeance, and satisfy my people's ashes!'
Thus I cried, as I rushed along with raging mind,
when suddenly I saw my mother, the gentle goddess:
more clearly than ever before she shone through the dusky night   590
without concealing her divinity, exactly
as she appeared in Heaven. She caught me by the hand
and held me, and said these words with lips the color of roses:
  " 'What overwhelming grief, my son, arouses such anger?
Why do you rage? And where is your concern for us?   595
Will you not look to see where you have left Anchises
your aged father, or if your wife Creusa still lives,
and Ascanius your son? The Greeks are swarming round them;

without my protecting hand the flames would have long since
consumed them,
the weapons of the enemy would have drunk their blood.   600
It is not the hateful beauty of Helen, Tyndareus' daughter,
nor the fault of Paris, but the relentless gods
—the gods, I say, who have uprooted noble Troy!
Behold! for I shall dissipate the opaque cloud
that veils your sight and dulls your mortal gaze with mist.   605
Fear not, Aeneas, to obey your mother's commands;
do not refuse, my son, to give heed to her counsels.
There, where you see massive stones torn apart from stones,
and smoke and dust all whirling around in the destruction,
Neptune is shaking the walls of Troy with his savage trident   610
and overturning Ilium from her foundations.
Here cruel Juno holds the ranks at the Scaean Gates,
and armed with sword she summons her allies the Greeks
to come from the ships . . .
And look you! on the citadel, Tritonian Pallas   615
sits resplendent in her cloud with the Gorgon's head.
The Father himself gives strength and courage to the Greeks
and stirs the gods himself against the arms of Troy.
So haste away, my son, and finish your vain struggle.
I will stay with you and take you to your father's house.'   620
    "She spoke, and disappeared into the inky night.
The awful faces of the gods, unfriendly powers,
come into view, opposed to Troy . . .

    "And then it seemed to me that Troy was falling in flames;
that Neptune's city was being uprooted and overturned;   625
just as an ancient ash-tree high up in the mountains,
battered by blow after blow of the farmers' iron axes,
as they attempt to dislodge it—the tree begins to tremble,
and, shaken by the blows, the crest and branches waver,
until at last it is conquered, and with a final groan   630
it crashes down the mountainside in a trail of ruin.
I climbed down, with the goddess as my guide, I went
between the flames and the foe; the weapons and fire made way.

"But when I reached the threshold of my father's house
and the ancient building, Anchises, whom I wished to carry   635
aloft into the mountains—this was my first concern—
refused to continue living in exile after Troy
had fallen. 'You,' he said, 'whose blood runs fast,
whose bodies still have all your youthful strength and vigor,
it is for you to flee . . .   640
If the immortal gods had wished me to live any longer,
they would have spared my house. Already I have seen
Troy sacked, and have survived it: that is enough, and more.
Now bid one last farewell to me as a corpse laid out,
and then depart. My hand will find a death for me: 645
the Greeks, from pity or greed, will despatch me: I need no tomb.
Too long already, hated by the gods, have I delayed,
yes, ever since the father of gods and king of men
blasted me with his thunder and touched me with his fire.'

"Thus Anchises persisted and he remained unshaken,   650
while we implored with streaming tears, Creusa my wife,
Ascanius, and all the household, that he should not
weigh down the scale of Fate and involve us in his doom.
But he refused, and sat unchanged and adamant.
I rush to battle: in misery I hope for death,   655
for what can either counsel or chance avail me now?
'What?' I said, 'shall I flee, and leave you alone, my father?
Such sacrilegious words can come from a parent's lips?
If it is Heaven's will that nothing of Troy survives,
if this is your fixed resolve and purpose, to add your doom   660
and ours to that of Troy, the door to death is open,
and Pyrrhus, bathed in Priam's blood, will soon be upon us,
who kills the son before the father's eyes, and slays
the father at the altar. Is this why you saved me, Mother,
from sword and flame: to see the enemy in my house?   665
To see my father, my son Ascanius, and my wife
Creusa, slaughtered, lying in one another's blood?
To arms, my friends, to arms! The last light calls the conquered!
Return and find the Greeks. Let us renew the battle.
For we shall not all perish this day unavenged!'   670

"Thereupon I gird on my sword and fit my left hand
into the handle of my shield, and go from the palace.
But on the threshold my beloved wife clings to my feet
and holds the little Iülus up for me to see.
" 'If you are going to die,' she said, 'take us with you   675
But if you have any hope for a successful resistance,
begin by defending your house. To whom will you leave Iülus?
To whom your father? Or me that once was called your wife?'
She cried: the entire house resounded with her weeping,
when suddenly there came to our eyes a miraculous omen: 680
between the hands, before the eyes of his desperate parents,
behold! above Iülus' head a light appeared,
a soft and lambent flame that did not harm the child
but flickered and played on his curly locks and around his temples.
We were afraid and hurried to extinguish the fire.   685
and quench the sacred flame with water from the spring.
But father Anchises raised his eyes to the starry heavens,
and joyfully he shouted with uplifted hands:
" 'Almighty Jove, if you are swayed by human prayers,
look this once upon us, if our goodness deserves it,   690
and help us, Father, give us a sign in confirmation.'

"The old man had scarcely spoken when a crash of thunder
resounded on the left, and gliding through the heavens,
a shooting star made a trail of light appear in the gloom.
We watch it as it gleams above the palace roof   695
until it buries its brilliance in the forest of Ida.
A long and luminous furrow shines across the night,
and all about the place there is a smell of sulphur.
My father's reluctance left him when he saw the omen.
He rose, invoked the gods, and adored the holy star: 700
" 'Now, now no more delay: I follow where you lead.
Paternal gods, protect my house, protect my grandson.
This omen came from you and Troy is in your hands.
I yield, my son, and no longer refuse to go with you.'
He finished. More clearly now we heard the roaring flames: 705
the conflagration echoed nearer through the city.

" 'Come, dear father,' I said, 'place yourself upon my neck.
My shoulders will carry you; the burden will not be heavy.
Wherever Fate shall lead us, we live or perish together.
Little Iülus will take my hand and walk beside me;   710
Creusa will follow my footsteps a pace or two behind.
And you, my servants, give heed and remember what I tell you:
there is a mound and an old deserted temple of Ceres
as you leave the city. Nearby is an ancient cypress
preserved for many years by our ancestral religion.   715
This will be our rendezvous: here we will gather.
You, my father, take the household gods and relics:
I may not touch them yet, for my hands are fresh from slaughter,
nor may I lay these bloodstained hands on sacred objects
until I have washed in flowing streams . . .'   720
    "Thus I spoke, and spread upon my neck and shoulders
the skin of a tawny lion; and with this for protection
I bent to lift my burden. Little Iülus followed,
his hand in mine; with unequal steps he kept beside me.
My wife was behind us, and thus we passed into the shadows.   725
And I, whom lately no kind of weapon had moved or frightened,
unterrified by thronging hosts of Greek invaders,
now am afraid of every breath, of every sound,
fearing alike for my companion and my burden.
    "Now we approached the gates, and thought we had escaped,   730
when suddenly there came to my ears the sound of footsteps
of many men. My father, peering through the gloom,
cried: 'Flee, my son, my son! Already they are upon us!
I see the gleam of their shields and the shining of their bronze!'
    "But now some hostile god bereft me of my senses: 735
I turned away from the road, traversed unfamiliar streets
in my confusion. Meanwhile my wife Creusa, alas!
malignant fates snatched her away from her wretched husband,
or else she lost her way, or fell from sheer fatigue.
I know not. All I know is: I never saw her again.   740
I did not even look for her, or think of looking
until we had reached the ancient mound and shrine of Ceres.
But when we reached the rendezvous at last, one was missing,

missing from her companions, her husband, and her child.
What man, what god did I not accuse in my deep despair? 745
What sight more cruel was seen in the overthrow of Troy?
I left my friends to guard Ascanius and Anchises
and the Trojan gods, having hid them in a winding glen,
while I myself returned to Troy in my shining armor,
determined to retrace my steps, to renew my danger, 750
to offer once again my head to all the perils.

"First of all I regained the walls and the dark gateway
from which I had departed; scanning every footprint,
I tried to trace my path with searching eyes in the darkness.
My soul was filled with horror and terrified by the silence. 755
I tried my house to see if perchance she had gone there;
the Greeks had poured into it and occupied the place.
The hungry fire was borne aloft by the wind, and reached
the very rooftops: the towering flames surge into the air.
I passed the citadel and looked at Priam's palace, 760
and there, besides the columns of Juno's deserted temple,
old Phoenix and accursed Ulysses, the chosen sentries,
were guarding the loot. And all about were the Trojan treasures,
snatched from the burning temples: tables of the gods,
cups of solid gold were heaped, and stolen garments. 765
Little children and their mothers, trembling, stood nearby
in long and silent lines . . .
I even dared to raise my voice and cry in the darkness,
filling the streets with shouting: I called and called again,
repeating, all in vain, the beloved name of Creusa. 770
And as I sought and endlessly rushed from house to house,
a melancholy spectre appeared before my eyes,
the ghost of my Creusa herself, but larger than life.
I could not move, my hair stood up, my voice was choked.
She spoke these words to me, seeking to still my fears: 775
'Why abandon yourself to this mad passion of sorrow,
O my dear husband? For these things could not have happened
unless the gods had willed them so. It is not fated
for you to take Creusa hence: Jove will not allow it.

A long exile awaits you, and weary stretches of sea.   780
At last, one day, you will arrive in the land of Hesperia,
where Lydian Tiber gently flows through the fertile fields.
There good fortune awaits you: prosperity and a kingdom,
and royal bride. So weep no longer for your Creusa.
At least I shall never be a prize of the Myrmidons   785
or Dolopians, or a slave to haughty Grecian women,
I, a Trojan, daughter-in-law of royal Venus.
The mighty Mother-Goddess keeps me in this land.
And now farewell, and never cease to love our son.'
    "She spoke; I wept and wished to say so many things,   790
but she departed and vanished into empty air.
Three times I tried to put my arms around her neck;
three times the image, vainly grasped, fled from my hands,
intangible as the wind, elusive as a dream.

    "At last the night was spent, and I returned to my friends,   795
and here I found, to my surprise, a vast assembly
of new recruits had now arrived: there were men and mothers,
a people prepared for exile, a miserable crowd.
From all directions they came, in heart and resources ready
for any land or any sea where I chose to lead them.   800
And now the Morning Star rose over Ida's ridges
and ushered in the day. The Greeks now held the city;
for us there was no hope. I yielded to my fate
and lifting up my aged father, I sought the mountains."

'End of Book II.'

BOOK III

THE WANDERINGS OF AENEAS

"After it pleased the gods to uproot Asia's power
and Priam's blameless people; when proud Ilium had fallen,
and all of Neptune's city lay smoking on the ground,
divine portents drove us into a scattered exile,
to seek deserted lands. And so we built a fleet   5
below Antandros and the hills of Phrygian Ida,
not knowing where the Fates would lead us, where we could settle.
We mustered our forces together. Summer had scarcely begun
when Father Anchises told us to spread the sails to Fate.
Weeping, I left the shores and harbors of my country,   10
the fields that had once been Troy. I put to sea, an exile,
with my companions, my son, and the divine Penates.

"The land of Mars with outspread fields is at a distance,
cultivated by Thracians; once Lycurgus' kingdom,
an old ally of Troy, and having kindred Penates,   15
while Fortune was with us. Hither I sail; on the curving shore
I build my first ramparts (but Destiny was against me),
and call the place Aeneadae, from my own name.
I was making sacrifice to my mother Venus
and other gods, to bless the undertaking; to Jupiter   20
I was slaughtering a snow-white bull upon the shore.
There chanced to be a mound nearby with cornel-bushes
on its top, and bristling shafts of myrtle spears.
I approached and tried to tear the leafy branches
from the earth, as decoration for the altar,   25
when lo! I see a portent terrible and wondrous:
for as the tree is torn away from its broken roots,
dark drops of blood come oozing down to stain the earth
with streaming gore; an icy terror shakes my limbs,

and all my blood runs cold with horror in my veins.   30
Again I try to pluck a second reluctant branch,
to find the hidden reasons for this mystery,
and once again dark blood comes flowing from the bark.
Shaken in my mind, I pray to the woodland Nymphs,
and Mars Gradivus, protector of the Thracian lands,   35
to bring the omen to a favorable issue.
I make a third attempt, with even greater force,
struggling on my knees against the stubborn ground.
I hear (shall I speak or be silent?) a pitiable groan
arising from the mound, and a voice comes to my ears: 40
" 'Why do you wound a miserable wretch, Aeneas?
spare me in the tomb: keep your hands from sacrilege.
For I am a Trojan, not a stranger, and this blood
is human. Flee from this cruel land and greedy shore;
for I am Polydorus. An iron crop of spears   45
transfixed my body; similar spears have taken root here.'
"Then my mind was overcome with fear and doubt:
I could not move, my hair stood up, my voice was choked.
Unhappy Priam once had sent this Polydorus
secretly to Thrace, with a great treasure of gold,   50
to be brought up by the Thracian king, for he mistrusted
the Trojan arms; he saw his city besieged and surrounded.
The Thracian, when Troy was conquered and her fortunes failed,
went over to the side of victorious Agamemnon,
broke the laws of Heaven, murdered Polydorus,   55
and stole the gold by force. To what crimes men are driven
by the cursèd lust for gold! When the terror left me,
I showed the omens to the leaders of my people,
Anchises first, and asked them to tell me their opinion.
They all agreed: we must leave the accursed land at once,   60
polluter of hospitality, and set sail again.
We perform the funeral rites for Polydorus, and build
a massive tomb of earth, with altars for the Manes,
with dark fillets for mourning, and black cypresses.
The Trojan women stand nearby with streaming hair.   65
Foaming bowls of warm milk are offered, and cups of blood

from sacrificial victims; we lay the spirit to rest
in the tomb; with loud voices we say a last farewell.

"As soon as we can trust the sea, and the winds are calm,
and the gently whispering breezes call us to the deep,   70
my companions launch the waiting ships and fill the shore.
We leave the harbor; lands and cities fade from sight.
In the middle of the sea there is a holy island[1]
beloved by the Nereids' mother and the Aegean Neptune;
which, as it was wandering about the coasts and shores,   75
Apollo the Archer bound to high Myconos and Gyaros;
an immovable home for men, scorning the winds and waves.
Hither we sail, and we are welcomed in the harbor.
We disembark and pay homage to Apollo's city.
Anius, king of the people and also priest of Phoebus,   80
his temples bound with fillets and the sacred laurel,
greets us, recognizing his old comrade Anchises.
We join our hands in friendship and enter under his roof.
I went into the old stone temple and I prayed:
"'Give us a home, Apollo; give walls to weary men,   85
descendants, a lasting city. Preserve this second Troy,
left by the Danaans and pitiless Achilles.
Whom shall we follow? Where can we go? Where fix our abode?
Father, grant us an omen, and come into our hearts.'
"Scarcely had I spoken: the ground began to tremble,   90
the threshold and laurels of the god, the entire mountain;
the tripod gave a groan as the doors of the shrine came open.
We all fell to the ground and a voice came to our ears:
'Enduring Trojans, the land which first gave you your birth,
your ancestors' land, shall now receive and welcome you   95
into its fertile fields. Seek your ancient mother:
there the house of Aeneas shall rule over all the world,
his children's children, and those who will be born to them.'
Thus Phoebus spoke. A shout arose of jubilation.
We ask each other which are the walls the god has told of;   100

---

[1]Delos, the legendary birthplace of Apollo.

whither does Phoebus tell the wanderers to return?
Then my father, remembering tales from men of old,
says: 'Listen, Trojan leaders, and learn from me your hopes:
Jove's island Crete lies in the middle of the sea;
there is Mount Ida and the cradle of our race.   105
There are a hundred cities, there is fertile land.
If I remember rightly, Teucer, our first ancestor,
sailed from Crete to the Trojan shore and chose the site
for his new kingdom; Ilium and the citadel
of Pergamum had not yet been built; they lived in the valleys.   110
From Crete came Mother Cybele, Corybantes' cymbals,
the grove of Ida and the secret mysteries,
and lions yoked to the chariot of the Mighty Mother.
Come, let us follow where the god's commandment leads us:
let us appease the winds and seek the land of Cnossus.   115
It is not far away; if Jupiter favors us,
in three days we shall anchor our ships on Cretan shores.'
    "So he spoke, and on the altar he slaughtered victims:
a bull to Neptune and a bull to glorious Apollo,
a black sheep to the Storm God, a white one to the Zephyrs.   120
A rumor flies about that Idomeneus, the ruler,
has left his fatherland, in exile: Crete is deserted,
the houses empty of foes, the dwellings all abandoned.
We leave Ortygia's harbor and fly across the sea,
skirting the hills of Naxos' revels, and green Donysa,   125
Olearos and snowy Paros, the Cyclades
scattered over the sea, and many turbulent straits.
The sailors raise their voices in varied competition;
the crews keep shouting: 'On to Crete, the land of our fathers!'
A wind springs up astern and follows us as we go.   130
At last we glide to the ancient shores of the Curetes.
Avidly I begin to build new walls for a city
and call it Pergamum, and urge the happy people
to love their hearths and raise a lofty citadel.

    "The ships had only just been drawn up on the beaches;   135
the youth were occupied with weddings and with farming,

and I was giving laws and homes, when suddenly,
out of a poisonous sky, a pestilence fell upon us,
attacking men and trees and crops, bringing death to all.
The men gave up sweet life, or dragged sick bodies about,   140
the Dog-Star scorched the fields and dried up all the crops;
the grass was parched, the harvest denied us sustenance.
My father urged us to retrace our path to Delos,
to ask the oracle of Apollo for indulgence,
and learn what end there would be for all our weary labors,   145
and where we should seek aid, and whither turn our course.
    "Now it was night, the time when all creatures are asleep.
The holy images of the gods, the Trojan Penates,
whom I had brought away with me from burning Troy,
came to me in my sleep and stood before my eyes,   150
clearly visible in a flood of brilliant light,
where the moon was shining through the inset windows.
They spoke to me, and with these words removed my fears:
'Apollo sends us of his own will to your very door,
and what he would have told you at Delos, he tells you now.   155
We followed you and your arms when Troy was consumed by
                                                            flames,
and on your ships we came across the swelling sea;
we shall exalt to Heaven your grandsons yet unborn,
and give empire to their city. Build great walls
for great men; do not fear the long labor of flight.   160
You must change your dwellings, for Delian Apollo
never intended you to settle here in Crete.
There is a land—the Greeks call it Hesperia—
an ancient land, mighty in arms and rich in soil.
Oenotrians inhabited it, but now men say   165
that their descendants call it Italy, after their king.
That will be our home, for Dardanus came from there
and father Iasius, from whom the Trojans are descended.
Arise now; go and tell your aged father, gladly,
these unmistakable tidings: he must seek Corythus   170
and the Ausonian fields, for Jove denies you Crete.'
    "I was thunderstruck at the vision and voice of the gods

(for it was not only a dream: I recognized
their faces and hair and fillets and their living expressions
and straightway an icy sweat came trickling down my limbs).   175
I leaped out of my bed and raised my hands to the sky
and lifted my voice and offered up a pure libation
upon the hearth. When I had performed this duty
I gladly told Anchises of the whole event.
He saw the double meaning of the twofold race,   180
and how he had been mistaken about the ancient lands.
He said: 'My son, harassed by Trojan destiny,
this is exactly what Cassandra told me once:
I remember her foretelling our people's fate;
she often named Hesperia and Italy.   185
But who could believe the Trojans would reach Hesperia's shores,
and who ever paid attention to what Cassandra said?
Now let us yield to Phoebus and follow better fates.'

    "So he spoke and we joyfully obeyed his words.
We left these homes as well—a few were left behind—   190
and spread our sails; the hollow ships plied the vast sea.
When we were on the deep and out of sight of land,
with only sea and sky to be seen in all directions,
a black cloud suddenly came looming overhead,
bringing night and tempest and stirring up the waves;   195
the winds disturb the waters and mighty billows break;
the ships are scattered by the storm over all the ocean;
clouds blot out the day; rainy darkness hides the sky,
and lightning flashes crackle through the broken clouds.
Driven off our course, we wander in the blind waves.   200
Even Palinurus could not tell night from day,
nor could he plot his course in the middle of the ocean.
For three uncertain days and as many starless nights
we wandered, shrouded in darkness, over the raging sea.
But on the fourth day land appeared upon the horizon,   205
with distant mountains; wisps of smoke were curling skyward.
The sails are lowered, we bend to the oars; without delay
the sailors churn the water and sweep the sea into foam.

"Saved from the ocean, I landed on the Strophades
(that is their Greek name), islands in the Ionian Sea,   210
the dwelling-places of the terrible Celaeno
and the other Harpies, after Phineus' palace
was closed to them, and they left their former tables in fear.
No monster is more grim, no curse from Heaven more awful,
no plague more fierce has ever arisen from Stygian waves.   215
These Harpies are birds with maidens' faces, and they drop
disgusting filth over everything; their hands are clawed,
their faces always pale with hunger . . .

"As we are carried thither and we enter the harbor,
behold! fine herds of cattle are grazing on the plain,   220
and flocks of goats on the grass with no one tending them.
We rush upon them with drawn swords, calling the gods
and Jove himself to share the booty; then on the beach
we raise the couches and we feast on the rich banquet.
But suddenly the Harpies come down from the mountains,   225
swooping fiercely, flapping their wings with frightful clatter;
they snatch the food, befouling everything with their touch.
Their raucous screams are mingled with a hideous stench.
A second time, in a recess under a hollow cliff
closely surrounded by trees and bristling shady bushes,   230
we spread the tables and rekindle fire on the altar;
again from out of the sky and from their hidden den,
the raucous flock hover about their prey with their claws,
and spoil the food with their mouths. I call my friends to arms
and tell them to do battle with the frightful creatures.   235
Quickly they do as they are bid, concealing swords
in the deep grass and hiding their shields away from sight.
When next the Harpies gathered, swooping and screaming down
over the curving shore, Misenus sounded his trumpet
from his high watch-point. My comrades rush to the strange battle,   240
trying with their swords to wound the filthy sea-birds.
But they could not feel the blows on their feathers, nor any wounds
upon their backs. They fly away on rapid wings,
leaving the half-eaten food and filthy droppings.
But one, Celaeno, perches on a lofty rock,   245

an ill-boding prophetess, and these are the words she screams:
  " 'So you wage war, you Trojans, over stolen cattle
and butchered bullocks? For these you are prepared to fight
and drive the blameless Harpies from their father's land?
Then listen to my words and take them to your hearts.   250
What the Great Father told to Phoebus, and Phoebus Apollo
told to me, I, the eldest Fury, now tell you:
you are seeking Italy: wafted by the winds
you will arrive in Italy and enter its harbors,
but never will you surround with walls your promised city,   255
until fierce hunger and your sin in attacking us
have driven you to gnaw and eat your very tables.'
  "She finished speaking and flew away into the forest.
The blood of my companions froze with sudden fear.
Their spirits flagged, and now, no longer by force of arms   260
but with vows and prayers, they all wish me to sue for peace,
whether these are goddesses or fierce, dread birds.
And Father Anchises, on the beach, with outstretched hands
calls the powerful gods and proclaims the sacrifice:
'O gods, ward off these threats and turn this doom away,   265
and graciously spare a pious folk.' He tells the men
to rip the hawsers from the shore and loosen the sheets.
The winds fill out the sails. We fly through foaming waves
upon the course directed by the winds and pilot.
Now amid the waves the wooded Zacynthus appears,   270
Dulichium and Same and craggy Neritus.
We pass the cliffs of Ithaca, Laertes' realm,
cursing the land that has given birth to cruel Ulysses.
Soon we see the cloud-capped peaks of Mount Leucata,
and the shrine of Apollo, dreaded by all sailors.   275
We wearily make for port and approach the little town.
The anchors are cast from the prows; the sterns rest on the shore.

  "Having at last arrived on land, beyond our hopes,
we cleanse ourselves for Jove and kindle votive altars.
On Actium's shore we celebrate the Trojan games.   280
The men all strip, and glistening with olive oil,

engage in native wrestling, glad to have escaped
so many Argive towns, glad to have fled the foe.
Meanwhile the sun revolves in its mighty annual course
and icy winter makes the waters rough with winds.   285
A shield of hollow bronze, once carried by great Abas,
I fasten to the pillars, marking it with a verse:

'AENEAS DEDICATES THESE ARMS FROM VICTORIOUS
                                                GREEKS.'

I gave commands to man the benches and leave the port.
They lash the sea in rivalry and sweep the water.   290
Soon we see the heights of Phaeacia recede;
we skirt the shore of Epirus, and come into port
at Chaonia, and the high citadel of Buthrotum.
    "And here an incredible rumor comes to fill our ears:
Helenus, Priam's son, is reigning over Greeks,   295
succeeding to the throne of Pyrrhus the Aeacid,
and Andromache once more is married to a Trojan.
I was amazed and burned with desire to see Helenus
and speak with him and learn of his remarkable fate.
I left the harbor and walked away from the shore and fleet,   300
when by chance I met Andromache herself
in a grove nearby the city, at a river 'Simois,'
offering libations to the ghost of Hector,
calling his spirit at an empty mound in the turf,
where she had built twin altars as a place of mourning.   305
When she saw me approaching with my Trojan weapons,
she was dazed and distracted by the marvellous sight;
she stiffened as she looked at me; the warmth left her bones,
she swooned, and only after a time was she able to speak:
'Is it really you? Do I truly behold Aeneas?   310
Son of a goddess, are you alive? Or if you are dead,
where is Hector?' She spoke, and shedding floods of tears,
filled the place with her laments. I could hardly speak
to her in her frenzy; I gasped a few interrupted words:
    " 'Indeed I live, but it is a life of great afflictions.   315
Have no doubts. For I am real, and not a ghost.

Alas, what evil fates have befallen you, deprived
of such a husband? Or what good fortune is yours,
Hector's Andromache? Are you still married to Pyrrhus?'
  "She lowered her eyes and spoke to me in a soft voice: 320
'O happy above all others, Priam's maiden daughter,
slain at the enemy's tomb beneath the walls of Troy,
Polyxena, who never was awarded by lot,
who never went, a captive, to the conqueror's bed!
I left burning Troy and sailed across the seas,   325
enduring the youthful insolence of Achilles' son,
bearing children in slavery. But afterwards,
seeking Leda's Hermione and a Spartan marriage,
Pyrrhus gave me to Helenus: one slave to another.
Orestes, however, burning with love for his stolen wife,   330
and driven to frenzy by the Furies of his crimes,
took him unawares and killed him at the altar.
On Neoptolemus' death, a part of his kingdom
came to Helenus, who named the fields Chaonian,
calling the region Chaonia after Trojan Chaon,   335
and built a Pergamum and Trojan citadel.
But you, Aeneas—what winds, what fates have brought you here?
What god has driven you, unknowing, to our shores?
What of your son Ascanius? Does he live and breathe?
Whom now, indeed, when Troy . . .   340
Does he still remember and love his mother Creusa?
Do his father Aeneas and his uncle Hector
arouse in him ancestral virtues and manly spirit?'
  "She spoke, and poured out floods of bitter tears and laments.
But Helenus, the son of Priam, now approached,   345
coming from the city with a goodly crowd.
He recognized his friends and led us to the gates,
rejoicing, but interrupting every word with tears.
As I advanced, I saw a little 'Troy,' and a replica
of 'Pergamum' and a little river called the 'Xanthus,'   350
and I embraced the portals of the 'Scaean Gates'.
My Trojan companions all rejoiced in the friendly town.
The king received them all in an ample colonnade.

Libations are poured to Bacchus in the midst of the hall.
They hold the goblets; the banquet is served on golden dishes.   355

"Now many days had passed. The breezes called the sails.
The canvases are filled and belly out in the wind.
I go to Helenus the seer with this request:
'O Trojan interpreter of the gods, who know the will
of Phoebus, the tripods, the Clarian laurel and the stars,   360
the language of the birds, and all the wingèd omens,
tell me (for the gods have spoken of my voyage
and all the oracles have told me of Italy,
the distant land that I must seek out and explore;
only Celaeno the Harpy foretold an evil doom,   365
and threatened dreadful anger and ill-omened famine):
which dangers shall I first avoid? What course shall I follow,
if I am to overcome all these dire afflictions?'
"Helenus slaughtered bullocks in the usual manner,
and begged the gods' indulgence and unbound the fillets   370
from his sacred brows; and led me by the hand
to Apollo's temple and the presence of the god
and spoke these words from his divinely inspired mouth:
"'Son of a goddess, since it has been clearly proven
that you travel across the sea by divine consent,   375
(for such is the order of things that Jupiter decrees)
I shall unfold to you a few things out of many,
so that you may more safely traverse the seas, and settle
in the Ausonian harbor, for the Fates forbid
that Helenus should know more, and Juno stays my speech.   380
First of all: Italy, which you think is very near,
whose neighboring ports, all ignorant, you prepare to enter,
—a long and pathless path intervenes, with weary stretches
of land; and first you must sail around Trinacria's[2] waves,
and in your vessels cross the salty Ausonian sea,   385
the Infernal Lakes, and Aeaean Circe's island as well,
before you can build your city in a safe domain.

---

[2]The Homeric name for Sicily (lit. "Three-cornered").

I shall give you a sign; remember it in your mind:
when in your anxiety, near secluded waters,
you find a sow beneath the oaks by a river's bank,   390
newly delivered of a litter of thirty offspring
(and both the mother and the suckling young are white),
this is the site of your city; here you may rest from your labors.
  " 'And do not fear the gnawing of your tables to come;
the Fates will find a way, and Apollo, if you call him.   395
But the Italian lands that border on this sea—
the nearer coasts, washed by the same tides as our kingdom—
avoid them, Aeneas! for evil Greeks inhabit them.
Here the Narycian Locrians have built a city.
And Cretan Idomeneus has peopled the plain with soldiers;   400
there is the small Petelia, Philoctetes' town,
the harbor of Meliboea with its encircling walls.
when you have passed them all, and your ships are safely anchored,
and votive altars have been raised upon the shore,
you must veil your head and hair with cloth of purple   405
lest any hostile face among the sacred fires
intrude and spoil the omens of the sacrifice.
These are the rites that you and your comrades must keep
and may your descendants show the same chaste piety.
But when, on your departure, the winds have carried you   410
to Sicily's coast, and the Pelorian narrows open,
seek the lands on the left side, and the waters too,
though it be longer; avoid the lands and seas on the right.
These lands, men say, were torn by violent convulsions
(such changes can occur in the long span of ages)   415
and separated, when the two lands were formerly one;
the ocean's might came in between, and with its waves
it cut Hesperia off from the coast of Sicily:
a narrow strait now washes the severed fields and cities,
with Scylla on the right, and implacable Charybdis   420
on the left; and from the depths of her gurgling whirlpool
three times each day she sucks the waves into her abyss,
and then she spews them forth, striking the stars with spray.
But Scylla hides unseen within her gloomy cavern;

thrusting forth her heads she drags ships onto the reefs. 425
Above, her shape is human: a maiden down to the waist,
fair of bosom; below, she is an enormous whale
with tails of dolphins growing from the belly of wolves.
Better to circumnavigate the entire island,
turning at Cape Pachynus, redoubling your course, 430
than once to see the ugly Scylla in her cave,
the rocks resounding with the barks of the sea-green dogs.
   " 'Moreover, if Helenus is a wise and trustworthy seer,
and if Apollo has inspired him with the truth,
this one thing, O son of a goddess, I prophesy: 435
this before all else I tell you again and again:
Do not fail to worship Juno's mighty power.
Seek Juno's favor first with prayers and libations
and suppliant offerings, for then and only then
shall you leave Trinacria and come to Italy. 440
But when you do arrive in that land, go first to Cumae:
the sacred lakes and rustling forests of Avernus.
There you will see the frenzied prophetess in her cave,
who chants the oracles, writing down the words on leaves.
Whatever she has written on these leaves, the maiden 445
arranges carefully and stores away in the cavern;
and they remain in place, unmoved and undisturbed.
But when the door is opened and a light breeze stirs them,
the delicate leaves are scattered all around the cave;
the Sibyl never thinks to catch them as they flutter, 450
or to rearrange them into coherent form;
therefore questions go unanswered and men are angry.
Do not be so concerned about the long delay
(no matter how much your friends complain, or your vessels call
for winds to fill the swelling sails and continue the voyage) 455
that you fail to see the Sibyl, and to request her
to chant the responses herself, and willingly open her lips.
For she will tell you of the peoples of Italy,
the future wars, and how to flee and withstand each labor;
if you beseech her well, she will grant a prosperous passage. 460
These are all the warnings that I am allowed to give you.

Now go, and by your deeds, exalt our Troy to Heaven.'
"When the seer had spoken thus with friendly words,
he commanded that gifts of heavy gold and ivory
be carried to the ships. The hulls are loaded down 465
with weighty silver and with cauldrons from Dodona;
a breastplate woven with a three-ply chain of gold;
and a magnificent helmet, pointed, with crested plumes,
which Neoptolemus had worn. My father, too,
has gifts. Helenus gives us horses and guides . . . 470
he gives us weapons and oarsmen to complete the crews.
"Meanwhile Anchises tells us to make ready the sails
so that we will be prepared for favorable winds.
The seer of Phoebus speaks to him with great respect:
'Anchises, a husband worthy of the goddess Venus, 475
care of the gods, twice rescued from the Trojan ruins,
Italy is before you: seize it with full sails!
But you must sail around beyond the nearest shore:
the Ausonia that Apollo reveals is far away.
Go, blessed in the love of your son. Why should I say more 480
and with my words delay the favoring South Wind?'
Andromache as well was saddened by our departure
and brought embroidered garments woven with threads of gold,
and a Phrygian scarf for Ascanius, a worthy present!
She loaded him with gifts of cloth, and spoke to him: 485
'Take these, my child, remembrances of my handiwork,
witnesses of the love of Hector's Andromache;
the last gifts you will ever receive from your relations.
O sole surviving relic of my Astyanax—
your eyes and hands and face—they all remind me of him, 490
and if he had been allowed to live, he would now be your age.'
"As I spoke words of farewell, my eyes were full of tears:
'Live happily, you whose fortunes are already achieved!
We are being called from one fate to another,
but you have earned your rest: no further seas to plow, 495
and no elusive Ausonian fields for you to seek.
You have your second Xanthus and another Troy
which you have built, under better auspices, I pray,

and well beyond the reach of Greek hostility.
If ever I reach the Tiber and its neighboring fields,   500
and if I see the citadels destined for my people,
your land and mine will be allied as sister-cities:
Epirus and Hesperia, with a common ancestor,
and common sorrows, we shall make one Troy in spirit:
this bond will be transmitted to our children's children.'   505

"We sailed across the waves, near the Ceraunian cliffs;
there is the road to Italy and the shortest passage.
The sun set; and the mountains were enveloped in darkness.
Drawing lots for oars, we disembarked and rested
near to the sea; we relaxed our bodies on the beach   510
and slumber came and flowed into our weary limbs.
Night, driven by the Hours, had not yet reached her mid-point,
when the alert Palinurus leaps up from his couch
exploring the winds, and straining his ears for the slightest breeze.
He looks at all the constellations in the sky,   515
Arcturus and the rainy Hyades and the twin Bears,
the hunter Orion, resplendent with his golden armor.
When he sees that all is calm and the sky serene,
he gives a signal from the stern: we break our camp,
and venture on our way, and spread our wingèd sails.   520
And now the rosy Dawn had put the stars to flight,
when we beheld afar, hills and a low-lying coast.
'Italy!' Anchises is the first to cry out.
'Italy!' the sailors echo with joyous shouts.
Then Father Anchises puts garlands in a massive bowl   525
and fills it with pure wine and calls upon the gods,
standing on the lofty stern . . .
'Gods who rule the seas and earth and winter storms,
grant us favoring winds and waft us with your breath!'

"A breeze springs up behind; a harbor lies ahead.   530
A temple comes into view: Minerva's citadel.
My comrades furl the sails and swing the bows to land.
There is a harbor shaped like a bow by Eastern tides

with jutting crags all foaming in the salty spray,
hiding the inner part; two walls come down like arms.   535
The temple itself is at some distance from the shore.
Here, the first omen: I see four horses on the grass,
grazing at large over the plain, as white as snow.
Anchises said: 'You bring us war, O Stranger-land!
For horses are a sign of war: these herds mean war.   540
And yet,' he said, 'horses are sometimes also yoked
to chariots, and bear the reins and bit in peace and concord.
So there is also hope of peace.' We pray to Pallas,
goddess of clashing arms, who welcomed our first approach.
We veil our heads with Phrygian cloaks before the altar,   545
and following the advice that Helenus had given,
we worship Argive Juno with due sacrifice.

"As soon as we had performed the votive offering,
we point our vessels' yardarms out to windward again,
and leave the Grecian land and the suspected fields.   550
Next is the Gulf of Tarentum, Hercules' town, they say,
and opposite the temple of Lacinian Juno
and Caulon's fort, and ship-destroying Scylaceum.
In the distance Trinacrian Aetna rose from the sea.
We heard from afar the crashing of the ocean's waves,   555
the pounding of the billows breaking on the shore,
the shallow water hissing on the sandy beach.
Father Anchises said: 'This must surely be Charybdis:
these are the rocks and cliffs that Helenus warned us of,
so free yourselves, my men, and bend to the oars together.'   560
The men all did as they were told, and first Palinurus
swung the groaning prow to the left amid the waves;
we all followed him, with oars and sails to the left.
We are raised aloft to the skies on top of the rolling waves;
and sink down, as the wave recedes, toward Hades' realm.   565
Three times the cliffs and caves sent off their echoing cry,
three times we saw the foaming spray and dripping stars.
The sun set and the wind died down. We all were weary;
in our ignorance we drifted toward the Cyclopes.

"There is a harbor, safe from the approach of winds   570
a spacious haven, but Mount Aetna thunders nearby,
and now and then an inky cloud comes belching forth,
smoking with pitchy whirlwinds and with blazing sparks,
and globes of fire fly to the heavens and lick the stars;
and rocks and mountains' ripped-out entrails are vomited forth,   575
and streams of molten lava burst out with a roar;
the volcano seethes and boils down to its very depths.
The story is that Enceladus' thunderstricken form
lies beneath the mighty mass of this Mount Aetna;
hence the flames that breathe forth from the ruptured furnace,   580
and every time the weary giant turns around,
all Sicily groans and trembles and hides the sky in smoke.

   "That night we hid in the woods, afraid of monstrous things,
nor did we know the reason for the awful noises,
for neither were there any stars nor constellations,   585
but the whole sky was overcast with gloomy mist;
the moon was hidden by the overhanging clouds.
But when the Morning Star arose the following day,
and when Aurora dissipated the humid shadows,
suddenly out of the woods there came an unknown man,   590
emaciated with hunger, piteous to behold,
he stretched out his hands, in suppliant fashion, on the beach.
We looked at him. He was hideous, squalid, with unkempt beard,
covered all over with thorns. But still he was a Greek,
one who had marched with his father's arms against our city.   595
When he saw the Trojan weapons and our garments
from a distance, he was frightened and checked his step,
but then he rushed headlong to meet us on the beach,
and cried, with tears and prayers: 'I beg you, by the stars,
by all the gods in Heaven, and by the air we breathe,   600
to take me away, Trojans! It does not matter where,
but only take me away! I know I am a Greek;
I freely admit that I came bearing arms to Troy.
For this fault, if I have done you such injuries,
cut me up and scatter me in the waves, or drown me: 605
if I must die, I had rather it were by human hands!'

"He finished and clasped my knees and clung there grovelling.
We urged him to tell us who he was, and of what race;
what sufferings he had undergone at Fortune's hands.
Soon afterward my father Anchises gave his hand   610
to the young man, and reassured him with this pledge.
He puts aside his terror and he makes this answer:
" 'I come from Ithaca, a companion of poor Ulysses.
My name is Achaemenides; Adamastus my father
was poor (if only we had remained thus!); I sailed for Troy.   615
Here my friends in their haste to leave this cruel threshold
forgot me and left me here in the Cyclops' monstrous cavern.
It is a house of bloody banquets, stained with gore,
huge and dark within. The Cyclops is a monster,
towering to the stars. O gods, keep this plague from earth!   620
No man can dare to look at him or speak to him:
he feeds on entrails and black blood of wretched mortals.
I myself have seen him seize two of my comrades
with his monstrous hand, as he lay there in his cave,
and smash them on a rock till the floor was swimming with blood.   625
I saw him chewing their limbs all dripping and clotted with gore,
and their flesh, still warm, was quivering between his teeth.
But not with impunity, for Ulysses would not allow it;
even in such dire straits he remained true to himself.
For when the Cyclops, gorged with food and immersed in wine,   630
laid down his head and stretched across the cavern's floor,
and in his sleep he vomited gore and morsels of food
and blood and wine all mixed together, we prayed to the gods,
and drew our lots, and then we all surrounded him
and with a sharpened stake, we pierced his one huge eye   635
that lay deep-set beneath the giant's savage forehead,
an eye as big as an Argive shield or Apollo's sun!
And this is how we gladly avenged our comrades' ghost.
" 'But you poor strangers, flee! make haste to escape from here
and cut your hawsers from the shore . . .   640
For there are a hundred other monstrous Cyclopes
exactly like Polyphemus who milks his fleecy sheep
penned in the rocky cavern; they live by the curving shore,

these giants, and they wander all about the high mountains.
This is the third time the moon has filled her horns with light   645
since I began to drag my life out in these woods,
the lonely haunts of savage beasts, and from a rock
I saw the giants and trembled as they walked and spoke.
A meager fare has been mine: berries and stony cornels
and branches feed me, and grasses torn up by the roots.   650
Scanning the sea all over, at last I saw your ships
approaching the shore, and so, whoever you might be,
I gave myself up; enough to have escaped these monsters;
here I am: you may kill me any way you wish.' "
    "Hardly had he spoken when on the mountain's top   655
we saw the giant himself, the shepherd Polyphemus,
moving his bulk among his sheep, seeking the shore:
a horrid monster, hideous, immense, and blind.
He held a pine trunk in his hand to guide his steps.
His fleecy sheep, his only joy, accompanied him;   660
they were his only consolation . . . .
As soon as he reached the water's edge and felt the waves,
he washed away the oozing blood from his sightless eye,
gnashing his teeth and groaning. He strode into the sea,
but the water did not even wet his towering sides.   665
We hastened from the place in terror, taking with us
the worthy suppliant. We silently cut the cables
and bent to the oars and swept the waves in competition.
The giant heard us and he moved toward the sound.
But when he realized that he could never catch us,   670
that even he could never wade the Ionian Sea,
he gave a frightful bellow that made the waters shudder.
The whole of Italy was terrified by the sound
and Aetna gave an answering roar from its hollow caverns.
    "The tribe of Cyclopes, roused from the woods and mountains,   675
came running to the harbor and crowded along the beach.
We saw them there with their single glaring eyes, frustrated,
the Brothers of Aetna—their heads went towering to the sky,
a horrible assembly; as on the mountain top
the lofty oak trees or cone-bearing cypresses   680

stand in a line: a forest of Jove or grove of Diana.
In our headlong terror we flee, it does not matter whither.
We spread our sails to whatsoever wind may come.
But Helenus had warned us of Scylla and Charybdis,
and of the danger of death that was equal on either side,   685
so we resolved to trim our sails and to turn back.
Happily, a North Wind came from Pelorus' strait.
I was carried past the harbor of Pantagias,
of living rock, and Megara's bay, and low-lying Thapsus.
Achaemenides, the friend of luckless Ulysses,   690
pointed out the landmarks where he had passed before.
    "In front of the Sicanian bay there is an island
near the wave-girt Plemyrium (or Ortygia,
as it was formerly called). Hither they say that Alpheus
the river of Elis, having run beneath the sea,   695
mingled with the Sicilian waves at Arethusa.
We worshipped the mighty gods of the place as we had been
                                                    bidden.
And next we came to the rich soil of marshy Helorus.
From there we skirt the projecting rocks and reefs of Pachynus,
and Camerina appears in the distance—the oracle said   700
it never could be moved—and then the plains of Gela
and Gela itself, which took its name from the laughing river.
Then the steep Acragas, which once was a breeding-place
for the most excellent horses, reveals its mighty walls.
Wafted by friendly winds, we pass the palmy Selinus   705
and Lilybaeum with its treacherous hidden rocks.
We find a harbor, the joyless shore of Drepanum
and here, alas! after so many stormy seas,
I lost my father Anchises, my greatest consolation;
here, O best of fathers, you left your weary son,   710
snatched in vain from so many dangers and disasters!
Even the prophet Helenus, with all his warnings,
did not foresee this sorrow, nor did the fierce Celaeno.
This was the last blow, the end of all voyages,
for as I sailed from Sicily, Fate drove me to Carthage."   715

Thus Father Aeneas, to an eagerly listening throng,
told of his wanderings, and of Heaven's destiny,
He ceased at last and was silent, for his tale was ended.

End of Book III

BOOK IV

THE TRAGEDY OF DIDO

But Dido, long since wounded by the shafts of love,
feeds the wound with her life-blood; consumed with secret fire,
she thinks of Aeneas' courage and his heroic deeds
and splendid race; his features and his words are implanted
in her heart; love's sickness grants her no repose.   5
    Next morning, just as Dawn was lighting up the land
with Phoebus' torch and dissipating the humid shadows,
she spoke, distracted, to her sympathetic sister:
"Anna my sister, I have had such frightful dreams!
What an extraordinary guest has come to our house: 10
he is so handsome, so brave—he has done such glorious deeds!
I really think he is descended from the gods,
for fear is the mark of lowly birth. Alas, what fates
pursue him—what wars and horrors he has seen and told!
Ah, if I had not sworn an inviolable oath   15
never again to let myself be bound in marriage
—since death betrayed and cheated me of my first love—
if I did not despise the thought of the marriage bed,
I might have yielded, perhaps, to weakness, for this one man;
for I confess, dear Anna, since Sychaeus' death,   20
since my brother stained the hearth with kindred blood,
this is the first and only man who ever moved me:
I recognize the traces of the ancient flame.
But I wish the earth would open up and swallow me,
or else that Jupiter would blast me with his lightning   25
and send me to the pallid shades of Erebus
before I violate my honor and break my oath.
The first man that I married took away my love;
well, let him have it: let him keep it in the grave."
So speaking, she bedewed her robe with bitter tears.   30

Anna said: "Dido, dearer to me than the light of day,
is your entire youth to be thus consumed with mourning?
Will you never know the joys of love and motherhood?
Do you really think dead ashes have regard for our oaths,
once they are in the tomb? No previous suitors, granted,   35
have won your heart, in Libya or Tyre: so be it;
you have refused Iarbas and other African chieftains,
but will you now reject a man you really love?
Have you forgotten what sort of people now surround you?
On one side the Gaetulians, a dauntless tribe,   40
unbridled Numidians, and inhospitable Syrtes,
and on the other, a barren thirsty desert-land,
and marauding Barcaeans. Need I remind you again
of all the threats of war your brother has been making?
By favor of the gods, I think, and with Juno's blessing   45
the winds have blown the Trojan vessels to these shores.
Just think, my sister, what a city you would have
with such a husband! Accompanied by Trojan arms
how high the Carthaginian fortunes then would rise!
Go, ask the gods for indulgence and make offerings.   50
Be hospitable; keep making new pretexts for delaying:
the savage winter; the stormy seas and rainy Orion;
his ships all battered by the tempest; unfriendly skies."
    These words gave fuel to the fire which burned poor Dido,
and put some hope in her anxious heart, and dissolved her shame. 55
First they went to the temples and sought peace at the altars;
according to ancient custom they sacrificed chosen rams
to Ceres the lawgiver, and to Phoebus, and Father Bacchus;
especially to Juno, preserver of marriage ties.
Holding a goblet in her hand, the beautiful Dido   60
pours the wine between the horns of a snowy heifer,
or walks with stately step around the bloodstained altars.
And at the newborn day, with gaping mouth she consults
the throbbing entrails of the sacrificial victims.
Alas, deceptive omens! How could vows and temples   65
aid such an impassioned soul? The fire devours her marrow:
the silent wound lives on and festers in her heart.

The miserable Dido burns and wanders distracted
throughout the city, like a doe unwittingly wounded
by a random arrow among the Cretan forests;   70
the shepherd who pursues her has left his shaft in her flesh
and as she flees amid the marshes and the woodlands
the fatal wingèd arrow still adheres to her side.
   She proudly takes Aeneas on a tour of Carthage
and shows him the walls, the wealth and resources of her city.   75
She starts to speak, but stops in the middle of a word.
When evening comes, she insists upon another banquet:
again she wants to hear about the fall of Troy,
and as he speaks, again she hangs on Aeneas' lips.
When they separate, and the pale moon begins to set,   80
and the declining stars are counseling men to slumber,
sad and lonely, she lies on the couch he just has left;
she sees his face and hears his voice, though he is not there.
She holds Ascanius on her lap (he looks so like his father!)
and tries thereby to deceive the love she dares not speak of.   85
The towers no longer rise; the soldiers drill no more;
the work on harbor and battlements comes to a stop,
and all construction on the walls is interrupted;
the scaffolds and the high machines are all deserted.

   As soon as Saturn's daughter, Jupiter's dear wife,   90
sees how Dido is afflicted: how her honor
cannot fight her madness, she goes and speaks to Venus:
"You and that son of yours have done a noble deed,
and won a glorious victory: you should be very proud—
two gods subduing with your tricks one helpless woman!   95
I know how you hate and suspect the walls of Carthage;
it has not escaped my notice how you fear us;
but where will it end? How long must we two go on fighting?
Would it not be better to arrange a marriage
and so have peace? You have accomplished what you wanted: 100
for Dido burns with love—the passion has entered her bones.
Let us unite our peoples: let us rule together.
Let Dido serve a Phrygian husband, and bring her subjects,

the Tyrians, into your power, as a dowry."
But Venus knew that Juno really had other plans,   105
and that she meant to divert to Africa the men
destined for Italy, and so she said: "I would be mad
to turn down such an offer and run the risk of war.
If only Fortune will approve the plan you propose.
For I am worried about the Fates: does Jupiter wish   110
the Tyrians and the Trojans to hold the city in common?
And does he want our peoples to be bound in alliance?
But you are his wife: you have the power to sway him with prayers;
begin, then, and I will follow." And royal Juno answered:
"I will arrange the matter: now listen to my words   115
and I will tell you briefly how it may be accomplished:
tomorrow morning when the sun begins to illumine
the dusky world, Aeneas and the unhappy Dido
propose to go a-hunting in a nearby forest.
Now, while the beaters sweep the marshes with their nets,   120
I shall send a gloomy cloud: a shower of hailstones
will fall upon them, and the sky will shake with thunder.
The party will be scattered by the murky darkness.
Aeneas and Dido will take shelter in a cave;
I shall also be present, and if I can rely   125
on your support, the two of them will be united
in everlasting wedlock." And Venus smiled at her,
unwilling to oppose her, agreeing with her ruse.

Meanwhile Dawn arose and left her bed in the Ocean,
and as the sun appeared, a selected band of youths   130
made ready their equipment—nets and snares and spears,
Massylian horsemen and keen-scented hunting dogs.
They all await the Queen in front of the royal palace
while she delays within. Her horse, in purple and gold,
paws the ground and champs at the bit with foaming mouth.   135
At last Dido appears, with a crowd of her retainers,
dressed in a Sidonian cloak with figured border;
with a golden quiver; her hair is bound in a golden knot,
her purple robe is fastened with a golden brooch.

Her Tyrian companions and the happy Iülus   140
advance together. Aeneas, handsomest of all,
joins forces with the Queen and takes his place at her side.
As when Apollo leaves behind the wintry Lycia
and Xanthus' stream, to see again his birthplace Delos;
renewing the dance; and mingling round his sacred altar,   145
the Cretans and Dryopes rage, and painted Agathyrses—
the god himself walks Cynthus' ridges; his flowing hair
is bound with tender garlands and diadem of gold—
his arrows clang on his shoulders—with the same sprightly step
Aeneas walked; the same beauty shone from his noble face.   150
And when they reached the mountains where the pathways ceased,
behold, wild goats were leaping from the craggy peaks
and jumping down the slopes, while in another direction
a herd of deer were galloping across the plain:
as they left the hills they raised a mighty cloud of dust.   155
Ascanius in the valley spurs his lively steed
and happily overtakes them, but in his heart he wishes
instead of this uninteresting game, to find
a foaming boar or tawny lion from the mountains.
Suddenly a crash of thunder comes from the heavens,   160
and rain begins to fall, mixed with a spatter of hailstones.
The Carthaginian escort and the Trojan youth
and Venus' grandson, all disperse across the fields
as they seek shelter; torrents come pouring down the hills.
Dido and Aeneas arrive in a cave together.   165
Earth and Juno, goddess of marriage, give the signal.
Lightning flashes from the sky to witness the union,
and nymphs scream from the mountain-tops in celebration.
     That day was the beginning of Dido's woes; that day
the seeds of death were sown; no longer does she think   170
of her reputation; she dreams no more of secret love:
she calls it marriage, and with that name conceals her sin.

     Straightway Rumor begins to run through Libya's cities:
Rumor, the swiftest of all the ills that plague mankind.
She thrives on speed and gains new strength from her rapid motion. 175

First she is small and fearful, but soon she rises to Heaven;
her feet are on the ground but she hides her head in the clouds.
They say that Mother Earth, in anger against the gods,
brought Rumor forth, the last of her children, sister to Coeus
and Enceladus; she is swift of foot and wing,   180
a huge and horrid monster. For each feather on her body
she has a watchful eye beneath (wonder of wonders!)
and as many tongues and hissing mouths and pricked-up ears.
At night she flies midway between the earth and heavens,
screeching, and never closes her eyes in gracious sleep.   185
By day she sits, a sentinel upon a rooftop
or palace tower, terrifying the greatest cities—
equally fond of wicked lies and simple truth.

  And now, rejoicing in her malicious gossip, she filled
the people's ears, and sang alike of fact and fiction: 190
telling how Trojan Aeneas had arrived in Carthage,
to whom fair Dido had deigned to join herself in marriage,
and how the two of them were whiling away the winter,
forgetful of their kingdoms, slaves of shameless passion.
This sort of talk the foul goddess spread in people's mouths,   195
and then she turned her lightning course to King Iarbas,
and with her words inflamed his mind and aroused his anger.
Hammon had ravished a Garamantian nymph, and Iarbas,
their son, had built a hundred temples to Jupiter,
in his broad lands, and a hundred altars with watchful fires   200
to honor the gods; the grounds reeked with the blood of victims,
the portals hung with garlands of many-colored flowers.
Distracted and incensed by the bitter rumor, they say
Iarbas stood before the altar in Jupiter's presence
and frequently besought the god with suppliant hands: 205
  "Almighty Jupiter, to whom the Moorish people
on broidered couches now are pouring Bacchic libations,
do you see what is happening? Or do we vainly tremble
when thunder resounds, and are they blind and aimless fires
that terrify our minds, mingled with meaningless noises?   210
This woman, wandering to my land, with my permission
has leased a piece of coastline to build her tiny town.

I have given her land to plow and terms of tenure—
she spurns my offer, but takes Aeneas as her lord!
And now this Paris with his effeminate retinue,   215
with perfumed hair and Phrygian hat tied under his chin,
has snatched another's prey, while I bring gifts to your temple,
and worship and do homage to your pretended power."
And as he clasped the altar and pleaded with these words,
the Almighty Father heard him and turned his eyes to Carthage;   220
the royal walls, the lovers forgetful of nobler fame.
He spoke to wingèd Mercury, giving these commands:
   "Go, my son, and call the Zephyrs—glide on your wings;
speak to the Trojan prince who lingers now in Carthage
unmindful of the cities the Fates have granted him.   225
And carry down my words to him through the swift winds:
It was not this his beautiful mother promised him,
it was not for this she saved him twice from Grecian weapons,
but to rule over Italy, a land fertile in empire
and raging in war; to carry on the Trojan stock   230
and bring the entire world beneath the rule of law.
If he is not inflamed with desire for such glory,
if for his own sake he will not shoulder the burden,
will he begrudge Ascanius the walls of Rome?
What is he doing? Why does he dally in enemy lands,   235
without a thought for his children, or for Italy's fields?
Let him take to his ships; this is my message for him."
   He spoke, and Mercury prepared to obey his commands.
First he binds on his feet his lovely golden sandals
that carry him aloft, swift as the breath of the wind,   240
over land and sea alike; then he takes his wand
with which he calls the pallid ghosts from the Underworld
and sends others on their way to gloomy Tartarus,
gives sleep or takes it away, and unseals the eyes in death.[1]
With this wand he drives the winds and skims the clouds,   245
and in his flight he sees the peak and the steep sides
of enduring Atlas carrying Heaven on his head—

---

[1]Cf. Odyssey V 43-49. This is an almost verbatim translation.

Atlas, whose pine-clad head is crowned with clouds and mist
perpetually, and beaten by the wind and rain;
his shoulders are covered with snow, rivers run down his chin,   250
his rough and shaggy beard is frozen stiff with ice.
Here, balancing on his wings, Cyllenian Mercury stopped.
From here he plunged toward the waves with his whole body,
headlong, like a bird which round the shores and fishy rocks
flies, skimming low above the surface of the waves.   255
Exactly so Cyllenian Mercury was flying
between the earth and sky, to Libya's sandy shores,
cutting through the winds as he came from his mother's father.
And when at last he reached the huts, with his wingèd feet,
he saw Aeneas building walls and planning houses.   260
His sword was decorated with stars of golden jasper;
a cloak of brilliant Tyrian purple hung from his shoulders—
a gift which generous Dido had wrought with her own hands,
picking out the thread with gold. And Mercury spoke:
    "Why are you busy laying foundations here for Carthage—   265
building a noble city, forsooth, but for your wife?
Have you forgotten all about your fated kingdom?
The ruler of the gods, and of the earth and sky—
Jove himself has sent me to you from shining Olympus;
Jove himself bade me take this message through the air.   270
What are you planning? Why are you wasting your time in
                                                    Carthage?

If you are not aroused with desire for such glory,
if for your own sake you will not shoulder the burden,
you should at least have a care for growing Ascanius,
and for his legacy—Italy and the Roman Empire."   275
Thus Cyllenian Mercury spoke his father's commands
and even as he spoke, he vanished from mortal sight
and disappeared from the eyes of men into empty air.
    And now Aeneas was dumbfounded at the sight:
his hair stood up on end and his voice stuck in his throat.   280
He burns with a desire to flee from that pleasant land,
thunderstruck by this warning from the immortal gods.
Alas, what could he do? How could he tell poor Dido

in her passion? With what words could he best begin?
He turns his mind this way and that, and now one plan   285
seems best for him to follow, but soon he thinks of another.
And as he wavered in his mind, this seemed the best:
He calls Mnestheus to him and Sergestus and brave Serestus
and bids them secretly prepare the ships and crews,
make weapons ready, concealing the cause of the change in plans. 290
And he himself, meanwhile, since Dido does not suspect,
in her innocence, that so great a love can ever be broken,
will seek the best approach, and wait for the proper moment,
and try to find a tactful way to tell the Queen.
The men all gladly obey and speedily do his bidding.   295

But Dido guessed (for who can fool a woman in love?)
and rapidly she caught the news of the coming departure,
suspecting even when there was nothing to suspect.
That same evil Rumor told her the fleet was being prepared.
She raged throughout the city, all aflame, like a Maenad,   300
frenzied as the Bacchanalian symbols are shaken,
when, every second year, the name of the god is called,
and she is summoned to Cithaeron's nocturnal revels.
At last she speaks to Aeneas, denouncing him as follows:
"Traitor, did you really think you could deceive me,   305
conceal so wicked a crime, and leave my land in silence?
Can neither our love dissuade you, nor the promises made,
nor Dido about to perish by a cruel doom?
What, even in the wintry storms you prepare your ships?
You hasten to set sail in the teeth of northern winds?   310
If you were not in search of foreign lands and homes
unknown, and if ancient Ilium herself were standing,
would you set out even for Troy through such a stormy sea?
Are you running away from me? Oh please, by the tears I am
                                          shedding,
and by your own right hand (for these are all I have left)   315
and by our marriage which has just begun, I implore you,
if ever I have deserved well of you, or if I ever
was good to you or made you happy, oh, take pity

on a house in ruins; change your mind, if prayers can persuade you!
It is all your fault the African chieftains hate me so,   320
yes, and the Tyrians too; it is all because of you
that I have lost my honor and my reputation,
my only hope of fame. With whom will you leave me to die,
O Guest (for I cannot call you Husband any longer)?
What do I wait for now—my brother Pygmalion   325
to come and overthrow the city? for Iarbas to take me?
If only I had conceived a child before you left,
if only a tiny Aeneas were playing in my house,
who would recall your face to me by his own likeness,
I might not feel so utterly conquered and forlorn."   330
    And so she spoke. Aeneas, warned by Jupiter,
kept his eyes steadfast, and mastered the pain in his heart.
At last he spoke: "I shall never deny that you deserve
anything of me that you could ever mention,
and I shall never think of you with bitterness   335
as long as I have life and breath and memory.
I have only this to say: I did not try to deceive you
(please do not believe that of me) or escape by stealth.
But neither did I ever promise to marry you.
If Fate had permitted me to choose my course of life,   340
if I had any choice at all of joy or sorrow,
my thoughts would be of Troy, my home, the sweet remains
of my own family. Priam's palace would still be standing;
a new citadel would have been built by my own hands.
But now Apollo with his Lycian oracles   345
has bidden me to set my course for Italy.
There is my love and my fatherland. If you, a Phoenician,
are now content to make your home in Libyan Carthage,
why should not Trojans settle on Italian soil?
Why is it unlawful for us to seek new homes?   350
For every time the dewy darkness veils the earth
and fiery stars arise, I see the unhappy ghost
of my father Anchises in my dreams; he frightens and warns me.
I think of young Ascanius, and the wrongs I do him
by cheating him of Italy, his destined kingdom.   355

And now the messenger of the gods has come to me—
(by your head and mine I swear it) sent by Jove himself—
I saw him with my own eyes in the clearest daylight
within these walls; with my own ears I heard him speak;
so stop tormenting both of us with your complaints.   360
Not of my own accord do I seek Italy."
    As he was speaking, the Queen had darted sidelong glances
but now she rolled her eyes up and down with silent gaze;
scanning him from head to foot, she cried out in anger:
"Wretched traitor, you are not the son of a goddess;   365
Dardanus never founded your line, but the Caucasus Mountains,
harsh and rugged, begot you; Hyrcanian tigers nursed you.
Why should I hide my feelings? What further wrongs do I wait
          for?
Did he but groan or look at me as I was weeping?
Did he shed one tear of pity for me who loved him?   370
What more can he do? Now neither the powerful Juno
nor Jove himself can look on this with eyes unmoved.
No one can be trusted! I found him, a shipwrecked beggar,
and took him in (what a fool I was!) and shared my throne,
rescued his missing ships, and saved his friends from death.   375
Oh, I am driven mad by Furies! And now Apollo
with 'Lycian oracles' and a 'messenger from Jove'
comes through the air with this abominable command.
Fine work for immortal gods, indeed, to disturb their rest!
Well, go then! I'll not hold you back or argue with you.   380
Go, look for Italy! Seek your kingdom over the waves!
But this I pray: if there is any justice in Heaven,
you will be punished on a jagged reef, and then, oh then
you will remember Dido. And from afar, I'll be near you
with funeral torches, and when death has claimed my body,   385
my ghost will haunt you wherever you go. You shall pay, you
          wretch!
Even from the depths of the world below, I shall hear ..."
    She breaks off in the middle of her words, in anguish;
she flees the light of day and tears away from his sight,
leaving him in fear and hesitation, wishing   390

to say many things. Her servants carry her in a swoon
and lay her down upon her bed in her marble chamber.
But good Aeneas, although he longed to allay her grief
and turn away her bitter sorrow with soothing words,
sighing deeply, and much shaken by his love,   395
obeys the god's command nonetheless, and returns to his ships.
The Trojans fall to work, and all along the shore
they launch the vessels: the keels are turned and set afloat;
the sailors, eager to be gone, bring leafy branches
and unhewn logs for oars ...   400
   From all the city one could see them streaming forth,
just as when the ants, mindful of coming winter,
plunder a heap of grain and store it up in their houses ;
a black column moves across the field as they carry their booty
through the grass in a narrow track; some push with their
                                       shoulders   405
against the bigger grains, while others close up the ranks,
rebuking the stragglers. The whole track is aglow with work.
What were your feelings, Dido, on seeing such a sight?
What sighs and groans did you utter, seeing from the fortress
the beach astir with men from far and wide, all working   410
and shouting along the seashore, right before your eyes?
O cruel Love, what terrible things you drive men to!
Again she bursts into tears, again has recourse to prayer,
again she swallows her pride, a humble suppliant,
lest she leave anything undone, and die in vain.   415
   "Anna," she said, "you see them bustling on the shore:
from everywhere they come. The sails are inviting the breezes;
the happy men are crowning the vessels' sterns with garlands.
If I was able to foresee this terrible sorrow,
I shall also have the strength to bear it. But oh, dear Anna,   420
grant me one last service; for the traitor was your friend—
to you alone the wretch entrusted his inmost thoughts,
and you alone know when and how best to approach him—
go, my sister, and entreat this haughty foe:
I am not the one who conspired to conquer the Trojans,   425
I never sent a fleet against his citadel,

nor did I disturb the ashes and grave of old Anchises;
why, then, does he refuse to listen to my prayers?
Where is he rushing off to? At least for his wretched lover
let him grant one last small boon, and wait for better winds.   430
I do not ask him to honor the marriage vows he has broken,
nor that he renounce fair Latium, or give up his empire;
I only beg for a little time to give rest to my passion,
till Fortune teach my conquered heart to bear its sorrow.
This last indulgence I beg—have pity on your sister—   435
if granted, it shall be repaid with interest at my death."

  This was her plea, and her unhappy sister, weeping,
conveys poor Dido's message. Aeneas remains unmoved:
he will not yield, he will not listen to her entreaties;
the gods and Fates prevent him from hearing with kindly ears.   440
Just as when the northern Alpine winds together
try with all their might to uproot a stubborn oak tree,
battering it on this side and that; with a loud noise
the trunk begins to shake and leaves fall to the ground,
but still the aged tree clings to the rock, for its roots   445
extend as far toward Tartarus as its top to Heaven—
just so the hero is battered by their constant pleas,
but though in his mighty heart he deeply feels the pain,
his will remains unshaken: their tears have no effect.

  Then the unhappy Dido sees that all is lost: 450
she prays for death; she wearies of looking at the sky.
And as if to strengthen her resolve to leave the earth
as she laid her gifts on the incense-burning altars,
she saw the holy water blacken(horrible sight!);
the wine she poured was turned to sinister, loathsome blood!   455
She spoke of this to no one, not even to her sister.
And furthermore, there was in the palace a marble temple
sacred to her former husband—she cherished it dearly,
bedecking it with snowy fleeces and festal branches.
From here she thought she heard the voice of her dead husband   460
calling to her at night, when the earth was held in darkness.
And then the lonely owl would hoot at night from the housetop,

an ominous, foreboding, gloomy note of death.
And oracles and sayings from the ancient prophets
terrified her with their warnings. She often had nightmares: 465
Aeneas himself pursuing her madly; then she was left
alone, without companions, walking an endless path,
searching for Tyrian friends in a deserted land.
Just as the mad Pentheus sees the band of Furies
with twin suns in the sky, and a double image of Thebes,   470
or when Orestes, Agamemnon's son, is driven
across the stage by his mother armed with flaming torches
and coal-black serpents, and Furies waiting on the threshold.
And so, worn out with sorrow, Dido yields to her madness;
resolved to die, fixing the time and place and manner   475
she goes and speaks to her grieving sister: her expression
conceals her dreadful plan beneath a placid face.

"I have found a way, dear Anna—congratulate your sister!
which will either bring him back or release me from my love:
near the limits of Ocean and the setting sun   480
is the distant land of Ethiopia, where great Atlas
turns on his shoulders the sphere inset with blazing stars.
I have seen a Massylian priestess from that place,
the guardian of the Hesperides' temple, she who gave
food to the dragon, guarding the tree with its sacred branches,   485
sprinkling dewy honey and slumber-giving poppies.
This priestess can, by means of her spells, release the hearts
of whomsoever she wills, while she can make others suffer,
stop rivers in their beds, and turn the stars in their courses.
She can raise nocturnal ghosts, and you will hear the ground   490
rumbling under your feet as ash-trees come down from the
                                  mountains.
As Heaven is my witness, sister, and your dear head,
against my will do I resort to magic spells.
Now go in secret and raise a pyre in the inner courtyard,
where I can burn the weapons which that wicked man   495
left in my chamber, all his garments, the bridal bed
(my curse and my undoing). I must destroy all things
that remind me of that scoundrel. Thus the priestess bids."

So speaking, she fell silent; her face was deadly pale.
But Anna never suspected that her sister's death   500
was the reason for these weird rites. Her mind cannot conceive
such frenzy: she fears nothing worse than when Sychaeus died,
and does as she is bidden ...

    The Queen, seeing the funeral pyre rise to Heaven,
constructed of oak and pine logs in the inner courtyard,   505
bedecks the halls with flowers and with funeral garlands.
She puts Aeneas' garments and the sword he left
and his image on the pyre, knowing well the end.
Altars are placed around. The priestess with streaming hair
calls in a thunderous voice the names of three hundred gods,   510
Erebus, Chaos, triple Hecate, three-faced Diana.
She sprinkled water, said to be from the spring of Avernus.
Herbs, cut with brazen sickles by the light of the moon,
swollen with poisonous black milk, were sought and gathered;
and a love-charm, torn away from the brow of a baby colt   515
before its mother could take it ...
Dido stands by the altar, with sacred meal in her hands,
one foot unsandalled, robe unbound, and thus she prays
calling on gods in her hour of death, and on the stars,
witnesses to her fate, and to whatever power   520
has the task of watching over mismated lovers.

    Night fell, and tired creatures enjoyed a peaceful slumber
over all the earth. The woods and seas were at rest.
The rolling constellations were in their midnight course.
The fields were quiet; animals and colored birds   525
from near and far, from limpid lakes and wooded forests
were all asleep beneath the silence of the night,
their hearts relieved of all their troubles and their sorrows.
But not the miserable Phoenician: she could not sleep,
relax, or welcome the night into her eyes and heart.   530
Her torture was renewed and doubled; her love swelled up
and burned within her; her bosom heaved with rage and passion.
She turns about her thoughts and speaks in her inmost mind:
"What shall I do? Be mocked by all by previous suitors?

Go on my knees and plead for some Numidian husband,   535
when I have scorned them all so many times before?
Or shall I follow Trojan ships and Trojan orders;
will they be pleased to think of me with gratitude,
remembering all the things that I have done for them?
But even if I wished it, would these arrogant ships   540
receive such a hated guest? Do you not see, you wretch,
even now, the full extent of Trojan duplicity?
What then? Shall I go alone with these exultant sailors?
Or shall I take with me my Carthaginian subjects
whom I could scarcely tear away from Phoenicia?   545
How can I tell them to put out to sea again?
No! Die as you deserve, and end your grief with the sword!
It was you, my sister, vanquished by my tears and madness,
who brought this woe on me, and put me at his mercy.
Why could I not have lived my life without any marriage,   550
blameless, like some animal, without such sorrows?
Why did I break the oath I made to Sychaeus' ashes?"
Such laments broke from the Queen's unhappy heart.

Aeneas meanwhile was asleep on the lofty deck
with everything made ready for the coming departure.   555
And as he slept the form of the god appeared to him,
coming again to warn him as he had done before.
The voice was the voice of Mercury, the complexion too,
the brilliant golden hair, the graceful limbs of youth.
"Goddess-born," he said, "how can you sleep in such danger?   560
Do you not see the perils that surround you, madman?
Do you not hear the sound of favorable Zephyrs?
The Queen is plotting tricks and wicked crimes in her heart:
resolved to die, she rouses all the tides of passion.
Will you not flee at once, while flight is possible?   565
Soon the sea will be full of wreckage and cruel torches,
soon the entire shore will be ablaze with flames,
if tomorrow's dawn still finds you lingering in this land.
But come, no more delays! Women are capricious,
fickle creatures!" So speaking, he vanished into the night.   570

Aeneas is startled by the sudden apparition.
He shakes the sleep from his limbs and rouses all his comrades:
"Quickly, my men, awake and seat yourselves on the benches.
Unfurl the sails: make haste; a god sent from high Heaven
tells us to begin our flight and cut the hawsers   575
and twisted cables. We follow you, O blessed god
whoever you are; we gladly obey your will once more:
remain with us and help us with favorable stars."
And as he speaks, Aeneas draws his sword from its sheath
and cuts the cable with his sharp and shining blade.   580
The others are seized with ardor. They all rush to and fro.
The shore is left deserted; the sea is hidden by ships.
They bend to the oars and churn the foam and sweep the blue
                                                          waters.

And now the Dawn departed from the saffron bed of Tithonus,
arose, and sprinkled early light over all the world.   585
As soon as Dido saw from her tower the light of day,
and all the ships under full sail moving out to sea,
and knew the shore and harbor were stripped of fleet and oarsmen,
she struck her lovely breast thrice and four times with her hand,
and tore her golden hair and cried: "O Jupiter!   590
this stranger is to depart, having mocked me and my kingdom?
Will they not fetch arms and follow, all the Tyrians?
and launch the ships from the dockyards in pursuit? Go, then!
Bring torches quickly, find your weapons, pull your oars!
But what am I saying? Where am I? What folly unhinges my
                                                    mind?   595
Poor Dido, only now your sins come home to roost?
You should have thought before, when you offered him your
                                                    crown.
So this is the faith of the man who carries his country's gods,
who lifted on his shoulders his father, worn out with years.
Could I not have torn him limb from limb, and scattered   600
his body in the waves—killed him and all the Trojans,
and served Ascanius up to eat for his father's banquet?
It would have been an uncertain fight. But what did it matter?

Whom should I have feared, who was about to die?
I should have burned his camp, set fire to his ships,   605
father and son and all the rest, and myself along with them!
O Sun, who with your light illuminate the world,
and Juno, witness and sharer of all my grief and sorrow,
and Hecate, invoked by night with screaming at the crossroads,
Avenging Furies, and all the gods of dying Elissa,   610
hear my prayers and turn your powers to my grief;
if that unspeakable wretch is fated to land safely,
if he is destined to float his ships to foreign shores,
if this is the goal determined for him by the Fates of Jove,
at least let him be harried by wars and savage peoples,   615
an exile from his land, and torn from his son's embrace,
let him beg for aid and see his friends all dying,
and when he has capitulated in unjust peace,
let him not live to enjoy his kingdom and the daylight,
but let him die before his time and lie unburied.   620
This is my prayer: these words I pour out with my life's blood.
And you, my Carthaginians, pursue his descendants
with wars and hatred. Make this offering to my ashes:
let there never be friendship or alliance between you!
May some unknown Avenger[2] rise from out of my bones   625
to hound the Trojan colonists with fire and sword,
now and hereafter, at any time when strength shall be given;
let seacoast fight with seacoast, I pray, and wave with wave,
and arms with arms; let them fight, and all their descendants."

    She ceased, and turned her frenzied mind in all directions,   630
seeking to put a speedy end to her hateful life.
She briefly spoke to Barce, the old nurse of Sychaeus
(for her own nurse was dead and buried in Phoenicia):
"O dearest nurse, call my sister Anna to me,
tell her to sprinkle my body with water from the river,   635
and bring the sacrificial victims for atonement.
So let her come; and veil your brow with a sacred fillet.

---

[2] A reference to Hannibal and the Punic Wars.

The rites to Stygian Jove that I have duly begun
I now shall finish, and make an end to all my woes,
entrusting to the flames the pyre of the Trojan scoundrel."   640
So she spoke. The nurse hurried with an old woman's zeal.

    But Dido, mad and trembling with her great decision,
rolled bloodshot eyes; her cheeks were flushed and quivering,
her face was pale with the pallor of impending death.
She bursts into the courtyard, climbs the lofty pyre,   645
and in her furor she unsheathes the Trojan sword—
a gift Aeneas had given her—not, alas, for that purpose!
Then, looking at the Trojan garments and well-known bed,
she paused a moment, giving way to tearful thoughts,
then lay upon the couch and spoke these final words: 650
"O relics dear to me while God and Fates allowed,
take my spirit; release me from my suffering.
I have lived: I have run the course that Fortune gave me;
now let a queenly shade pass to the world below.
I have built a famous city and seen my walls arise;   655
I have avenged my husband and punished my wicked brother.
Happy, alas! too happy I would have been, if only
the Trojan ships had never landed on my shores."
She spoke, and buried her face in the bed. "I die unavenged,"
she said, "but let me die. Thus gladly I go to Hades.   660
And may the cruel Trojan see the flames from his ship
and take with him the evil omen of my doom."

    As she spoke, she fell upon the sword. Her servants
saw her fall, and saw the blade covered with blood;
her hands were spattered with it; a loud wail rose to the rooftops, 665
and Rumor madly raced throughout the shaken city.
The palace walls resounded with lamentations of women,
and sobs and screams from all the city rose to Heaven,
as if Carthage had been invaded by the foe,
as if ancient Tyre were in ruins, and hungry flames   670
were now devouring the houses of men and temples of gods.
Her sister heard, and in a swoon she rushed through the crowd,
tearing her face with her nails and beating her breast with her
                                                                     hands:

she called the dying woman by name in her anguish:
"So that was it, my sister? This is how you deceived me?   675
This is why you wanted a pyre and altar and flames?
What shall I first bewail? In dying you scorned your sister;
you might at least have permitted me to share your doom.
The same blade and the same hour would have taken us both.
Was it for this I built the pyre and invoked the gods: 680
that while you lay in death, I should be far away?
You have killed yourself, my sister, and me, and all your people;
you have destroyed the city! Give me water for her wounds,
and let me catch her dying breath with my own lips."
With these words she climbed the steps to the funeral pyre   685
and threw her arms about her already dying sister,
weeping, and stanching the dark blood with her own garments.

The Queen attempted to raise her heavy eyelids, but failed.
The deep wound made a gurgling sound beneath her breast.
Three times she tried to raise herself upon her elbow;   690
three times she fell back on the couch. Her rolling eyes
sought the sky, and when she found it she groaned aloud.
    Then mighty Juno, taking pity on her anguish
and difficult death, sent Iris down from high Olympus,
to free her struggling spirit from the imprisoning limbs.   695
For since she did not die by Fate or natural death,
but wretchedly, before her time, in sudden frenzy,
Proserpina had not yet taken from her head
the golden lock assigning her to Stygian Orcus.
And so, on saffron wings, and sparkling with the dew,   700
Iris comes trailing a thousand colors from the sun
and hovering over her head she says: "This offering
I take, as bidden, to Pluto, and set you free from the body."
And as she spoke, she cut the lock of hair with her right hand.
Then all warmth leaves the body; life passes into the air.   705

End of Book IV.

BOOK V

THE FUNERAL GAMES

Aeneas meanwhile holds the middle course with his fleet
and cuts a path straight through the waves made dark by the
          North Wind.
He looks back at the walls of Carthage aglow with the flames
of wretched Dido's funeral pyre. No one knows the reason
for such a fire. But they know the cruel agonies   5
of love that is turned to hate, and what frenzied women can do;
and so the Trojans' hearts are full of gloomy forebodings.
  When the ships are in mid-ocean and out of sight of land,
with only sea and sky to be seen in all directions,
a black cloud suddenly comes looming overhead   10
bringing night and storm, and stirring the dark waves.
The pilot Palinurus cries from the lofty stern:
"Alas! Why have such dreadful clouds blotted out the heavens?
What are you planning, Father Neptune?" and as he speaks
he bids them shorten sail and bend to the heavy oars,   15
and steers an oblique course into the wind and says:
"Noble Aeneas, even with Jupiter helping us
I never could reach Italy under such a sky.
The wind has changed and now it blows athwart our course;
it comes from the dark west; the sky is overcast.   20
We neither can resist nor sail into the storm.
Since Fortune is victorious, let us follow her:
wherever she leads us, thither let us set our course.
Sicily is not far, the land of your kinsman Eryx,
if I remember rightly, and can retrace the stars."   25
And good Aeneas said: "I have known it for some time now:
the winds will have their way. In vain we steer against them.
So change your course; indeed, what land would I rather see,
to what shores would I rather take my weary ships

than that in which my Dardan friend Acestes lives,   30
and where my father Anchises' bones are laid to rest?"
When he had spoken thus, they seek the harbor. The West Wind
fills the sails; the ships run swiftly with the tide;
at last they happily put in at the well-known shore.

Acestes from a distant hilltop sees and wonders   35
at the approach of friendly ships, and goes to meet them,
armed with javelins and a hide of Libyan bear;
Acestes, born of Trojan mother to Crinisus
the river-god; remembering his parentage,
he greets the Trojans joyfully with rustic splendor   40
and he consoles the weary men with friendly resources.

The following day, when Dawn had put the stars to flight,
Aeneas called his comrades together from the shore
and to the assembled men he spoke from a little hill:
"Noble sons of Dardanus, sprung from the race of gods,   45
a year has now gone by with the passing of the months
since we laid the mortal remains of my father Anchises
to rest in the ground and consecrated the sorrowful altars.
The day is now at hand, if I am not mistaken,
which I shall keep in grief and honor; the gods have willed it.   50
If I were in exile today in the Gaetulian Syrtes,
or on the Argolic Sea, or in the town of Mycenae,
I still would perform the yearly vow with solemn rites
and heap the altars high with the appropriate gifts.
But now, the ashes of my dear father (not, I think,   55
without the mind and will of the gods) are buried here,
right in our presence, and we are in a friendly harbor.
Come, let us celebrate the day with joyful rites.
Let us pray for winds, and when our city is founded,
may he grant us to offer these rites each year in temples.   60
Acestes, born of Trojan stock, gives you two oxen
for every ship. Invite to the feast your own Penates
and whatever gods our host Acestes worships.
And further, when the ninth Dawn lights the world for mortals
and with her rays dispels the darkness from the world,   65

I shall hold contests for the Trojans: first, a boat-race,
then a trial of speed with feet, and next a test
of strength and skill with javelins or with light arrows,
and then will come the contest with the rawhide gloves.
Let all appear and try to win the victor's palm.   70
And now, be silent all, and wreathe your brows with leaves."
    He speaks, and crowns his temples with his mother's myrtle.
Likewise Helymus and Acestes, ripe with age,
the boy Ascanius and the other youths do the same.
He went from the assembly, amid many thousands,   75
to the mound, the center of a thronging crowd.
And there he made libation, pouring on the ground
two goblets of undiluted wine, two of fresh milk,
and two of victims' blood. He scattered flowers and said:
"Hail, blessed father, once again! Hail to your ashes,   80
rescued in vain; all hail, my father's spirit and shade!
Since it was not allowed to have you at my side
as I seek the fated fields of Italy and the Tiber."
    As he finished, a gigantic, slippery serpent,
with seven monstrous coils, crept from the foot of the shrine.   85
It circled the mound benignly, gliding past the altars.
Its back was spotted with blue markings, and its scales
blazed with gleaming gold like a rainbow in the sunlight,
reflecting a thousand brilliant colors through the clouds.
Aeneas was astonished at the sight; the serpent,   90
gliding with its long body among the bowls and goblets,
tasted the offerings, then crept harmlessly away
beneath the tomb, leaving the altars where it had fed.
Aeneas begins again the interrupted rites
for his father, not knowing if this is the Genius of the place   95
or Anchises' attendant spirit; he kills two sheep,
two swine, and two dark-backed bullocks, according to the
                                                custom,
and pours the wine from bowls, calling upon the spirit
of great Anchises, and the Manes from Acheron.
His friends, too, gladly bring gifts, whatever each one has,   100
they pile the altars high and sacrifice the bullocks,

while others in turn place the cauldrons, and lying on the grass
put live coals beneath the spits and roast the meat.

The awaited day was at hand: the steeds of Phaëthon
conveyed the ninth Dawn forth into a cloudless sky.   105
The name and reputation of the great Acestes
aroused the countryside; they merrily came to the beach,
some to see Aeneas' men, and some for the contest.
And first the prizes are set out for all to see
in the middle: holy tripods, verdant crowns and palms,   110
the prize for the victors, and armor, and garments dyed with
                                                         purple,
and talents of silver and gold. Then from a mound in the center
the trumpet's blare proclaims the beginning of the games.
    First four well-matched ships with heavy oars begin
the contest; ships selected from the entire fleet.   115
Mnestheus on the "Sea-Serpent" with his eager crew
(soon Mnestheus the Italian, from whom comes Memmius' line);
and Gyas on the great "Chimaera", a mighty ship,
a floating city; she was rowed by Trojan youth
in triple tiers, with threefold banks of oars arising;   120
Sergestus (ancestor of the house of Sergius)
sails in the huge "Centaur", and in the sea-blue "Scylla"
Cloanthus, from whom your line stems, Roman Cluentius.
    There is a rock far out beyond the foaming surf;
it is sometimes lashed and overwhelmed by the surging waves,   125
when winter gales roar overhead and hide the stars;
but when the sea is calm it raises its tranquil bulk
in silence, a friendly roosting place for sun-loving seagulls.
Here Father Aeneas places a bough of leafy oak
as goal-post for the sailors, so that they may know   130
where they should steer the ships and then retrace their course.
They draw the lots for position, and on the lofty sterns
the captains shine from afar with gold and purple splendor.
The members of the crew are crowned with poplar garlands;
their naked shoulders glisten from the olive oil.   135
They sit upon the benches, with eager arms at the oars;

intent, they await the signal; in each exultant heart
anxiety is vying with the passion for glory.
Then at the trumpet's sound they all leap forth at once
from their starting places. A shout goes up to the sky   140
as straining muscles churn the waters into foam.
They plow the sea in furrows; the sea-lanes open wide,
swept by the oars and triple-pointed beaks of ships.
No such headlong speed when two-horse chariots
shoot out from the barrier and race across the plain;   143
not so fervently do charioteers shake the reins
as they flick the whips across the loosened steeds.
Applause and shouting from the cheering spectators
fills the nearby forest and the sheltered beach;
the hills are struck by the sound and send the echo back.   150
     Gyas takes the lead and skims across the waves
amid the shouts and tumult. After him Cloanthus,
who has a stronger crew, but yet he is retarded
by his ship's weight. And after them the Serpent and Centaur
are running neck and neck, each striving for the lead.   155
Now the Serpent is out in front, now the huge Centaur
overtakes her, and now they are racing side by side,
both plowing through the salty spray with their long keels.
And now they were approaching the rock that marked the turn,
when Gyas, who still was in the lead at the halfway point,   160
loudly called out to Menoetes, the ship's pilot:
"Why are you steering so far to starboard? Change your course,
keep to the shore, graze with your oars the rocks on the left.
Let others hold the deep!" He finished, but Menoetes,
fearing hidden rocks, steered out to the open sea.   165
"You are away off your course! Steer for the rocks, Menoetes!"
Gyas shouted again, to call the pilot. And now
he sees Cloanthus behind him, on the nearer course.
Between the ship of Gyas and the loud-sounding rocks
he slips through on the left and now is out in front,   170
and, having passed the goal, is out of dangerous waters.
Then the young man's bones begin to burn with rage.
Tears run down his cheeks; forgetful of his pride

and of his comrades' safety, he throws the timid Menoetes
off the lofty poopdeck headlong into the sea.   175
And he himself, not only captain but also pilot,
takes the helm, cheers on the crew, and steers for the shore.
Old Menoetes rose at last from the ocean's bottom
with difficulty, soaking wet, his garments drenched,
and climbed up on the rock and sat where it was dry.   180
And all the Trojans laughed to see him fall and swim,
and laughed to see him spitting the salt water out.
    And now the other two began to have great hopes,
Sergestus and Mnestheus, of passing the tardy Gyas.
Sergestus takes the lead and now comes near the rock,   185
but his precarious lead is less than one boat's length.
The rival Serpent almost is abreast with her prow.
The captain Mnestheus urges on his crew, amidships,
and cheers them: "Come, you loyal followers of Hector,
bend to the oars! You whom I chose to be my comrades   190
in the final hours of Troy. Come, show the same strength now,
the same courage you showed in the Gaetulian Syrtes,
in the Ionian Sea, and in Malea's dashing waves.
I do not ask to win—no first place now for Mnestheus—
let those win to whom Neptune has granted it—   195
but to be last is disgraceful: win only this, my men,
escape this infamy!" The men strain at the oars,
and to their mighty strokes the brazen stern is a-quiver;
the ocean's surface skims by, the men all pant for breath,
their mouths are parched and dry; their bodies stream with sweat.   200
The glory that they seek is won for them by chance:
for as Sergestus in a frenzy approached the rocks,
beginning to navigate the dangerous inner lane,
the poor man ran aground upon a hidden reef,
the rocks were shaken and the oars' blades hit and snap   205
upon the flinty crag. The ship's bow hung suspended.
The crew jump up and, shouting at the long delay,
try to push her off with pikes and grappling hooks,
and pick the broken oars out of the whirling waters.
The happy Mnestheus, made keener by this same success,   210

with quickened oars, and offering prayers to the winds,
seeks the level waters and skims to the open sea.
Just as a dove, when suddenly startled in her cave,
whose nest and fledglings are hidden in the rocky cavern—
at first she loudly flaps her wings as she seeks the fields, 215
frightened away from her home, but soon she begins to glide
upon her liquid path without moving her swift wings;
so Mnestheus, so the Serpent cut through the home stretch,
so her very momentum carries her in flight.
And first he leaves behind Sergestus, aground on the reef, 220
struggling, calling in vain for help in the shallow waters,
trying to learn to row a ship with broken oars.
Then he overtakes Gyas and the huge Chimaera
with all her bulk; she yields, because she has no pilot.
Now they are almost at the goal; there is only Cloanthus, 225
whom he strives to pass, straining with all his might.
The spectators begin to shout, cheering them on,
encouraging the pursuers, making the heavens resound.
These think it would be a disgrace to lose the glory
which they have won; they would gladly give their lives for honor; 230
those thrive on success: they are able, because they think they
                                                    are able.
And now perhaps they would have won, for the prows are abreast,
had not Cloanthus, stretching both his hands to the sea,
poured forth prayers and called the gods to hear his vows:
"Gods who rule the ocean over which I sail, 235
I shall gladly sacrifice to you a white bullock
before your altars on the shore, and throw the entrails
into the salty waves, and pour you flowing wine."
He spoke, and in the depths of the sea the Nereids,
the band of the Phorci and the maiden Panopea, 240
heard him, and Father Portunus pushed him with mighty hand.
Swifter than the South Wind or a wingèd arrow
she speeds to land and comes to rest in the deep harbor.
  Then Anchises' son summoned them all together
according to custom; the herald's cry proclaims Cloanthus 245
the victor; his temples are garlanded with wreath of laurel.

And as prizes for the ships he is asked to choose
and take three bullocks, wine, and a large talent of silver.
And the leaders themselves are given special prizes:
the winning captain receives a golden cloak with border   250
of Meliboean purple with double wavy lines;
the royal boy[1] is woven in, on leafy Ida,
tiring the swift deer with his feet and javelin,
alert and panting; the eagle, armor-bearer of Jove,
has caught him in his talons and carries him up from Ida: 255
in vain the aged retainers stretch their hands to the sky;
the air resounds with the savage baying of the dogs.
The captain whose skill had won for him the second place
was given a coat of mail, with hooks of triple gold
which he had taken with his own hands from Demoleos   260
when he conquered him by the rapid Simois.
This was his gift—a glorious defense in battle.
The servants Phegeus and Sagaris could scarcely carry it
with its many folds, on their shoulders, yet Demoleos
once had worn it as he scattered the fleeing Trojans.   265
And for the third prize there was a pair of brazen cauldrons
and silver bowls with figures wrought in high relief.

  Now the gifts were all bestowed, and the men were departing,
proud of their prizes, their temples bound with purple fillets,
when, hardly wrested from the rock by means of his skill,   270
without his oars, one whole tier disabled, lo! Sergestus
limped in with his dishonored ship, amid much laughter.
As when oftentimes a serpent, caught on the roadway,
run over obliquely by a brazen chariot wheel,
or hit with a rock by a traveller and left for dead,   275
trying in vain to escape, it drags its heavy coils,
part ferocious with blazing eyes and hissing neck
held on high, part crippled by the wound, and retarded,
it struggles and gets itself entangled in its own coils—
in such a manner did the ship creep painfully;   280
yet with sails hoisted, she reached the harbor under full sail.

---

[1]Ganymede.

Aeneas presented Sergestus with the promised gifts,
happy that the ship and crew are brought back safely:
he receives a slave named Pholoë, a Cretan woman,
skilled in Minerva's crafts, nursing her twin offspring.   285

Once the boat race is finished, the good Aeneas goes
to a grassy field, surrounded by the rolling hills
and forests; in the center of this little valley
was the circle of a theater. Here, amid many thousands,
the hero came with his men and sat in a raised seat.   290
Here were invited all who wished to contend in the foot-race.
The prizes were set out as an incentive to courage.
From all directions Trojans and Sicilians throng,
Nisus and Euryalus the first . . .
Euryalus famous for his beauty and his youth,   295
and Nisus for devotion to the boy. There followed
Prince Diores, of the noble family of Priam,
and Salius and Patron together, one Acarnanian,
the other an Arcadian, born of Tegean stock,
and two Sicilian youths, Helymus and Panopes,   300
accustomed to the woods, companions of old Acestes,
and many others besides, whose fame has been forgotten.
Then Aeneas spoke as follows in their midst:
"Listen to my words, you men, with happy minds,
for no one shall depart without a gift from me.   305
I shall give to each two Cretan arrows of iron,
and a battle-axe wrought with silver to carry away.
All shall have the same reward, and the first three
will also receive prizes and pale olive garlands.
This is the winner's prize: a horse with splendid trappings.   310
The second prize will be an Amazonian quiver
full of Thracian arrows, bound with a golden belt,
and for the clasp a buckle made of polished jewels.
The third shall go away content with an Argive helmet."
    When this was said, they took their places. Suddenly   315
the signal sounded; they shot away from the starting-post,
pouring like a rain-cloud, their eyes fixed on the goal.

Nisus takes the lead at once over all the others,
swifter than the wind, or a wingèd bolt of lightning.
Next to him, but only a poor second, Salius;   320
then after another long interval comes the third,
Euryalus...
Helymus follows next, and just in back of him
Diores flies, his foot grazing the other's heel,
almost at his shoulder; and if more laps had remained,   325
he would have passed him by, or left a doubtful issue.
Now they were on the last lap, near the goal itself,
panting and weary, when, alas! the unlucky Nisus
slipped and fell in a pool of blood, where cattle were slain
by chance, and grass and ground were soaked all through with
                                                  blood.   330
For even as he was about to win, the youth
could not keep his balance, but fell right on his face,
in all the filth and gore and slime of the sacrifice.
But even now he did not forget his friend Euryalus;
for as he rose he threw himself right in the path   335
of Salius, who fell and rolled in the bloody sand.
Euryalus runs by, the victor by grace of his friend.
Taking the lead, he crosses the line amid shouts and cheers.
After him Helymus, and Diores the third.
Now Salius protests the decision with loud cries   340
before the whole crowd and all the elders in the theater,
claiming it was a foul, and demanding the first prize.
Public opinion sided with Euryalus,
for his tears and virtue, always fairer in a fair form.
Diores is on his side too, making loud protests: 345
in vain had he, Diores, come in third, if the first
and highest honors should be given to Salius.
Then Father Aeneas says: "Your rewards are assured, my lads:
no one shall change the order of the first three prizes.
yet I may show my pity for my friend's mishap."   350
So speaking, he gives to Salius the enormous hide
of an African lion, with shaggy mane and gilded claws.
Then Nisus says, "If this is the reward for the loser,

and you have such pity for the fallen, what is my prize?
For I would surely have been the one to win the race   355
if I had not met with the same bad luck as Salius."
And as he spoke he showed to all his face and limbs
wet with filth and gore. And Father Aeneas smiled
and ordered a shield brought out, the work of Didymaon,
taken from Neptune's sacred temple by the Greeks.   360
This is the noble prize he gives to the excellent youth.

    When the race was ended and the prizes given,
Aeneas said: "Now, whoever has courage and a stout heart,
let him come forth and try his skill with the rawhide gloves."
and he set up a double prize for the boxing-match: 365
for the winner, a steer bedecked with fillets and with gold;
and to console the loser, a sword and splendid helmet.
Without delay Dares arose, with mighty muscles
and shows himself amid resounding roars from the crowd.
Dares, the only man who had ever fought with Paris;   370
the same who at the tomb where valiant Hector lay,
struck great Butes of Amycus' Bebrycian race,
the champion, an enormous giant of a man,
and left this Butes dying on the yellow sand.
This was Dares who raised his hand, eager for battle,   375
showing his broad shoulders, flexing his bulging biceps,
sparring to the left and right with mighty blows.
A match is sought for him; but no one of the crowd
has the courage to face this man with the boxing gloves.
So Dares, elated, thinking that the prize was forfeit,   380
did not delay any longer, but stood before Aeneas,
and grasping the horn of the bull with his left hand, he said:
"Son of a goddess, if no man dares to fight with me,
must I stand here forever? What sense is there in waiting?
Let me take my prize!" And all the assembled Trojans   385
shouted that the promised reward should be given to Dares.
    But Acestes spoke reproachful words to old Entellus,
who was sitting next to him on the green seat of grass:
"Entellus, once the greatest of heroes, but in vain,

will you allow so great a prize to be carried off 390
without a fight? Where is your godlike teacher Eryx,
of idle reputation? And what about your fame
throughout all Sicily? And the trophies in your house?"
Entellus said: "Neither love of fame nor glory has gone,
driven away by fear; but my blood runs cold and numb 395
with sluggish age; my strength of body is chilled and gone.
If I still had the strength I once had, as this lout
with his noisy bragging, if I were a few years younger,
there would be no need of prizes or of bullocks
as an incentive." So speaking, old Entellus 400
threw into the ring a pair of boxing gloves
of massive weight, the ones that Eryx used to fight with,
in olden days, binding his arms with the tough hide.
All were astonished, so great were the gloves: of seven hides,
and they were stiff with lead and iron sewn into them. 405
Dares, aghast above all, shrank back and would not fight,
while the noble son of Anchises examined the gloves,
turning them about to see the heavy folds.
  Then the old man Entellus said these words from his heart:
"What if a man had seen the very gloves and arms 410
of Hercules himself, and the sad fight on this shore?
Your brother Eryx used to wear these boxing gloves
(you can see how they are spattered with blood and brains)—
with these he fought the great Alcides;[2] and I used them too
when I was young and strong, and the blood ran hot in my veins, 415
and envious age had not yet made my temples white.
But if the Trojan Dares declines to use our arms,
and good Aeneas and lord Acestes both approve,
let us make it an equal fight. So have no fear,
I'll not use Eryx's gloves, nor you the Trojan ones." 420
So speaking, he threw the double cloak from off his shoulders
and bared his giant frame with its great bones and muscles,
and stood there towering in the center of the arena.
Then Anchises' son brought gloves of equal weight

---

[2]Hercules: see Glossary.

and bound the hands of both the men with similar arms.   425
   Immediately each of the fighters stood upon his tiptoe,
fearlessly, and lifted both arms high in the air.
They raise their heads up high, rolling with the punches,
sparring and boxing, trading blow for deadly blow.
The one is quick of foot, and confident in his youth,   430
the other mighty of muscle and limb, but his knees are shaking
and trembling, and a painful panting shakes his limbs.
Many blows are given and taken on both sides,
ringing out on hollow flanks, making their chests
resound, and punches rain on ear and head alike,   435
and cheeks and faces smart beneath the heavy blows.
Entellus stands there motionless, with dignity,
dodging the blows with body and with vigilant eyes.
The other, as if he were besieging a lofty city,
or storming a well-armed fortress high up in the mountains,   440
darting, and trying now this approach and now the other,
making attack upon attack, but all in vain.
Entellus rises up and aims a killing blow
with his right hand, but Dares, alert, sees it coming
and steps aside with agile body to avoid it.   445
And Entellus, whose strength was wasted on the air,
loses his balance and topples heavily to the ground,
just as, sometimes, on Erymanthus or Mount Ida,
a lofty hollow pine tree is uprooted and falls.
Then the Trojan and Sicilian youth arise;   450
a shout goes up to the sky. Acestes first runs forward,
and taking pity, lifts his aged friend from the ground.
The hero is not frightened or deterred by his fall.
He eagerly returns to the fight with violent anger;
his shame and righteous indignation give him new strength,   455
and furiously he drives Dares about the arena,
striking him now with a right-hand blow, now with a left.
Without ceasing the blows come down like rain on a rooftop,
giving the other no rest, so thick and fast are the punches,
as with both fists the Sicilian hero pummels Dares.   460
   Then Father Aeneas did not let their fury go further,

nor did he allow Entellus to rage any more in anger,
but put an end to the fight, and saved the worn-out Dares,
speaking soothing words to console the exhausted fighter:
"Unlucky man, what madness has you in its grasp?   465
Do you not see that his strength and all the gods are against you?
Yield to the gods!" Thus did Aeneas stop the fight.
　But Dares' friends led him to the ships; he could hardly walk,
his battered head was swaying from one side to the other,
and he spat out clots of blood and teeth all mixed together.   470
They were summoned and took the sword and helmet for him,
leaving the palm and bullock for the winner Entellus.
Then the victor, rejoicing in spirit, and proud of the bull,
said: "Son of a goddess, and Trojans, now you all shall see
what strength there used to be in my body when I was young,   475
and what a dreadful fate you rescued Dares from!"
When he had spoken, he set himself facing the bull
which stood there, the prize of battle, and lifted his right fist
and struck the beast with his glove directly between the horns,
shattering the skull and dashing out the brains.   480
The bull falls lifeless and quivering upon the ground.
Entellus stands above it and he speaks these words:
"This better life I give you, Eryx, instead of Dares,
and now, the champion, I lay down my gloves and my art!"

　Straightway Aeneas invites all those who may desire   485
to enter the archery contest, and sets out the prizes.
With his strong hand[3] he raises the mast of Serestus' ship
and from the very top he suspends a fluttering dove
attached to the masthead by a cord, as a mark for their arrows.
The contestants met; the lots were thrown into a helmet   490
of bronze; the first turn went, amid many rousing cheers,
to one Hippocoön the son of Hyrtacus.
And Mnestheus, who had only just now won the boat-race,
followed him; Mnestheus, his temples wreathed with the green
　　　　　　　　　　　　　　　　　　　　　　　　olive.

---

[3]or, according to some editors, "with a large throng".

Third was Eurytion (your brother, famous Pandarus,   495
who long ago, when ordered to upset the truce,
were the first to shoot your arrow into the Achaeans).
Finally, in the helmet's bottom was the lot
of old Acestes, who dared compete in a sport for youth.
    Now they flex their muscles and they draw the bows,   500
each with all his might, and take the shafts from the quivers.
And first the arrow of Hyrtacus' son sped on its way;
leaving the twanging bowstring, it whistled through the breeze
and came to rest, fixed firmly in the wood of the mast.
The masthead trembled, the dove was frightened and fluttered
                  her wings,   505
and the whole place resounded with cheers and loud applause.
Next the eager Mnestheus stood with bow bent back,
aiming on high, with eyes and arrow in a straight line.
Alas! he could not hit the bird with his iron-tipped shaft,
but instead the arrow cut the knot and severed the cord   510
of linen, which tied the dove by the foot to the lofty masthead,
and she swiftly flew away into the dark clouds and the wind.
Then speedily Eurytion, whose bow was drawn
and shaft was ready, invoked his brother with a vow;
he took quick aim at the dove now flying in the free sky,   515
and pierced her as she flapped her wings beneath a black cloud;
leaving her life with Heaven's stars she plummeted downward,
and as she fell she brought down the deadly shaft that had pierced
                  her.
    Only Acestes was left and he had lost the prize;
Nevertheless he aimed an arrow high in the air,   520
to show that an old man still could draw the ringing bow.
And now a sudden omen met the eyes of all,
a future portent, later shown by the awful outcome,
when frightening soothsayers read the riddle, but too late.[4]
    For as it pierced the transparent clouds, the shaft caught fire,   525
and made a blazing trail, and vanished into thin air,
just as often happens when a shooting star,

---

[4]Perhaps a reference to the burning of the ships, or the Punic Wars.

detached from Heaven, speeds through the sky with streaming
tresses.
Sicilians and Trojans were amazed and stood there rooted,
praying to the gods on high, but the great Aeneas   530
did not reject the omen; embracing the happy Acestes,
he loaded him down with magnificent gifts and spoke as follows:
"Take them, father. For the mighty King of Olympus
has by these portents willed for you especial honors.
This is a gift which once belonged to Anchises himself: 535
a mixing-bowl engraved with figures, a princely present
which Cisseus of Thrace once gave my father Anchises
as a remembrance and a pledge of his esteem."
So speaking, he wreathed the old man's brow with green laurel,
proclaiming him the winner, first above them all.   540
The good Eurytion did not begrudge the prize,
although it was he alone who had brought down the bird.
After him a prize for the man who had cut the cord,
and finally the one who hit the mast with his arrow.

But Father Aeneas, even before the contest is over,   545
calls Epytides to him, the guardian and companion
of the boy Iülus, and speaks to his loyal ear:
"Go and tell Ascanius, if his youthful troops
are ready to show their skill in maneuvering their horses,
to parade them now, in honor of his grandfather,   550
and show himself in arms." He tells the streaming crowds
to leave the long field and the arena clear for action.
And now the boys appear before their parents' eyes
in even ranks, resplendent on their bridled steeds,
and as they pass, Sicilians and Trojans cheer them on.   555
As is the custom, they wear their hair with clipped garlands,
and each one carries two spears of cornel tipped with iron;
some have polished quivers hanging from their shoulders,
with golden circlets around their necks and over their chests.
There were three troops of horsemen with three captains to lead
them;   560
each troop was subdivided into two bands of six,

as with equal ranks and leaders they gaily rode by.
One troop of boys was proudly led by a little Priam,
noble son of Polites, renewing his grandfather's name,
destined to add many offspring to the Italian glory;   565
he rides a noble Thracian pinto dappled with white;
and white pasterns and white forehead held on high.
Atys leads the second troop (whence the Latin Atii);
Atys, a little boy, beloved by the boy Iülus.
Last and handsomest of all came Iülus himself,   570
riding a Sidonian horse which beautiful Dido
had given him as a remembrance and token of her love.
The other boys were riding on the Sicilian horses
belonging to old Acestes . . .
    The Trojans greet the timid boys with joyful cheers,   575
recognizing in their features their parents of old.
When they had gaily ridden round the stadium,
beneath their loved ones' eyes, Epytides from afar
gave the awaited signal with a crack of his whip.
They rode apart in equal ranks; then the three squadrons   580
broke ranks on either side, separating the columns,
then came together at a call, with levelled spears.
Next they went into other formations and counter-formations
in opposite groups, weaving circles with alternate circles
and simulated a real battle with their weapons,   585
turned their backs in flight, levelled their spears and charged,
finally making peace and riding in even ranks.
Just as they say of old in the Cretan Labyrinth
the paths were woven with blind walls and deceptive ways,
a thousand different turnings to break the follower's tracks—   590
a baffling puzzle and an irretraceable maze—
so the Trojan children tangled and knotted their steps,
playfully weaving terrified flight and make-believe battle,
like a school of dolphins swimming through the waves,
merrily cleaving the Carpathian and Libyan seas.   595
Ascanius later revived this custom and the contests,
when he surrounded Alba Longa with its walls,
and taught the early Latins to celebrate the games

just as he had done in his youth with the Trojan boys;
The Albans taught their children, and from them, in succession,   600
great Rome inherited and preserved the ancestral custom.
Even today the boys are called "Troy" and the squadron
                                                    "Trojan".
And thus ended the games in honor of blessèd Anchises.

Now for the first time Fortune changed and broke her faith.
While at the tomb they celebrate the various games,   605
Saturn's daughter Juno sends Iris down from Heaven
to the Trojan fleet, wafting her with breezes,
thinking many thoughts, her old grudge unforgotten.
So, moving swiftly on her thousand-colored rainbow,
Iris runs, invisible, along her path.   610
She spies the huge assembly, looks about the shore,
and sees the deserted harbor and abandoned fleet.
Far away the Trojan women on the shore
are weeping for Anchises' death, and as they weep
they look at the deep sea. "Alas, what seas remain   615
for a weary people!" This is the lament of all.
They long for a city; one and all they are sick of the sea.
And so into the women's midst, well-versed in malice,
Iris throws herself, but not with the face and dress
of a goddess; she becomes old Beroë, the wife   620
of Tmarian Doryclus, who once had fame and family
and children; in this guise she joins the Trojan matrons.
"Alas for us poor wretches," she said, "whom Achaean hands
did not drag to slaughter beneath our country's walls!
Unhappy race, for what destruction does Fate reserve you?   625
This is the seventh summer since the fall of Troy,
and we have measured all the seas and all the lands,
inhospitable rocks and stars, as over the ocean
we pursue a fleeing Italy and toss on the waves.
Here is the land of our kinsman Eryx and host Acestes: 630
who prevents us from building walls and founding a city?
O Fatherland and gods saved from the foe in vain,
shall there never be another Troy? Shall I never see

another Xanthus and a Simois, Hector's rivers?
Nay rather, come and burn with me these accursèd ships!   635
For I have seen the prophetic Cassandra in a dream
and she gave me blazing torches, saying: 'Here seek your Troy:
this shall be your home.' Now is the time for deeds;
such omens admit no delay. See, four altars to Neptune!
The god himself is giving us the will and torches!"   640
    She finished and first of all she snatched the fatal flame
and held it high aloft and threw it with all her might.
The Trojan women were amazed and stupefied.
One of them, the eldest of all, whose name was Pyrgo,
the royal nurse of Priam's many children, spoke: 645
"I tell you, mothers, that is not Beroë, the Rhoetian,
the wife of Doryclus. Look at those flashing eyes,
the signs of heavenly beauty, look at the radiance,
the features, hear her voice, see her step as she walks!
I myself left Beroë a little while ago,   650
sick and unhappy because she was the only one
who could not take a part in Anchises' funeral rites."
so she spoke . . .
    But the women began to look at the ships with doubtful gaze
and jealous eyes, wavering between a sad desire   655
for the present land and the far-off destined realm,
when the goddess poised herself on her wings and flew away,
cutting the enormous rainbow beneath the clouds.
Then indeed, amazed by the omen and mad with frenzy
they shout and some seize fire from the hearths within;   660
while others strip the altars and throw on leaves and branches
and torches; Vulcan rages madly with loosened reins
among the benches and oars and decks of painted fir.
    Eumelus brings the news about the burning fleet
back to the tomb of Anchises and the theater seats.   665
They look and see the billowing clouds of inky smoke.
First Ascanius, just as gaily he had led
his parading squadrons, spurred his horse to the shaken camp;
the worn-out trainers are powerless to hold him back.
"What is this new madness?" he cries, "what are you doing,   670

unhappy women? This is not the enemy camp
that you are burning, but your own hopes! Look, it is I,
your Ascanius!" He threw his helmet at his feet,
the one he had been wearing for the make-believe battle.
Aeneas hastens to the spot with the other Trojans.   675
The women are terrified and scatter over the shore
and hide themselves in whatever woods and caves they find.
They are ashamed of the deed, having now regained their senses;
they recognize their kin, and Juno is gone from their hearts.
But this is not enough to put the fire out;   680
it burns with unchecked fury; under the wet oak
the caulking slowly belches smoke, the hulls are eaten
by smoldering flames that devour the entire vessel;
the heroes' strength and floods of water are in vain.
Then good Aeneas tore the cloak from off his shoulders,   685
raised his hands to Heaven and called the gods for aid:
"Almighty Jupiter, if you do not hate the Trojans,
and if your ancient kindness has any regard for men
and all their suffering, let my ships escape the flames.
Now, Father, snatch the Trojan fortunes from destruction,   690
or else, if I deserve it, with your thunderbolt
destroy what little remains to us, right here and now."
   Hardly had he spoken when it began to rain;
torrential showers poured from the sky, and thunder grumbled,
shaking hill and plain. A steady patter of raindrops   695
falls from the heavens, inky black with clouds and south winds.
The ships are waterlogged, the half-burned timbers soaked
until the fire is quenched at last and the heat subsides
and all the ships save four are rescued from the flames.

   But Father Aeneas, shaken by this bitter fate,   700
pondered in his heart, considering weighty problems,
turning this way and that: should he forget the Fates
and settle in Sicily, or aim for Italian shores?
Then the aged Nautes, whom Tritonian Pallas
had taught above all men, and imbued with craft and skill   705
(for she would give him answers about the wrath of the gods

and what it portended, and what the course of Fate required),
tried with these words to comfort Aeneas: "Son of a goddess,
let us follow Destiny as she calls or recalls us;
whatever happens, fortune is overcome by enduring. 710
Here is the Trojan Acestes, sprung from blood divine;
make him the willing partner and sharer of your counsels;
entrust to him the men whose ships are lost, and those
who are weary of your great adventures and fortunes;
pick out the aged men, and the women sick of the sea, 715
the weak, the sick, and those who are terrified of danger,
and let these weary souls find rest in Sicily;
let them build a city here and call it Acesta."
Aeneas is fired by these words of his aged friend,
and he is truly torn apart by his many troubles. 720
Now dusky night came in her chariot through the sky
when down from Heaven glides the spirit of Father Anchises,
all of a sudden, and he speaks the following words:
  "O my son, dearer to me than life itself,
while life remained, my son, harassed by the Fates of Troy, 725
I come to you by command of Jove, who drove the fire
from your ships and pitied you from Heaven on high.
Obey the excellent advice that aged Nautes
has given you: take to Italy only chosen youths,
only the stoutest hearts. A harsh and rugged people 730
must be overcome in Latium. But first of all
come to me in the infernal regions of Dis;
visit the gloomy depths of Avernus; for I am not
among the sad shades of Tartarus, but in Elysium,
the pleasant dwelling of the Blessed. The chaste Sibyl 735
will lead you here, after black sheep have been slaughtered.
Then you shall learn of your race and the walls that will be
                                                     yours.
And now farewell: damp Night revolves in her mid-course;
the panting horses of cruel East have breathed on me."
  He spoke, and vanished into thin air like a wisp of smoke. 740
Aeneas said: "Where are you rushing and hurrying away?
Whom are you fleeing from? Why may I not embrace you?"

So speaking, he stirs up the coals of the sleeping fires,
and with sacred meal and incense he makes the sacrifice,
humbly, to Trojan Lar and the shrine of white-haired Vesta.   745
Speedily he calls his comrades, Acestes first,
telling them of Jove's command and his father's counsel,
having resolved in his mind upon a course of action.
The conference is short: Acestes does not refuse.
The matrons are enrolled for the city, and on the shore   750
are left all those who wish, who are not desirous of glory.
They repair the ships' benches and the charred wood of the hulls,
refit the vessels, make new oars, refurbish the rigging
—a small number of men, but brave and belligerent.
Meanwhile Aeneas marks out boundaries with a plow,   755
assigning houses by lot, here Ilium and here Troy.
Trojan Acestes is delighted with his new kingdom;
he proclaims a forum, calls the Senate and gives them laws.
Then on the summit of Mount Eryx, close to the stars,
a shrine to Idalian Venus is founded, and a priest   760
assigned to Anchises' tomb with a broad and sacred grove.
    After nine days of feasting and offerings at the altars,
the gentle breezes have calmed and lulled the angry sea;
the South Wind breathes upon them and calls them to the deep.
A loud lament arises from the winding shore.   765
They all embrace each other and wait a night and a day.
Even the mothers now, and those to whom the sea
had recently seemed a cruel and unspeakable terror,
want to go and suffer all the hardships of exile.
The good Aeneas comforts them with friendly words   770
and tearfully commends them to his kinsman Acestes.
He orders three steers slain to Eryx, and a lamb
to the Tempests, then the lines are duly cast off.
Aeneas himself, his temples crowned with olive garlands,
stands alone at the prow and holds the cup, and throws   775
the entrails into the salty waves, and pours the wine.
A wind springs up astern and follows them as they go.
They lash the sea in rivalry and sweep the water.

Meanwhile Venus' heart is gnawed by anxious cares.
She speaks to Neptune, pouring forth her heart's lament: 780
"The cruel anger and unrelenting heart of Juno
compel me, Neptune, to descend to every prayer.
Neither the lapse of years nor piety softens her.
Unbroken by Jove's will and Fate, she will not rest.
She is not satisfied with having devoured Troy   785
and dragged its sorry remnants through every punishment;
she now must needs pursue the ashes and the bones.
She alone can know the reason for such hatred;
you yourself have witnessed the tremendous storm
she recently created in the Libyan Sea.   790
She mingled sea and sky, relying on Aeolus
and his storms, in your domain she dared this . . .
Yes, and she fiendishly drove on the Trojan women
and made them burn the ships (a monstrous deed!) and forced
                                                              them
to leave their friends and kinsmen on an unknown shore.   795
I pray you, allow the rest to sail across your waves
in safety; let them reach at last the Laurentian Tiber,
if what I ask is right, if the Fates allow those walls."
     Then Saturn's son, the ruler of the sea, speaks thus:
Cytherea, it is right for you to put your faith   800
in my kingdom, your birthplace: I have earned your trust,
and often calmed the raging waters and the heavens.
On land as well (witness Xanthus and Simois)
my care has been for Aeneas. When the pursuing Achilles
forced the stricken Trojan armies back to the walls,   805
slaying many thousands, making the rivers groan
—so full were they of corpses—when Xanthus was unable
to find his way to the sea, then I, in a hollow cloud,
snatched up Aeneas as he confronted Peleus' son
—an uneven, ill-omened match—though I myself desired   810
to uproot perjured Troy, which my own hands had built.
My purpose has remained unchanged, so have no fears.
Just as you wish, he shall safely reach Avernus' haven.
Only one shall you seek in vain amid the waves,

one life shall be given for many . . ."   815
    With these words he soothed the goddess and made her **glad**,
then yokes his steeds with golden bridles and foaming bits
and lets the reins fly freely in his loosened hands
and skims above the surface in his sea-blue car.
The heavy waves subside beneath the thundering axle,   820
the swollen sea is calmed; clouds vanish from the sky.
Then come his varied companions, the enormous whales,
the aged band of Glaucus, Ino's son Palaemon,
the speedy Tritons and the whole army of Phorcus;
Thetis and Melite on the left, the maid Panopea,   825
Nesaea and Spio, Thalia and Cymodoce.
    Now in turn Father Aeneas' anxious heart
is filled with soothing joys; he orders all the masts
to be raised up, and all the sails to be unfurled.
The crew all hasten to the task and set the sails   830
now to the right, now to the left, and turn the yard-arms
this way and that; the steady winds are favorable.
Palinurus, first of all, leads the close-packed column,
the others all take their signals for the course from him.

Now dewy Night had reached the midpoint of the heavens;   835
the members of the crew were stretched out on the benches
beneath the oars, relaxing on the wooden seats,
when Sleep came gliding lightly down from the stars of **Heaven**,
cleaving the gloomy sky and parting all the shadows,
seeking you, Palinurus, bringing evil dreams   840
to the innocent; the god sat on the lofty stern,
in the guise of Phorbas, and he spoke these words:
"Palinurus, son of Iasus, the sea itself
is guiding the ships; the wind is steady, 'tis time for rest;
lay down your head and rest your weary eyes from labor.   845
I myself will take your turn for a while at the rudder."
Scarcely even lifting his eyes Palinurus makes answer:
"Can you be telling me to trust the quiet sea
and placid waves? Shall I put my faith in such a monster?
Shall I entrust Aeneas to the treacherous winds   850

when I myself have been so often deceived by them?"

    These words he spoke without relaxing his hold on the **tiller**
and never taking his eyes away from the guiding stars.
But the god shook on his temples a branch of Lethe's **dew**
steeped in soporific Stygian strength; his eyes   **855**
began to swim; no longer could he keep them open.
Hardly had his limbs relaxed in sudden slumber
when, leaning above him, Sleep threw him overboard
still holding on to the rudder, into the clear waves,
calling often on his comrades, but in vain.   **860**
The god then flies away into the balmy air.
Nevertheless the fleet glides safely on its course,
fearlessly, just as Father Neptune has promised them.
And now, as they sailed, they were approaching the Siren **Cliffs**,
always fraught with peril, and white with sailors' bones;   **865**
the rocks were pounded by the ceaseless roaring surf,
when Aeneas realized that Palinurus was gone
and that the ship was drifting; he took the helm himself
and steered her through the night, with many a heartsick groan:
"Alas, too confident in sea and sky, Palinurus,   **870**
all naked you shall lie upon an unknown shore."

End of Book V

BOOK VI

THE LOWER WORLD

Thus spoke Aeneas, weeping. He gives his fleet the reins,
and finally he glides to the shores of Euboean Cumae.
They turn the prows to face the sea, and secure the ships
with the firm teeth of anchors, and the rounded keels
fringe the beach. An eager band of youthful Trojans   5
leap to the Hesperian shore. Some look for seeds
of fire hidden in veins of flint; others raid the forest,
home of wild creatures, and they find and point out streams.
But good Aeneas seeks the heights and throne of Apollo,
and the huge cave nearby, home of the dreaded Sibyl,   10
into whom the god of Delos breathes his spirit
and mighty mind, revealing secrets of the future.
They reach the grove of Hecate and the golden roof.
   Men say that Daedalus, in his flight from Cretan Minos,
ventured to trust himself to the sky on swooping wings   15
and glided to the chilly North, on an unknown path,
hovering at last above the Chalcidian peak.
And here, restored once more to land, he dedicated
his wingèd oars to Apollo, and built a mighty temple.
On the doors is seen Androgeos' death; the Athenians,   20
condemned, alas! to pay as annual tribute, the bodies
of seven children. There was the urn with the lots all drawn.
Opposite, Cnossus' island rises from the sea;
the cruel passion of the bull, Pasiphaë,
her furtive mating, the hybrid shape of the Minotaur,   25
her two-formed offspring, monument of monstrous love.
Here was the artful Labyrinth with its intricate paths;
but Daedalus, in pity for Ariadne's love,
unwound the roundabout devices of the maze,
guiding the lover's sightless feet by means of a thread.   30

You too, O Icarus, would have had a share in the sculpture,
had grief permitted: twice had Daedalus attempted
to picture your fall in gold—twice failed the father's hands.
    The Trojans would have continued looking at these tales
had not Achates returned, and with him Deiphobe,   35
daughter of Glaucus, Apollo's and Diana's priestess.
She said; "This is no time for you to look at pictures;
better to sacrifice seven bullocks from unbroken herds,
and seven sheep selected according to ritual."
Thus she spoke to Aeneas; the Trojans swiftly complied.   40
Then the priestess summoned the men to her lofty temple.
The side of the Euboean cliff is hollowed out
into a cavern with a hundred mouths and tunnels,
through which as many voices emerge—the Sibyl's answers.
And as they reached the temple's threshold the maiden cried: 45
"Now is the time to consult the oracle. Lo, the god,
the god!" and as she spoke her face and color changed,
her hair fell in disorder, her bosom heaved and panted,
her heart swelled with wild frenzy; she seemed to become taller,
her voice no longer sounded human; the god was near her,   50
touching her with his breath. "Trojan Aeneas," she said,
"Why do you delay with prayer? For until you pray
the temple's mighty mouth will not be afraid and open."
She was silent. An icy shudder ran through the Trojans' limbs.
Aeneas, their king, begins to pray from deep in his heart.   55
"O Phoebus, you who have always pitied the woes of Troy,
who guided the hand of Paris and the Dardanian shaft
against Achilles, under your leadership I have sailed
to many lands and many seas, from the distant country
of the Massylians to the fields the Syrtes border.   60
Now at last we have reached the fleeting Italian shore:
may Troy's ill fortune not pursue us any further!
And all you gods and goddesses, who once were offended
by Troy and all her glory, Destiny now permits you
to spare this people. And you, O holy prophetess,   65
seer of the future, grant us (for I do not ask
a kingdom not promised by Fate) allow the Trojans to settle

in Latium, with the wandering, storm-tossed gods of Troy.
And I shall dedicate to Phoebus and Trivia
a solid marble temple, with festal days for Apollo.   70
You too, O Sibyl, shall have an ample shrine in our land,
where I shall place your oracles and mystic responses
that you will give my people, with chosen men as priests.
Only, I beg you, do not entrust your verses to leaves,
for they will fly about in wild disorder, the playthings   75
of greedy winds; but chant them yourself." He finished speaking.
But the prophetess, not yet submitting to Phoebus,
runs wildly through the cave, still trying to shake off
the power of the god. But Phoebus, all the more,
torments her mouth and tames her heart and molds her will.   80
And now the hundred mighty mouths, of their own accord,
opened and carried through the air the seer's response:
     "You who at last have overcome the sea's great perils,
the land holds even worse for you. The Trojans will come
into Lavinium's realm—dismiss this care from your mind—   85
but they will live to regret it. Wars, terrible wars
I see for you. The Tiber will run red with blood.
Another Simois and Xanthus and Grecian camp
await you there; and you shall find another Achilles,
also born of a goddess; and Juno still will hound you;   90
and you shall pray, a suppliant in desperate plight,
to all the peoples, and all the cities of Italy.
The cause of all these woes will again be a foreign bride,
again an alien marriage . . .
But do not yield to troubles, nay, face them even more boldly   95
than Fortune seems to permit you. For the road to safety
will come, where you least expect it, from a Grecian city."
These are the ambiguous words the Cumaean Sibyl
chants from her shrine, a roaring echo in the cavern,
shrouding truth in riddles. Such is the might of Apollo,   100
holding the reins, applying the goad to the priestess' mind.
But when her frenzy had passed and her raging mouth was silent,
the hero Aeneas began: "O maiden, no new trials
or unexpected labors are in store for me;

for I have foreseen them all within my mind.   105
One thing I pray: since this is said to be the entrance
to the Underworld—the gloomy marsh of Acheron,
allow me to see again my beloved father's face;
teach me the road and open for me the sacred portals.
I rescued him from flames and a thousand enemy spears;   110
I carried him on my shoulder through the Grecian lines;
he was my companion, sharing with me the dangers
of all the menacing seas and all the hostile skies—
a weak old man, endowed with strength beyond his years.
He is the one who told me to approach your temple,   115
in humble supplication. Take pity on son and father,
gracious lady, I beg you, for you can accomplish all things;
and not in vain has Hecate made you Avernus' mistress.
If Orpheus was allowed to redeem the shade of his wife,
trusting the harmonious strings of his Thracian lyre,   120
if Pollux was permitted to ransom his brother Castor
by dying in his stead, and comes and goes so often . . .
and Theseus and Hercules—but why mention them? I, too,
claim my descent from Jove." He spoke, and clasped the altar;
the priestess then replied: "Trojan, son of Anchises,   125
sprung from blood divine, the descent to Avernus is easy.
The doors of gloomy Dis stand open night and day.
But to retrace your steps and escape to the air above,
this is the task, this the toil. To a few, whom Jupiter loved,
or who were exalted by their virtuous deeds to Heaven,   130
sons of gods, this was permitted. Surrounded by forests,
inky Cocytus girds the place with sinuous folds.
But if you have in your heart such longing, such desire
twice to cross the Styx, and twice to see black Tartarus,
if you really wish to embark on such an insane adventure,   135
this is what you must do. There is a golden bough
hidden in the forest: both leaves and stem are of gold;
this bough is consecrated to infernal Juno,
and deeply hidden by shadows in the gloomy valley.
And no one is allowed to see Earth's hidden domain   140
who has not first plucked the golden foliage from its tree.

The fair Proserpina herself demands this gift.
Now when the branch has been taken away, another one
grows in its place, and shines with the same golden luster;
so search with lifted eyes, and find it, and pluck it off,   145
and it will easily come away of its own accord,
provided the Fates are willing; but otherwise, no force
will avail to conquer it—not even a blade of steel.

   Moreover, the body of your friend is lying there,
(alas, you know not!) defiling the fleet with the stain of death,   150
while you are busy here consulting oracles.
Begin by giving him the burial he deserves,
and bring black cattle for your first peace-offering.
Then and only then shall you see the Stygian forests,
the road no living man may walk." Then she was silent.   155

   Aeneas goes with grieving face and downcast eyes,
leaving the cave, and pondering within his heart
these dark events. And at his side the faithful Achates
walks, keeping step with him and sharing in his sorrows.
And as they walked they spoke of many different things,   160
wondering which was the dead comrade the priestess spoke of,
who was to be buried. Suddenly, on the beach, they saw
Misenus, cut off by a most untimely doom—
Misenus, son of Aeolus, without an equal
in stirring men to battle with his brazen trumpet.   165
He had been great Hector's companion; at Hector's side
he had fought, renowned alike for spear and trumpet.
And after victorious Achilles had slain his chief,
this hero had joined forces with the Trojan Aeneas,
becoming his friend, and serving no inferior leader.   170
But when he made the sea resound, blowing a sea-shell
and foolishly defied the gods to compete with him,
the jealous Triton (if the story can be believed)
seized him and drowned him in the waves amid the rocks.
And so they mourned Misenus with loud-voiced lamentation,   175
especially good Aeneas. Then they carried out
the Sibyl's commands, with tears; they build a funeral pyre,

like an enormous altar reaching to the sky.
They go into the ancient forest, home of beasts,
and pine trees fall, and oaks resound with the blows of axes,   180
and ashen logs and oaken beams are split with wedges,
and huge tree trunks come rolling down the mountainside.
Aeneas too takes part in the work; he leads his men,
urging them to the task, and even wielding the axe.
But as he looked at the forest, he pondered in his heart,   185
thinking about the task ahead, and he said a prayer:
"If only the Golden Bough would show itself to me
in this great dark forest! For all the prophetess said
came true—alas, too true! concerning you, Misenus."
Scarce had he spoken when two doves came flying down   190
out of the sky; before his very eyes, they alighted
on the green grass. Then good Aeneas was overjoyed
—he recognized his mother's birds, and thus he prayed:
   "O be my guides and find the way (if there be one);
direct your course through the deep wood where the Golden
                                                              Bough   195
casts its shadow on the ground. And you, immortal mother,
help me in my trouble." So speaking, he checked his steps,
watching the birds for a message, to see where they would go.
They flew away, and stopped to feed, and flew again,
keeping only as far ahead as the eye could follow.   200
And when they reached the entry-way of reeking Avernus,
they rose into the air and then came swiftly to rest;
having found the desired double tree they perch on its top,
and there the Golden Bough shone through the leafy greenness.
As in the winter's cold, the mistletoe in the forest   205
blooms with new foliage, not sown by its own tree,
surrounding the smooth tree-trunk with its yellow berries,
such was the appearance of the golden leaves,
so they tinkled in the breeze on the shadowy oak.
At once Aeneas seized and broke the reluctant bough   210
and carried it to the house of the prophetic Sibyl.
   The Trojans meanwhile were weeping on the shore for
                                                           Misenus,

offering the last rites to the ungrateful ashes.
First they raised a lofty pyre of resinous pine
and oaken logs, and they entwined dark foliage   215
on the sides, with funeral cypresses in front.
They decorated it on top with shining armor.
Some of them heated water in bubbling bronze on the fire,
and washed and anointed the frigid corpse with lamentation.
Sorrowingly they lay the limbs upon the couch   220
covered with purple garments, a familiar costume.
And some of them put their shoulders to the heavy litter
—a melancholy task—according to ancient custom
they held the torch with averted eyes. All burned together,
frankincense, food-offerings, bowls of olive oil.   225
When the ashes collapsed and the fire had died away,
they washed the thirsty dust of the remains with wine,
Corynaeus put the bones in a brazen urn,
and with fresh water he encircled his friends three times
and cleansed them, sprinkling dew from a fertile olive branch.   230
After he had pronounced the last words of farewell,
the good Aeneas erected an enormous barrow,
and placed on top of it the weapons, oar, and trumpet,
beneath a lofty mountain, which still is called Misenus,
preserving the hero's name for all eternity.   235
This done, he hastened to obey the Sibyl's commands.

    There was a deep and yawning cavern with rugged rocks,
sheltered by inky waters and a gloomy forest:
no birds could safely fly above this stretch of water,
winging their way—such was the noxious emanation   240
that poured from its black jaws into the arch of Heaven,
hence the Greeks called the lake Avernus: the Birdless Place.
Here first the priestess set in line four dark-backed bullocks
pouring upon their foreheads a libation of wine;
she cut the topmost bristles from between their horns   245
and laid them on the fire as the first offering,
calling aloud on Hecate, supreme in Heaven and Hell.
Others cut the victims' throats and caught the blood,

still warm, in bowls. Aeneas slew a black-fleeced lamb
to Night, the Eumenides' mother, and her mighty sister,   250
and sacrificed a sterile cow to Proserpina.
Then he begins nocturnal sacrifices to Pluto,
laying on the flames whole carcasses of bulls,
pouring rich olive oil over the blazing entrails.
And lo! at the appearance of the sun's first rays   255
the ground began to tremble right beneath their feet,
and wooded mountains shook and dogs howled in the gloom
at the approach of Hecate. "Away, unhallowed ones,
away!" the priestess cried, "Away from the sacred grove!
But you, Aeneas, forward: draw your sword from its sheath;   260
now is the time for courage, now for a stout heart."
So saying the Sibyl madly rushed into the cavern,
and he, with dauntless steps, followed in her path.

O Gods who rule the world of ghosts and silent shades!
Chaos and Phlegethon, and soundless realms of night,   265
allow me to tell what I have heard, and with your powers
let me reveal the secrets of the dark depths of earth!
They went their way in the darkness of the gloomy shadows
through the empty halls and the intangible world of Dis,
as when, by uncertain moonlight, a path goes through the forest   270
when the sky is obscured by Jupiter with shadows,
and when black night has robbed the world of all its colors.
Before the Entrance Hall, and in the jaws of Orcus,
Grief and Avenging Cares have made their dwelling place.
There dwell pallid Disease, and melancholy Old Age,   275
and Fear, and ill-advising Famine, and shameful Want,
all horrid shapes to behold, and Death and Suffering,
and Sleep, Death's brother, and all the guilty Joys of the soul,
and on the opposite threshold War, the bringer of Death,
the iron chambers of the Furies, and mad Discord   280
with bloody fillets that encircle her snaky locks.
And in the midst an ancient elm spreads out its branches,
an immense and shady tree, and here, they say, false Dreams
make their dwelling, clinging under every leaf.
And all manner of monsters with their various shapes   285

are stabled at the door: Centaurs, and two-formed Scyllas,
and hundred-armed Briareus, and the Lernaean Hydra,
hissing horribly, and the fire-breathing Chimaera,
and Gorgons and Harpies and triple-bodied Geryon.
Here, in sudden terror, Aeneas seized his sword   290
and turned the naked blade against the approaching monsters,
and, had he not been cautioned by his wise companion
that they were only phantoms without bodily substance,
he would have attacked them, vainly cleaving shades with steel.
Thence the road led to Tartarus and Acheron's stream.   295
A muddy whirlpool seethes and gurgles as the abyss
belches out its filthy sludge to choke Cocytus.
Here is the Guardian, watching over the horrid water:
Charon, squalid and repulsive, with unkempt beard
covering his chin, with staring, blazing eyes   300
and dirty clothing hanging, knotted, from his shoulders.
Alone he poles the boat and takes care of the sails,
as in his gloomy vessel he transports the dead;
an old man, but he has the green strength of a god.
The crowds of ghosts rush swiftly to the river-bank,   305
mothers and men, and bodies of great-hearted heroes,
finished with life, and boys, and maidens yet unmarried,
placed on the funeral pyre before the eyes of their parents;
they were as many as the leaves, that in the forest
flutter to the ground at the first chill of autumn,   310
as many as the birds that flock from sea to shore
when winter's frost drives them overseas to sunny lands.
They stood there, begging to be the first ones carried across,
and stretched their hands in longing for the other shore.
But the sullen ferryman took now some, now others,   315
while others still were thrust away from the sandy bank.
Aeneas marvelled and was disturbed by all the commotion.
"Tell me, maiden," he said, "why this thronging to the river?
What do the spirits want? By what discrimination
are some left behind, while others cross the leaden waters?"   320
The aged prophetess made answer briefly thus:
"Son of Anchises, truly an offspring of the gods,

you see the pools of Cocytus and the Stygian marsh,
a power even the gods are afraid to swear falsely by.
this crowd you see had no resource for burial;   325
the ferryman is Charon; those he takes have been buried.
He may not bear them over the banks and raucous waters
until their bones have found a final resting place.
They wander and flit about the shores for a hundred years
and only then are they admitted to these waters."   330

    The good Aeneas paused and checked his footsteps, thinking
many things, and pitying much their cruel plight.
He saw among them, sorrowful, lacking funeral honors,
Leucaspis, and Orontes, captain of his fleet,
whom the South Wind, as they came across the sea from Troy,   335
had overwhelmed, sinking the men and ships alike.
And lo! there was the helmsman also, Palinurus,
who only recently, on the way from Africa,
as he was watching the stars, had fallen overboard.
When Aeneas recognized his mournful shade,   340
he said to him: "What god was it, O Palinurus,
that snatched you from our midst and drowned you in the waves?
Come, tell me: Apollo never lied to me before,
but he deluded me with this one answer, saying
that you would escape the sea and safely reach the shore   345
of Italy. Is this how the god fulfills his promise?"
The other answered: "Apollo's tripod did not deceive you,
son of Anchises, my chief; no god threw me into the water.
The tiller which I was holding as I steered the ship
was wrenched away from my grasp, and I fell overboard,   350
taking it with me. I swear to you by these rough seas,
that I was less afraid for myself than for your ship
which now, bereft alike of rudder and of pilot,
was foundering amid the mighty surging waves.
Three stormy nights the wind drove me across the water,   355
carrying me on the crashing sea; but on the fourth day
from the crest of a lofty wave, I sighted Italy.
I slowly swam to land, and just as I reached safety,

weighted down by my dripping clothes, I grasped the rocks
with my fingernails, when suddenly, barbarians,   360
thinking me a rich prize, attacked me with their swords.
Now the waves hold me and the winds throw me on the beach.
I pray you, by the lovely light and air of Heaven,
and by your father and the hope of growing Iülus,
save me from these woes, unconquered one! Either heap earth   365
upon me, for you can, and seek the harbor of Velia,
or if there is a way, if your goddess-mother shows you
—for I cannot think that without protection of the gods
you are preparing to embark on the Stygian marsh—
give me your hand, wretch that I am, and take me with you   370
across the water, that I may find peace at least in death."
So he had spoken, and the prophetess began to answer:
"Whence comes this wild desire of yours, O Palinurus?
To see the River Styx without due burial,
and the Cocytus, and to approach this bank unbidden?   375
Think not the gods' decrees can ever be changed by prayer.
But listen to what I say, for it will allay your sorrow:
the neighboring peoples and their cities, far and wide,
driven by heaven-sent omens, shall appease your bones,
and build a tomb, and to the tomb give offerings;   380
the place will bear the name of Palinurus forever."
At these words, his cares are dispersed for a little while,
and he rejoices in the land that will have his name.

    They resume their journey, approaching near the river,
but when the ferryman sees them from the Stygian water,   385
passing through the silent grove and nearing the bank,
he speaks to them, addressing words of stern reproach:
"Whoever you may be, coming in arms to my river,
stop where you are, and tell me the reason for your coming;
this is the land of Shades, of Sleep and drowsy Night.   390
And living bodies may not cross in the Stygian boat.
Indeed, I had no joy in ferrying Hercules
across the water, and Theseus and Pirithoüs—
sons of gods they were, and invincible in strength:

for one tried to drag into chains by force Tartarus' watchdog,   395
from the King's very throne, and snatched him away all trembling;
the others tried to take our Queen from Pluto's chamber."
The soothsayer of Apollo briefly made an answer:
    "Fear not, Charon: we plan no trickery or deceit;
our weapons will not hurt you; Cerberus may bark   400
and frighten bloodless shades for all eternity,
and chaste Proserpina remain on her uncle's doorstep.
This is Trojan Aeneas, virtuous and brave,
descending to Erebus to see his father's shade.
If you are not moved by the sight of such great piety,   405
you know this branch, at least," and she showed the Golden
                                                        Bough
hidden in her robe. Charon's anger subsided.
He said no more, but marvelled at the holy gift
—the fateful wand, which he had not seen for a long time;
and turning his blue vessel's stern, he approached the shore.   410
The other spirits, sitting there upon the benches,
he dislodges, opening the gangplank; and receives
the great Aeneas. The leaky boat groans under the weight,
and marshy water begins to flood it through the chinks.
At last he brings the priestess and the hero across   415
and lands them safely on ugly mud and gray swamp-grass.
The huge Cerberus is here, barking with all three mouths,
crouching with his enormous body in the cavern.
The priestess, seeing the snakes all writhing on his necks,
throws him a morsel drugged with honey and doctored meal.   420
He catches it and gobbles it ravenously down
with triple jaws: straightway his monstrous limbs relax
and he sprawls along the ground for all the length of the cavern.
With the guardian asleep, Aeneas gains the entrance
and quickly leaves the shore from which there is no return.   425
    And soon voices are heard in wails and lamentation:
the souls of weeping infants, who, on the very threshold
of a sweet life they did not share, were snatched away
from their mothers' breasts, and plunged into an early death.
Nearby were those condemned to die on spurious charges.   430

But these places were not assigned without lot or judge:
for Minos presides and shakes the urn; he calls a council
of the voiceless, and learns of all their lives and deeds.
In the next place dwell those unhappy, innocent souls
who, hating the daylight, took their lives with their own hands.   435
How willingly they now would exchange their dreary lot
for all the poverty, toil and woes of the upper air!
But Fate stands firm: the ugly marsh and unlovely water
hold them fast, and the nine circles of Styx surround them.

Not far from here, and stretching out in all directions,   440
are seen the Mourning Fields (for such is the name they bear).
Here are all those who have wasted away from cruel love,
hidden in secret paths, concealed by myrtle groves,
even in death their bitter grief has never left them.
Here Aeneas saw Phaedra, and Procris, and sad Eriphyle,   445
pointing out the cruel wounds her son had made,
and Evadne, and Pasiphaë, and Laodamia,
and Caeneus, formerly a youth, but now a woman,
turned back again by Fate into her former shape.
Phoenician Dido, her wound still fresh, was there among them,   450
wandering in the forest. When the Trojan hero
came near and recognized her dim form amid the shadows,
just as, in the early part of the month, one sees
(or thinks he has seen) the new moon rising among the clouds—
he shed bitter tears and spoke to her in words of love: 455
"Unhappy Dido, was it true—this rumor I heard,
and are you really dead? Did you end your life with the sword?
Was I, alas, the reason for your death? I swear by the stars,
by the world above, by whatever is sacred in the grave:
against my will, O Queen, I departed from your shores;   460
but the will of the gods, which forces me now to walk in the
                                                                shadows
through this gloomy world of deep and endless night,
drove me with their dire commands. I never thought
that my departure would bring you such deep distress.
But stay your step, and do not withdraw from my sight.   465

Whom are you fleeing? This is the last word I may speak to you."
With such words and with tears, Aeneas tried to soothe
the blazing anger and the savage gaze of Dido,
but she turned away from him, with eyes fixed on the ground;
and the words he spoke had no more effect on her   470
than if she had been made of flint or Parian marble.
At last she tore herself away, and hating him still,
she fled into the shadows of the grove, where Sychaeus,
her former husband, gave her love and sympathy.
But none the less, Aeneas, shocked by her unjust fate,   475
watches her from afar with tears, and pities her.

He follows the difficult path, and comes to the distant fields
where those who were renowned in war dwell in seclusion.
Here Tydeus meets him; here too, Parthenopaeus
the great warrior, and the pallid shade of Adrastus;   480
and here the Trojan chiefs, much bemoaned in the upper world.
He sees them and laments: stretched out in long array
there were Glaucus and Medon and Thersilochus,
Antenor's three sons, and Polyboetes, priest of Ceres,
and Idaeus, who still had his chariot and arms.   485
They stand around him, crowding on the right and left,
nor is it enough to have seen him once: they want to linger
and walk along with him, and learn why he has come.
But the Danaan leaders, Agamemnon's army,
as they see the hero's gleaming arms in the darkness,   490
tremble in great alarm: some turn away to flee,
as in former days they sought the ships, and others
raise a tiny cry to mock their gaping mouths.
And here he saw the son of Priam, Deiphobus,
his whole body mutilated; his face was cruelly mangled—   495
his face and both his hands, his ears were torn from his temples,
his nostrils were lacerated with a repulsive wound.
Scarcely recognizing the trembling shade, that tried
to conceal his horrible torture, he spoke in familiar voice:
"Deiphobus, mighty in arms, descendant of Teucer's stock,   500
who had the will to punish you with such cruel revenge,

and who had the power over you? for Rumor told me
that on the last night, weary with killing Greeks so long,
you sank exhausted on a bloody heap of corpses.
I built an empty tomb for you on the Rhoetean shore,   505
and with a loud voice called three times upon your spirit.
Your name and weapons guard the place. But you, my friend,
I neither saw nor buried in your native soil."
Priam's son replied: "Nothing has been left undone
by you, my friend; you have paid every due to me and my ghost.   510
My fate and that Laconian[1] woman's murderous crime
plunged me into these woes; she left me these souvenirs!
For you know how we all spent that last fateful night,
in vain, deluding joys; you must remember it well!
When the deadly horse leaped over the Trojan walls,   515
carrying armed foot-soldiers in its hollow womb,
she, pretending to dance, led all the Trojan women
shouting in Bacchanalian rites: she held the torch,
inviting all the Greeks down from the citadel.
I meanwhile had sunk down, all overcome with cares,   520
in our ill-fated bridal chamber. Sweet, deep slumber,
the image of placid death, lay heavily upon me.
My excellent wife took every weapon from the house—
she had even stolen my faithful sword from under my head.
She called in Menelaus and opened wide the doors,   525
hoping, I suppose to do her lover a service,
and thus erase the memory of her ancient crimes.
What more is there to say? The Greeks broke into my bedroom;
Ulysses, author of crimes, came with them. O gods, if I pray
with pious mouth, let the Greeks pay equal penalties!   530
But what are you doing here—you who are still alive?
Is this a part of your wandering over the stormy seas?
Have the gods sent you? What destiny compels you
to visit this sad and sunless place of desolation?"

    As they talked together, Dawn with her rosy chariot   535
had crossed the sky's midpoint in her celestial course.

---

[1] i.e. Helen.

They might have spent the whole allotted time in this manner
but the Sibyl came to them and spoke brief warning:
"Night is coming, Aeneas; we waste the hours in mourning.
This is the place where the road divides into two parts: 540
on the right, as it goes beneath the walls of mighty Dis,
our path leads to Elysium, but on the left
the wicked find their punishment in Tartarus."
Deiphobus said: "Do not be angry, holy priestess:;
I will go and take my place and return to the shadows.   545
Go, glory of Troy, and find a better fate than mine!"
So Deiphobus spoke, and turned his steps away.

Aeneas suddenly looked back, and under a cliff
he saw broad battlements on the left, and triple walls:
surrounded by a rapid river of seething flames,   550
Tartarean Phlegethon went rushing by the rocks.
A massive gate in front, with columns of adamant;
no human might, not even gods can ever uproot it.
An iron tower rises upward; Tisiphone
is sitting there in front, girt with a bloody garment,   555
guarding the portal night and day, for she never sleeps.
And groans are heard within, and the sound of the cruel whip,
and the metallic clanking of dragging iron chains.
Aeneas stops in terror at the hideous din:
"Tell me, maiden, what crimes are these? What punishments   560
are inflicted here? What is this terrible uproar?"
The priestess answers him: "Leader of the Trojans,
no upright soul may ever cross this evil threshold,
but when Hecate placed me in charge of Avernus' groves,
she told me of all the penalties, and showed me the region.   565
Cretan Rhadamanthus rules this awful place:
he punishes and hears the evidence and confessions,
whenever a man, in the world above, rejoicing in crime,
delays repentance for his sins till the hour of death.
At once Tisiphone scourges the guilty with her lash,   570
for she is the Avenger, and she holds fierce serpents
in her left hand as she calls her savage band of sisters.

Then finally, creaking on its horrid, strident hinges,
the portal opens. Do you see the sentinel
sitting in the gateway? Do you see her form?   575
The Hydra, even more terrible, with fifty heads
and gaping black mouths, is within; and Tartarus itself
opens its yawning jaws twice as far in the gloom
as we see Olympus stretching upward in the sky.
Here the ancient race of Earth, the Titan offspring,   580
smitten by thunderbolts, are tortured in the abyss.
Here I have seen the huge bodies of the Aloides
who tried to tear the very sky down with their hands
and to expel Jupiter from his heavenly dwelling.
I have seen the cruel punishment of Salmoneus   585
who imitated the lightning and thunder of Olympus;
for he, drawn by four horses and brandishing a torch,
rode in triumph through the cities of Greece, and his town
in the middle of Elis, demanding divine honors.
Madman—to imitate the inimitable storm clouds   590
and thunderbolts with bronze and the pounding of horses' hoofs!
But the Almighty Father launched his own thunderbolt
from the cloudy sky—he needed no pitchy firebrand!
and drove the impostor headlong with a mighty cyclone.
And there is Tityos, foster-son of Mother Earth,   595
his massive body stretched out over nine full acres,
and an enormous vulture with a crooked beak
gnaws his immortal liver and his anguished entrails—
deep within his body it makes its loathsome banquet,
nor is there any respite, for the muscles are reborn.   600
Why speak of the Lapiths, Ixion, and Pirithous,
over whom a black rock hangs, that always seems
about to slip and fall? And golden, gleaming couches
stand before their eyes, with banquets of royal splendor
spread upon them; but the eldest Fury, nearby,   605
sits and prevents their hands from touching the banquet tables:
she leaps up, holding a firebrand, screaming thunderous cries.
    "Here are those who hated their brothers in their lifetime,
or beat their fathers, or cheated clients and dependents;

or misers who gloated in solitude over all their wealth,   610
and did not share it with their kin (there are many of them!),
and those killed in adultery, and those who waged
unholy wars, not fearing to betray their masters—
all are awaiting their doom within. Do not ask to learn
what punishments, and what dreadful doom is awaiting them.   615
Some roll a huge rock about; others are stretched on wheels;
unhappy Theseus is doomed to sit forevermore,
and the miserable Phlegyas admonishes all
bearing witness with loud voice amid the darkness:
'Be warned: learn to do justice and not to scorn the gods.'   620
This one sold his country for gold to a powerful tyrant;
another made laws and rescinded them—all for a price;
another invaded his daughter's bed with forbidden marriage.
All of them dared monstrous crimes, and accomplished them.
If I had a hundred tongues and a hundred mouths,   625
and a voice of iron, I could not tell of all their crimes;
I could not repeat the entire list of punishments."
Thus spoke Apollo's aged priestess, and she added:
"But come, let us be on our way, and complete the task;
let us hasten. Now I see the massive walls   630
built in the forge of the Cyclopes, and the arching gateway
where we have been commanded to lay the appointed gifts."
She spoke; they moved together on the gloomy path
and crossed the intervening space, and came to the doorway.

   Aeneas enters and sprinkles his body with fresh water   635
and plants the Golden Bough upright upon the threshold.
This done, the duty to the goddess was fulfilled.
They reached the happy land of the Elysian Fields,
the blessed dwelling places of the Fortunate Groves,
Here an ampler air envelops the fields in light—   640
a rosy light, with its own sun and its own stars.
Some spirits are exercising their limbs on grassy lawns,
or vying in games and wrestling on the yellow sand,
others are taking part in the dance, and singing songs.
Orpheus, the Thracian priest, is there in his long robe;   645

playing the harmonious lyre with its seven strings,
striking it now with his fingers, now with an ivory plectrum.
Here was the ancient race of Teucer: a beautiful family,
the great-souled heroes who were born in happier days,
Ilus and Assaracus, and Dardanus, Troy's founder,   650
He marvels from afar at the arms and phantom chariots.
Their spears are planted in the ground; unharnessed horses
graze on the plain; the same joy in chariots and arms
that was theirs in life, the same pride in their sleek horses
is still with them now, when they are dead and buried.   655
And lo! Aeneas sees others to the left and right,
feasting on the grass, and singing joyful hymns
within a fragrant laurel grove, whence the Eridanus
rolls through the forest with its stream, to the upper world.
Here are those who were wounded fighting for their country;   660
and those who in their lifetime were pure and pious priests
and trusted soothsayers, whose words were meet for Apollo.
And those who had made life better with their skill and inventions,
and those who were remembered for their kindly deeds.
They all wore snowy fillets bound around their temples.   665
And as they thronged about, the Sibyl spoke to them,
especially to Musaeus, for he was in the center
of the great crowd, towering head and shoulders above them:
"Tell me, Blessed Shades, and you, O best of poets,
where may we find Anchises: it is for his sake   670
that we have come here, crossing Erebus' rivers."
The hero made answer to her thus with a few brief words:
"No one has a fixed home; we live in the shady forests,
on the soft river-banks, in meadows fresh with streams.
But if your heart desires it, climb this little hill   675
and I will set you soon upon an easy pathway."
He spoke, and walked ahead, and from the top of the hill
pointed out the shining fields; they descend from the heights.

Now Father Anchises, deep within a verdant valley,
was earnestly examining the imprisoned spirits   680
about to pass to the world above. And, as it happened,

he was talking about his family, his beloved grandsons,
their destinies and fortunes and characters and deeds.
And as he saw Aeneas advancing over the grass,
he joyfully stretched out both his hands to greet him;   685
tears streamed down the old man's cheeks, and he cried aloud:
"Have you come at last? Has the love your father expected
conquered the terrible road? May I really see your face,
my son, and hear and speak in the familiar tones?
I hoped and felt in my heart the time would finally come,   690
and I have counted the days; my longing did not deceive me.
Over how many lands and oceans have you traveled
to come here to me! What perils have beset you!
How I feared for your safety when you were in Africa!"
Aeneas said to him: "Your grieving spirit, father,   695
came to me often, driving me to seek this place.
My ships are in the Tyrrhene sea. Give me your hand,
father, and do not withdraw from my embrace."
So speaking he wet his face with flowing streams of tears.
Three times he tried to put his arms around his neck: 700
three times the image, vainly grasped, fled from his hands,
intangible as the wind, elusive as a dream.

   Meanwhile, in a secluded valley, Aeneas sees
a solitary wood, with rustling sounds of bushes,
and the river Lethe flowing by the peaceful homes.   705
Around it were innumerable tribes and peoples,
like bees in the meadow on a lovely summer's day,
alighting on many-colored flowers, streaming about
the shining lilies: the whole field resounds with their humming.
Aeneas is thrilled at the sudden sight, and asks the reason   710
(since he does not know): what is the river yonder,
and who are all these people thronging on the banks?
Father Anchises answers: "These are souls who are destined
to live a second time in the body. The river is Lethe,
whose tranquil waters of oblivion they are drinking.   715
I have long desired to tell you of them, and show you,
and to describe the descendants of my line; so that you
may rejoice all the more with me in finding Italy."

"But, Father, am I to think these souls return to the air
and enter a second time into the sluggish bodies?   720
What is this mad desire the poor souls have for the daylight?
    "I shall tell you, my son, and not leave you in suspense,"
the old man said, and he revealed each truth in order.
    "First, the heavens and the earth, and the watery fields,
the shining globe of the moon, the Titanic sun and the stars   725
are nurtured by an inner Spirit, pervading their members;
a great Mind moves the universe and all its parts.
Thence the race of men and beasts and wingèd birds,
and monsters borne by the sea beneath its marbled surface.
The Spirit in these seeds of life is celestial Fire;   730
so far as harmful earthbound bodies do not hamper them,
nor limbs and mortal members dull their perceptions.
Whence come fears and desires, griefs, and joys: they cannot
perceive the sky, for they are imprisoned in gloomy dungeons.
And even when they leave the light, on their last day,   735
not all the ills and bodily plagues depart from them,
miserable wretches! but, of necessity,
many lie deeply imbedded in a marvellous fashion.
Therefore they are punished for their ancient sins
and they are schooled with suffering. Some hang suspended   740
to the empty winds; from others the sins are washed away
by huge gurgling whirlpools, or burned away with fire.
Each submits to his own Manes. Then we are sent
to Elysium, and a few remain in the Happy Fields
until the lapse of time and the revolving years   745
remove at last the ingrown stain, and leave the spirit
ethereal and pure, a spark of pristine fire.
And these souls, after a cycle of a thousand years,
are summoned by the god to drink the waters of Lethe,
so that they may forget, and revisit the upper vault,   750
and again they may desire to enter the body."
    So spoke Anchises; he took his son and the Sibyl with him
into the middle of the murmuring, thronging crowd;
he found a little hill, from which he could see them all,
the whole long line, and recognize the approaching faces.   755

"Come, my son," he said, "and I shall unfold to you
your destiny, the whole glory of the Trojan line,
the grandsons and descendants of Italian stock:
illustrious heroes who will be the heirs to our name.
That youth you see who is leaning on a headless spear—   760
his lot has placed him nearest to the light; he will be
the first to rise to the upper air of Italian blood:
he is Silvius (an Alban name), your last-born son,
whom Lavinia, your queen, will raise in the forest
when you are old, to be a king and father of kings: 765
from him our dynasty will rule in Alba Longa.
The next is Procas, glory of the Trojan race,
and Capys and Numitor and Silvius Aeneas
who will revive your name, outstanding in piety
and arms alike, if ever he gains the Alban throne.   770
What youths they are! See what mighty strength they display!
Look how their temples are shaded with the Civic Oak!
These shall build Nomentum, Gabii, Fidena's city;
they will crown the hills with Collatine citadels,
Pometii, and Castrum Inui, and Bola and Cora—   775
these shall be the names of the now nameless lands.
And Romulus, the son of Mars, will join his grandfather:
born by Ilia of Assaracus' blood.
Do you see the double plumes upon his helmet,
and how his father marks him for the world above?   780
Under his auspices, my son, illustrious Rome
shall bound her empire by the earth, and her soul by Olympus,
and with a single wall surround the seven hills,
blessed in her offspring, like the Berecyntian Mother
Cybele, crowned with towers, drawn in her chariot,   785
through the Phrygian cities, glad in her godly offspring,
embracing a hundred grandsons, all heaven-dwelling gods.
    "Look now in this direction and behold this people:
your own Romans. Here is Caesar, and all the line
of Iülus, destined to pass beneath Heaven's vault.   790
This is the man that you have heard so often promised:
Augustus Caesar, child of a god, who will re-establish

the Golden Age in Latium's fields where Saturn reigned:
he shall extend his empire beyond the Garamantians
and Indians, to a land that lies beyond the stars,   795
beyond the path of the year and the sun, where sky-bearing Atlas
turns on his shoulders the sphere inset with blazing stars.
Already at the news of his coming, the Caspian region
and the Maeotian land are trembling with terror;
the seven mouths of the Nile are in panic and confusion.   800
Not even Hercules traversed so many lands,
although he shot the bronze-footed deer, and pacified
the Erymanthian woods, and his bow made Lerna tremble.
Not even Bacchus the Conqueror, who drove his tigers
down from the heights of Nysa, steering with reins of vine-leaves.   805
Shall we hesitate, then, to assert our valor with deeds?
shall fear prohibit us from settling in Italy?
    "But who is that man apart, crowned with an olive wreath,
and bearing sacred objects? I recognize the hair
and the white beard of Numa, King of Rome, the first   810
to give laws to the newborn city; from barren Cures
he will achieve a mighty empire. And his successor,
Tullus, will break the country's peace, call sluggish men
to arms, arouse the ranks long unaccustomed to triumphs.
The boastful Ancus is the man who follows him,   815
already rejoicing overmuch in the popular favor.
Do you wish to see the Tarquin kings, and the proud spirit
of the avenger Brutus, and the recaptured fasces?
He will be the first to win the consul's power,
and cruel axes; and when his sons renew the war,   820
he, their father, will sacrifice them on liberty's altar:
unhappy man! however the future will praise his deeds;
love of country will conquer, and endless passion for fame.
    "And see! the Decii, Drusi, and Torquatus,
with savage axe, and Camillus, bearing home the standards.   825
And those whom you see shining with their matching armor,
harmonious spirits now, while in the realm of night,
alas! what bloody battles they will wage between them,
if ever they see the light of day! The father-in-law

descending from Alpine forts and Menoecus' citadel,   830
the son-in-law opposing him with Eastern armies.[2]
Oh, my sons, do not accustom your hearts to such warfare!
Do not turn your courage and strength against your country!
And you be the first to spare, who claim your descent from
                                        Olympus:
lay aside your weapons, blood of my blood!   835
    "That man will conquer Corinth, and drive his chariot
triumphant to the Capitol, famed for Achaean slaughter.
This one will overthrow Argos and Agamemnon's Mycenae,
and even a descendant of the mighty Achilles:
avenger of Troy and Minerva's desecrated temple.   840
and who would leave you in silence, great Cato, or you, Cossus?
or the Gracchan family, the twins of Scipio's line,
thunderbolts of war, and Libya's destruction?
or Fabricius, great though poor? or Serranus, planting his furrow?
Fabii, where do you hurry an old man's weary steps?   845
You, Maximus, who by delaying, alone will restore the State . . .
    "Others will fashion living bronze with softer lines,
or, as I believe, draw lifelike features from marble,
plead with greater eloquence, describe with a rod
the motions of the heavenly bodies and the stars.   850
But you, Roman, remember to rule the world with empire
(this shall be your art), to impose the law of peace,
to spare the subject nations, and tame the haughty in war."
Thus spoke Father Anchises, and added as they marvelled:
    "Look how Marcellus advances, glorious with his spoils,   855
and how he stands out victorious above all the others.
He, a knight, shall lift the State disturbed by tumult;
he shall smite the Phoenicians and the rebel Gauls,
and thrice hang up the captured arms to Father Quirinus."
    And now Aeneas said, for he saw, along with him,   860
a youth of outstanding beauty, shining in his armor,
but with a sorrowful countenance and downcast eyes:
"Who is that, my father, who walks beside Marcellus?

---

[2]Caesar and Pompey, who married Caesar's daughter.

Is it his son? or is it one of his many descendants?
What murmurs from the crowd! What a majestic bearing!   865
But black night flits about his head with gloomy shadow."
And Father Anchises answers him with welling tears:
"Do not ask, my son, of your family's great sorrow!
The Fates will only give the earth a glimpse of him
and then no more. Rome would have been too powerful   870
in your eyes, O gods, if this gift had been hers to keep!
What lamentations of men shall arise from the famous field
to the city of Mars! and what a funeral, O Tiber,
you shall see one day as you glide past the recent tomb!
No youth of Trojan stock shall raise so high the hopes   875
of his Latin ancestors. Never shall Romulus' land
take such great pride in any other of her children!
Alas for piety, pristine faith, and glory in war!
No one could have fought him with impunity,
whether he marched on foot against the enemy,   880
or urged his foaming steed, digging its flanks with spurs.
Alas, poor boy, if you could break the hard chains of Fate!
You shall be Marcellus. Give lilies with full hands;
let me scatter shining flowers; to my grandson's soul
let me give these gifts at least, and perform a useless service!"[3]   885

And thus they wandered through all the infernal region,
the broad and misty plain; they looked at everything.
And after old Anchises had shown all to Aeneas,
inflaming his soul with desire for the coming glory,
he told his son of the wars that he must wage hereafter,   890
and of the Laurentian peoples and city of Latinus,
and in what manner he should flee or withstand each danger.
   There are two gates of Sleep: one, they say, is of horn,
through which an easy way is given to the true shades;
by the other, which shines with the gleam of ivory,   895
the Manes send false dreams into the world above.
Anchises, speaking thus, conducts his son and the Sibyl

---

[3]See Introduction, page viii.

and sends them to the upper world through the ivory gate.
He speeds his path to the ships, and sees his friends again,
and sails along the shore to the harbor of Caieta.   900
The anchors are cast from the prows; the sterns rest on the shore.

End of Book VI

BOOK VII

THE WAR IN LATIUM

You, too, Caieta, nurse of Aeneas, by your death
have given eternal fame to our shores, and even now
your honor guards your tomb, and in great Hesperia
your name still marks your bones, if in that there is any glory.
But good Aeneas, when the funeral rites were completed,   5
and the mound was raised on high, and the raging seas were stilled,
spreads his sails once more to the winds and leaves the harbor.
The breezes blow in the night, and the palely gleaming moon
shows them the way; the sea shines with her glancing beams.
The Trojans narrowly skirt the shores of Circe's land,   10
where the Sun's rich daughter makes the deserted woods resound
with her unceasing songs, and in her splendid halls
she burns the fragrant cedar torches to lighten the gloom,
and weaves a fine-spun web across the noisy shuttle.
The growls of angry lions can be heard from there   15
protesting at their chains and roaring through the night;
the raging of bristly boars as well, and bears in cages,
and mournful howling from the forms of monstrous wolves,
all of whom the cruel goddess Circe had changed
from human shapes into the forms of animals.   20
Lest the good Trojans too should suffer such a fate,
and enter the harbor or approach the dreaded shores,
Neptune filled their sails and wafted them with winds,
so that they escaped and fled the raging shoals.
And now the sea began to glow with the light of dawn,   25
and saffron Aurora shone in her rosy car from the heavens,
when the wind died down and all the breezes suddenly stopped;
the oars began to churn the sluggish, marbled waves.
Aeneas sees a great forest rising from the ocean
and in the midst, the Tiber with its pleasant waters   30

140

rushes down with whirling rapids to the sea,
yellow with churned-up sand; and all around and above
the many-colored birds that dwell by the river-banks
delight the heavens with their song, and fly through the forest.
He tells his men to change their course, and make for land,   35
and happily he enters the mouth of the shady river.

Come now, my Muse Erato, tell me, who were the kings
and what events were taking place in ancient Latium
when first the Trojan ships arrived on Italian shores.
I shall now unfold the beginning of the war,   40
and you, Muse, give aid to your poet. I tell of savage strife,
and battle lines, and valiant kings going to death,
Tyrrhenian bands and all Hesperia in arms.
A greater story now is being born for me;
I begin a greater task.   45
               The aged king Latinus
ruled the lands and placid cities in lasting peace.
Latinus was the son of Faunus and the nymph
Laurentine Marica. Picus was the father of Faunus,
and his father was Saturn, founder of the race.
Now Fate had willed that old Latinus should have no sons   50
or male descendants—they were cut off in early youth.
The only offspring to preserve the house was a daughter,
and she had reached the age when she was ripe for marriage.
From Latium and Ausonia there were many suitors,
but handsomest beyond all other wooers was Turnus,   55
son of an old and noble family, whom the Queen-Mother
longed with a great desire to have as son-in-law.
But many portents from the gods stand in the way.
   In the palace courtyard was an ancient laurel
—a sacred tree, it had been preserved for many years,   60
for it was said that Latinus himself had found the tree
and dedicated it to Phoebus when first he built
his city; thence he gave his people the name Laurentes.
It happened once that to this tree (wonder of wonders!)
a swarm of bees buzzing loudly through the liquid air   65

came and made their home, with intertwining feet,
and there they hung in sudden swarm from the leafy branch.
The seer at once proclaimed: "I see a stranger coming:
from the same direction an army comes to this same place,
and here they hold their sway in the highest citadel."   70
And furthermore, as Lavinia stands near her father
while he kindles the altar with a hallowed torch,
it seemed (O horrors!) that her long hair caught on fire,
her headgear all began to burn with crackling flames,
her royal tresses burned, her crown was on fire, too,   75
with all its jewels; and surrounded with smoke and glare
she scattered flames of Vulcan all throughout the palace.
The omen was both wonderful and terrifying,
for she herself, they said, would have great fame and fortune,
but to her people she would bring disastrous war.   80

    The king, disturbed by the omens, seeks the shrine of Faunus,
his prophetic father, in Albunea's grove,
the greatest of the forests, whose sacred spring resounds,
breathing noxious vapors from the gloomy shadows.
Here the Italian peoples and all Oenotria   85
seek oracles in times of doubt, and here the priestess
brings her gifts and lies on the fleece of slaughtered sheep;
and, courting slumber in the silence of the night,
she sees all manner of ghosts and mysterious phantoms flying,
and hears strange, varied voices, and talks with immortal gods,   90
and shades from Acheron in the depths of dark Avernus.

    Here too, King Latinus himself came seeking an answer
and duly sacrificed a hundred woolly sheep,
lying down upon their outspread skins and fleeces.
Suddenly a voice came from the depth of the forest: 95
"Do not seek to join your daughter in Latin wedlock,
and put no trust, my son, in bridal-chambers prepared:
for foreign sons shall come, whose blood will exalt our name
up to the very stars; the offspring of their race
shall one day, where the revolving Sun looks on both oceans,   100
see the whole earth turn obedient at their feet."

    This answer from Father Faunus in the quiet night,

this warning is not kept shut within Latinus' lips;
but Rumor, darting to and fro through Italy's towns,
had already brought the tidings, by the time   105
the Trojans moored their vessels to the grassy bank.

  Aeneas and his captains and the fair Iülus
stretch their weary limbs under a high tree's branches,
and spread a feast, with cakes of meal along the grass
below the food (as Jupiter himself had advised them)   110
and on these cakes of meal they pile the fruits of the field.
Now, by chance, when all the rest had been consumed,
the lack of food compelled them to eat the little cakes—
to violate with hand and daring mouth the loaves,
and not to spare the fateful circles of the crust.   115
"Look! We are even eating the tables!" Iülus said,
only this, in jest. But that voice, when it was heard,
meant the end of their troubles. Aeneas seized on the words
and stopped the boy as he spoke, amazed at Heaven's will.
Immediately he cried out: "Hail, O promised land!   120
And likewise hail to you, O faithful gods of Troy!
This is our home, this our country. I remember Anchises
my father told me once about this secret of Fate:
'My son, when you are carried to an unknown shore,
and compelled by hunger to eat your very tables,   125
then, in your weariness, you may hope for a home, and there
begin to build your houses and ramparts of defense.'[1]
This is that hunger, this is the last of all our trials,
the end of all our afflictions . . .
And so, let us bestir ourselves: with the sun's first rays,   130
gladly let us explore the land, and learn who lives here,
and where their city is; let us search in different directions
from the port; and now pour wine to Jove, and call in prayer
my father Anchises, and place the wine back on the tables."
So speaking, he crowns his temples with a leafy branch,   135

---

[1]Actually, it was the Harpy Celaeno who made this prophecy, not Anchises. Cf. III, 255, ff.

and he invokes the Genius of the place, and Earth,
first of the gods, and Nymphs, and rivers still unknown;
he prays to Night, and to Night's rising constellations,
and to Idaean Jove, and to the Phrygian Mother,
and to his parents, one in Heaven, one in Erebus.   140
Thereupon the Almighty Father thundered thrice
from a clear sky, and displayed a burning cloud in the heavens
with his own hand, glowing with rays of golden light.
The rumor suddenly makes its way through the Trojan men
that the day has come at last to found their promised city.   145
Zealously they renew the feast, and cheered by the portent,
they set out mixing bowls and wreathe the wine with garlands.

Next day, when early Dawn was lighting up the land,
they set out on their separate ways to find the city,
the boundaries and coasts; here is Numicius' fountain,   150
here is the river Tiber, here live the hardy Latins.
Aeneas selects a hundred men, from every rank,
good speakers all, and bids them go to the monarch's walls
as envoys; every man is wreathed with Pallas' branches,
bringing the hero gifts and asking peace for the Trojans.   155
Without delay they do as are bidden; they go
at a rapid pace; while Aeneas makes a shallow ditch
to mark the walls, and he begins to build his ramparts,
camp-wise encircling his first site on Italian shores.
His envoys went their way until they espied the towers   160
and steep roofs of the Latins; they approached the walls.
Before the city, boys and youths in earliest flower
train on horseback, driving chariots in the dust,
bending tight-strung bows, hurling tough javelins,
challenging each other to race or boxing-match,   165
when a messenger rides up to tell the aged king
that men of mighty size, with unfamiliar clothing,
have just arrived. The king commands them to be brought in
and takes his seat in the midst on his ancestral throne.
Majestic and huge, the palace of Laurentian Picus,   170
towering on a hundred columns, crowned the city,

awe-inspiring with trees and ancestral sanctity.
Here the kings were wont to receive the scepter and fasces,
according to the omens, here was the shrine and the Senate,
here were the sacred banquets, when a ram was slaughtered,   175
and elders used to sit at the long line of tables.
Here, too, are statues of their ancestors, set in order,
made of ancient cedar: Italus and Father Sabinus,
Planter of Vines—the statue is holding a pruning-knife—
and aged Saturn, and an image of two-faced Janus;   180
they stand in the courtyard, with other kings from the very
                                                         beginning,
and heroes wounded in battle fighting for their country.
Weapons are also hanging from the sacred door-posts,
and captured chariots, and curving battle-axes,
and plumes from helmets, and mighty bars taken from gates,   185
and javelins and shields, and beaks torn from warships.
Picus, Tamer of Horses, holding the Quirinal Staff,
sat in a short toga, with the Sacred Shield
in his left hand—Picus himself, whom Golden Circe, his bride,
captivated by passion, had struck with her wand, and changed   190
with drugs into a bird with color-sprinkled wings.
   Such was the temple of the gods where Latinus sat
on his ancestral throne: he called the Trojans to him,
and as they entered he spoke to them with placid mien:
"Tell me, Dardans (for not unknown to us is your city   195
and your noble race, and all your travels on the seas);
what do you seek? What reason, what necessity
has borne you over the deep blue sea to Ausonia's shores?
Whether you wandered from your course or were driven by winds,
things that often happen to sailors on the ocean—   200
you have entered our rivers; your ships lie in our harbors.
Do not flee our hospitality; know that the Latins
are of Saturn's race: we are just men, not by compulsion or law,
but of our own free will we hold to the ways of God.
And indeed I remember (although it is a long time ago)   205
Auruncan elders told the tale of how Dardanus,
coming from this land, first went to Phrygian Ida

and Thracian Samos, or Samothrace, as it is called;
from Tyrrhenian Corythus came Dardanus;
now he has been received on a starry throne in the heavens,   210
and by his altars he increases the number of gods."
    He finished speaking, and Ilioneus made answer thus:
"O distinguished son of Faunus, no black tempest
has driven us through the waves to seek refuge in your land;
nor have we missed our course, misled by stars or coast.   215
Gladly and of our own volition we come to you,
expelled from a kingdom that was once the mightiest
seen by the Sun in his wanderings from high Olympus.
Our race was founded by Jove, the Dardan youth rejoice
in Jove as their ancestor; our king is related to Jove—   220
Trojan Aeneas, who has sent us to your gates.
How great the tempest was that poured from savage Mycenae,
overwhelming Ida's plain; how the worlds of Europe and Asia,
driven by destiny, collided in mortal combat—
all men have heard of these events, even those who live   225
by the circling stream of Ocean, the outermost edge of Earth,
or at its very center, scorched by the pitiless Sun.
From that disaster, we have sailed over all the seas,
and now we seek a small domain for our country's gods,
a safe bit of shore, and air and water, free to all.   230
For we shall bring no shame to your kingdom; no small glory
will come to you, and everlasting gratitude.
Nor shall Italy ever regret receiving Troy
to its bosom: I swear by Aeneas' fortunes and his right hand,
well known to many men in loyalty and war: 235
many are the peoples (you must not despise us
for coming to you with woollen fillets of suppliants)
who have courted us as friends and allies for themselves.
But Heaven's will has driven us by its commands
to seek your land. For Dardanus came from here, and now   240
Apollo with his stern decrees has sent us back
to Tuscan Tiber and Numicius' sacred fountain.
Moreover, Aeneas offers you a few small gifts,
relics of former wealth snatched from the flames of Troy:

Anchises used this golden cup to pour libations;   245
these belonged to Priam, he used them when he gave
laws to the Trojans, according to custom: a scepter and crown
and robes woven by the Trojan women . . ."
    As Ilioneus was speaking, Latinus held his face
and gaze fixed steadily on the ground; only his eyes   250
darted about as he thought: it was not the embroidered purple
nor Priam's scepter that moved the old king half so much
as did the thought of his daughter's wedding and bridal bed,
and in his mind he pondered over Faunus' oracle:
This must be the stranger that the Fates have sent   255
from distant lands to be my son-in-law, and share
my sovereign power; from Aeneas will spring the race
peerless in valor, which will conquer all the world.
At last he said with joy: "May the gods fulfill and prosper
our will and their intent. Trojans, your wish is granted: 260
I do not scorn your gifts. As long as Latinus reigns
you shall not lack for fertile soil and Trojan abundance.
As for Aeneas, if he longs for us so much,
if he is eager for our friendship and alliance,
let him come in person, and not fear a friendly face.   265
My terms of peace consist of shaking your leader's hand.
So take my answer now back to your Trojan prince:
I have a daughter, one whom I am not allowed
(as my father's oracles and Heaven's omens have told us)
to join in marriage to an Italian; a foreign bridegroom   270
will come—this is Latium's destiny—who will exalt
our name to the very stars. Such is my belief:
that Aeneas was sent by Fate, and such is my desire."
    So speaking, the aged king picks horses from his stable
—three hundred of them stood, well-groomed, in lofty stalls—   275
and commands them to be led out for all the Trojans in order,
swift of foot and gorgeous in their purple trappings,
with golden chains on their necks, and golden saddle-cloths,
and the bits they champ with their teeth are made of yellow gold.
For the absent Aeneas he chooses a chariot and two steeds: 280
they were of immortal race, breathing fire from their nostrils—

the clever Circe had bred the stock by stealing the stallions
from her father the Sun, and crossed them with a mortal mare.
With these words, and mounted on these gifts from Latinus,
Aeneas' men rode proudly back to him, bringing peace.   28

But lo! the cruel wife of Jove was now returning
from Inachus' Argos, flying through the air,
when out of the sky, from the Sicilian Pachynus
she saw the happy Aeneas and the Trojan fleet.
She sees them building houses, trusting in the land;   29
their ships are left behind. She is seized by keen chagrin.
She shakes her head and pours these words from deep in her heart:
"O hateful race, and Trojan fates, hostile to mine!
Could they not have perished on the Sigean plains?
Or could they not have been captured? Could burning Troy   29
not have consumed them all? No: through the flames and foe
they have found a way! My power is worn out and useless,
I suppose; my anger is sated and I must rest!
Why, when they were all exiled from their native land
I even pursued them with my hatred across the waves;   30
and I used all the resources of sea and sky against them!
But of what use has Scylla been to me, or the Syrtes,
or cavernous Charybdis? They are safe in Tiber's channel;
safe from me and the waves. Yet Mars was allowed to destroy
the mighty race of the Lapiths; the Father of the gods   30
gave ancient Calydonia to Diana's anger—
and what did Lapiths and Calydon do to deserve such a fate?
But I, great consort of Jove, who have left no stone unturned,
who have lowered myself to try every sort of trick against them,
I am conquered by Aeneas! Well then, if my own power   31
is not strong enough, I know where I must turn:
if I can find no aid in Heaven, I'll try in Hell!
Granted, I'll not be allowed to keep him from ruling Latium;
the Fates have decreed that Lavinia shall be his bride;
but at least I can cause delays and difficulties,   3
and tear up by the roots the peoples of both the kings.
They shall pay with their people's lives for uniting the races:

your dowry, maiden, shall be Rutulian and Trojan blood;
your bridesmaid the Goddess of War. Not only Hecuba
conceived a firebrand and gave birth to nuptial flames.　　320
No! Venus herself has given birth to another Paris;
another funeral torch for reborn Pergamum!"
　　She finished speaking and flew to earth, a terrible sight,
and from the Dread Goddesses' home and the infernal shades
she calls Allecto, Maker of Grief, who loves sad wars,　　325
and anger and treachery and all sorts of wicked crimes.
Even her father Pluto hates this monster, likewise
her sisters in Tartarus hate her; she takes so many forms,
so savage is her appearance, swarming with black snakes.
Juno goes to her and sharpens her hate with these words:　　330
"Maiden, daughter of darkness, do me this one service:
do not allow my honor and my fame to be conquered
and defeated: prevent the Trojans from courting Latins
with marriage plans, and occupying Italian lands.
For you can turn a brother against a loving brother,　　335
and overturn houses with hate; you can bring lashes and torches
of death into the house. You have a thousand names,
a thousand ways of mischief. Arouse your fertile heart:
break the peace, sow seeds of war; at the same instant
let their men all wish, demand, and seize the sword!　　340
　　Forthwith Allecto, steeped in her Gorgonian poisons,
makes for Latium and the lofty roofs of Latinus
and sits upon the silent threshold of Queen Amata
who already was burning with a woman's distress and anger
about the Trojans' arrival and the wedding of Turnus.　　345
The goddess flings on her a snake from her dark blue locks
and puts it into her bosom, deep in her inmost heart,
so that, frenzied, she will upset the entire house.
The serpent glides between her garments and her soft breasts,
winding its way without her feeling and knowing it;　　350
and breathing its poison, drives her mad: the snake becomes
the golden collar on her neck, it becomes her fillet,
twisting through her hair and sliding over her limbs.
And while the liquid poison, stealing through her body,

permeates her senses and fills her bones with fire,   355
but still before she is completely overwhelmed,
she softly spoke, in a mother's fashion, with many tears
over her daughter Lavinia and the Phrygian's wedding:
"Lavinia is to be given to Trojan exiles, Father?
Have you no pity for your daughter or yourself?   360
Nor for her mother whom, at the first northerly wind,
this wicked pirate will desert and make for the sea
taking the girl with him? Was not that how the Phrygian shepherd
stole into Sparta and carried Leda's Helen to Troy?
What of your promise? What of your care for your own people,   365
and your hand so often pledged to your kinsman Turnus?
If you really are seeking a foreign son-in-law,
if Faunus' commands are so important to you,
why then, I say that every land except our own
is a foreign land, and this, I think, is the will of the gods.   370
And Turnus, if his house is traced back to its origins,
is descended from Inachus, Acrisius, and Mycenae."

When she sees that her words are useless, that Latinus
is firm and obdurate; when the serpent's maddening poison
has entered her very vitals and spread throughout her body,   375
then the unhappy woman, goaded by monstrous frenzy,
rages madly through the city with wild abandon.
As sometimes a top, spinning under the twisted lash,
which boys intent on their game drive through the empty halls,
—driven by the whip it goes spinning round and round,   380
and the puzzled group of children gaze on it in wonder,
marvelling at the way the wooden toy is whirling,
renewing its life with blows: with no slower course, Amata
is driven through the midst of the city and proud people.
She even pretends to be a Bacchante and goes to the woods,   385
a prey to greater madness, embarked on a greater sin,
and then she hides her daughter among the leafy mountains,
to rob the Trojan of his bride and prevent the wedding.
"Evoë Bacchus!" she screams, "You alone deserve the maiden;
for you indeed she has taken up the supple thyrsus,   390
for you she joins the dance, and grows her sacred hair!"

Rumor flies, and the matrons, inflamed with the same frenzy,
are driven, one and all, to seek new dwelling places.
They leave their homes with naked neck and streaming hair.
Some of them fill their air with their resounding shrieks,   395
and dressed in fawn-skins, carry spears all wreathed with vine-leaves.
The queen herself in their midst is holding a blazing pine-torch
and singing a marriage song for Turnus and her daughter;
rolling her bloodshot eyes, she suddenly shouts in her frenzy:
"Listen, Latin mothers, wherever you may be: 400
if your good hearts still have love for wretched Amata,
if any care for a mother's rights still gnaws your souls,
come, let down your hair, and join me in the revels!"
Such has the queen become, amid woods and wild beasts' lairs,
as Allecto drives her on every side with the goad of Bacchus.   405

　　After she was satisfied with the madness she caused,
seeing the purpose and house of Latinus all upset,
the sullen goddess flies away on dusky wings
to the brave Rutulian's walls, where Danaë, they say,
with her Acrisian colonists, borne by the South Wind,   410
built her city; the place was once called Ardea
by our forefathers; the glorious name of Ardea stands
but its fortune is gone. Here Turnus, in his lofty palace,
was sleeping peacefully in the middle of the night.
Allecto puts aside her furious face and aspect,   415
changing herself into the likeness of an old woman,
with many wrinkles furrowing her loathsome forehead,
and white hair and a fillet wreathed with olive spray.
She becomes Calybe, aged priestess of Juno,
and stands before the young man's eyes, speaking these words: 420
"Turnus, will you allow your labors to go to waste,
and Trojan colonists to steal away your empire?
The king denies you your bride and dowry won with blood;
a foreign heir is being sought for Latinus' kingdom.
Go, you fool, and offer yourself to thankless perils!   425
Go, scattering Tuscan battle-lines, and protecting Latins
with peace; omnipotent Juno now has ordered me

to speak this message to you as you lie here asleep.
So up now, joyfully arm your men, and lead them through
the gates to battle! Set fire to the Phrygian chiefs   430
and painted ships at anchor in the lovely river!
The powers of Heaven command it: unless Latinus himself
is willing to keep his promise and give you his daughter in marriage,
let him at last know what it is to meet Turnus in battle!"
The young man laughed at the aged priestess and in his turn   435
began to speak as follows: "I am not, as you think,
unaware of the Trojans' landing in Tiber's waters;
do not invent such fears for me. Nor is Queen Juno
unmindful of our case . . .
But you, mother, old age made weaker by sloth, and barren   440
of truth, is troubling you with vain anxieties
and mocking you with false fears amid the wars of kings.
Your task is to guard the shrines and statues of the gods:
let those who fight the wars rule over war and peace."
    At these words Allecto burned with furious anger.   445
But a sudden tremor seized the young man's limbs as he spoke,
his eyes stared as the Fury hissed with all her snakes,
revealing herself in her true shape. Her flashing eyes
rolled, and she thrust him back as he tried to speak, but failed.
She made a pair of serpents rise up from her hair,   450
and cracked her whip, and spoke these words with raging mouth:
"Behold me, weakened by sloth, whom old age, barren of truth,
is mocking with false fears amid the wars of kings!
Look at these! I come from the home of the Dreaded Sisters,
bringing War and Death in my hand . . ."   455
    So speaking, she threw a torch at the youth, and fixed the brand
smoking with dark fire, in the breast of Turnus.
Terrified, he broke out of his sleep; his bones and limbs
were dripping with the sweat bursting from every pore.
Madly he calls for arms; he seeks them in bed and palace.   460
Love of the sword and madness for war are raging within him,
and anger most of all; as when crackling, burning sticks
are placed beneath a boiling cauldron, making the water
rage and bubble with the heat—a seething flood

dancing and steaming high with foam, until the torrent   465
contains itself no longer; dark steam rises to Heaven.
And so he violates the peace, and tells his soldiers
to march upon Latinus and to prepare their arms:
Italy must be defended, the enemy repulsed,
and he would be a match for Trojans and Latins together.   470
When he had spoken, he called the gods to hear his vows,
and all the Rutulans vie in exhorting each other to arms;
some are moved by Turnus' grace and youthful beauty,
some by his royal ancestry, and some by his exploits.

While Turnus fills the Rutulians with courageous ardor,   475
Allecto speeds on Stygian wings to the Trojan camp,
planning new tricks; observing where the fair Iülus
was hunting wild beasts on the shore with nets and horses.
The Fury from Hell imbues the hounds with sudden frenzy,
touching their nostrils with the familiar scent, and making them 480
dash in hot pursuit of a stag. This was the beginning
of all their troubles; this kindled the peasants' hearts to war.
There was a stag of outstanding beauty, with huge antlers;
it was taken unweaned from its mother and raised by Tyrrhus' sons
and Tyrrhus their father, keeper of the royal herds,   485
entrusted with the care of all Latinus' pastures.
Their sister Silvia had trained the stag to obey her,
and treated him as a pet and wreathed his horns with garlands,
grooming the wild creature and bathing him in the spring.
He had become quite tame, and used to his master's table.   490
He wandered in the woods, but of his own accord
returned to the well-known door, however late the night.
While this stag was roaming, the frenzied hounds of Iülus
started him as he was floating down the stream,
and cooling himself in the shade of the grassy river banks.   495
Ascanius himself, inflamed with passion for glory,
drew a pointed shaft and bent his curvèd bow.
His aim was guided by the goddess: the arrow sped,
whizzed through the air, and pierced the stag in flank and belly.
The wounded animal made his way to the well-known roof;   500

moaning, he found his stall. Bleeding and seeking help,
suppliant-like, he filled the house with pitiful cries.
The sister Silvia first, beating her arms with her hands,
called for help, arousing the hardy peasants nearby.
And they (for the Fury is hiding in the silent forest)   505
suddenly appeared: one was armed with a charred firebrand,
one with a knotty cudgel; whatever each one finds,
his anger makes a weapon. Tyrrhus calls his men
—he chanced to be splitting an oak in four by driving wedges—
and panting with a furious rage he seized an axe.   510

     The wicked goddess, looking for a chance for mischief,
flies to the roof of the farmhouse. From its topmost peak
she sounds the shepherds' call and on a curvèd horn
she blows a blast from Hell that makes the forest tremble,
and straightway every grove resounds to its very depths.   515
The far-off lake of Diana heard it; the sulphury spring
of Nar with its whitish waters; the fountains of Velinus;
and frightened mothers clutched their babies to their breasts.
And hastening to answer the dreadful horn's alarm,
the savage farmers seize their weapons from all sides.   520
Likewise the Trojan youth pour from the open gates
of the camp; they hurry one and all to Ascanius' rescue.
The battle lines are formed: this is no peasants' struggle
fought with heavy clubs and charred and pointed stakes,
but with two-edged steel they fight, and a black harvest   525
of drawn swords bristles, brazen weapons gleam in the sun,
reflecting light and sending it back into the clouds;
as when the white-caps form with the first breath of the wind,
and little by little the waves arise, becoming higher,
until at last they tower to the very heavens.   530
Now in the front line young Almo (who had been
the eldest of Tyrrhus' sons) is slain by a whistling arrow.
The deadly shaft sticks in his throat, choking with blood
the liquid path of voice and the slender breath of life.
Many corpses are on the ground: the old Galaesus,   535
slain as he tries to intervene and make peace—the most righteous
of all the Ausonians, and also the wealthiest.

He had five bleating flocks of sheep, five herds of cattle
in his pastures, a hundred plows turned up his soil.

And as they fight in equal strength across the plain,   540
Allecto, having kept her promise (bloody battle
and many deaths resulted from the first encounter),
departs from Hesperia and flies through the air to Heaven,
speaking to Juno triumphantly with haughty words:
"See, your quarrel has given way to gloomy war!   545
Now try to make them come together in friendly alliance,
seeing that I have poured Italian blood on Trojans!
I shall do even more, if such is your desire:
I'll spread the rumor, embroil the nearby cities in war,
and kindle their souls with lust for battle, so that they come   550
from everywhere; I'll sow war's seeds throughout the land!"
    And Juno answered: "Enough alarms and treachery:
the causes of war are firmly rooted. Hand-to-hand combat
rages; the weapons of chance are stained with recent blood.
Let them celebrate this alliance and these nuptials,   555
the excellent son of Venus and the great Latinus!
But the King of high Olympus would not wish
for you to wander freely through the upper regions,
so go now; whatever further tasks must still be done,
I shall do myself." These are the words of Juno.   560
The Fury raises her wings, all hissing with her snakes,
and leaving the upper air departs to her home in Cocytus.
There is a place in Italy's midst, beneath high mountains,
renowned and noble in its fame throughout the world—
the Valley of Ampsanctus. Dense forests all around   565
hem it in with their foliage, and in the middle
a rushing torrent flows in eddies amid the rocks.
There is a gloomy cavern, the window of Hell itself,
and an enormous gorge, where Acheron bursts forth,
and opens its noxious jaws. This is where Allecto   570
hid her despisèd power, relieving earth and Heaven.
    And Saturn's royal daughter puts the final touch
of her hand to the war meanwhile. From the battlefield

the crowd of shepherds come rushing back into the city
bringing the dead boy Almo and the mangled Galaesus,   575
calling on the gods and on their king Latinus.
Turnus is there, and amid the fiery passion caused
by the slaughter, redoubles the terror: "Trojans are called to
                                                        mingle
their blood with ours and rule us: Turnus is spurned from the
                                                        door."
And those whose mothers, driven mad by Bacchus, roam   580
the trackless woods in chorus (for great is Amata's name),
are coming from all sides demanding aid from Mars.
And all of them, despite the oracles and omens,
perversely throng, and clamor for an evil war.
They gather in noisy crowds about Latinus' palace.   585
And he resists them, like an immovable cliff by the sea
which, though the waves come crashing with their mighty roar,
stands unmoved in its bulk above the howling billows;
the rocks and foaming waters seethe in useless rage;
the seaweed, hurled against its side, is sent swirling back.   590
But when he sees that he cannot stop their blind purpose,
and all is going according to cruel Juno's will,
the king cries out to the gods and to the empty skies:
"Alas!" he says, "we are broken by Fate and swept by the
                                                        tempest!
And you, my poor children, will pay the price with blood   595
for sacrilege. You, Turnus, guilt and punishment
remain for you, and you shall pray to the gods, but too late.
My rest is near at hand, for I am on the threshold
of life; all I lose is a happy death." He spoke no more,
but shut himself in his palace and dropped the reins of state. 600

   There was a custom in Latium, held sacred by Alban tribes
forever afterwards, and now by Rome herself,
when first the people rouse the God of War for battle,
whether it be the Getae, Arabs, or Hyrcanians
against whom war is waged, or even India,   605
Land of the Dawn, to reclaim the standards from Parthians:—

there are two gates of War, for that is what they are called,
hallowed by religion and fierce dread of Mars;
they are closed by a hundred brazen bolts, and the lasting
                                        strength
of iron; the guardian Janus never leaves the threshold.   610
Now, when the leaders vote that war is to be declared,
the Consul himself, with Quirinal robe and Gabine cincture,
unlocks with his own hands the creaking Gates of War,
and calls for war with his own lips; then the other soldiers
follow, and brazen trumpets sound in raucous agreement.   615
This is how Latinus was asked to declare the war
on Aeneas' men, and to unbolt the gloomy gates.
But the aged king shrank with his hand, and he refrained
from the hateful duties, and hid himself in the darkness.
Then the Queen of the Gods came gliding from Heaven and
                                        opened   620
the lingering gates with her own hand; on their turning hinges
the Saturnian Queen burst open the iron Gates of War.
Ausonia, formerly sluggish and unmoved, is aflame:
some are preparing to march through the plain, some on tall
                                        horses
are stirring up the dust; they all cry out for arms.   625
Some are polishing their shields and javelins
with greasy fat, and honing axes on the whetstone,
rejoicing to carry banners and hear the blare of trumpets.
Five great cities set up anvils and make new weapons:
the powerful Atina and the haughty Tibur,   630
Ardea, Crustumeri, and towering Antemnae,
they make the hollow helmets and weave the wicker shields,
while others hammer breastplates out of gleaming bronze,
or fashion polished greaves from light and flexible silver.
All pride in sickle and plowshare, all love of agriculture   635
has come to this! They retemper ancestral swords in the smithy.
And now the trumpet sounds; the word goes forth for battle.
One swiftly snatches a helmet from the wall, another
yokes his excited steeds, and puts on shield and armor
of triple golden mail, and girds on his faithful sword.   640

Now, Muses, open the gates of Helicon and sing:
which kings were moved to war, what armies followed each
to fill the plain with battle; and what peoples flourished
in Italy in those days, and with what arms she burned.
For you remember, Muses, and you are able to tell;   645
to me, a mere faint breath of a rumor has drifted down.
   First, from Tuscan shores, the fierce Mezentius,
who scorned the gods, enters the war and arms his troops.
Next to him is Lausus his son, the handsomest
of all, except for Turnus, the Laurentian hero—   650
Lausus, tamer of horses and conqueror of beasts.
He leads a thousand men from Agylla's town, who followed
in vain; he deserved to be happier in his father's rule;
he merited a better father than Mezentius.
The goodly son of goodly Hercules, Aventinus   655
next displays on the turf his chariot crowned with palms,
and on his shield he wears his father's insignia:
a hundred snakes and the Lernaean Hydra surrounded with
                                                    serpents.
In the woods of the Aventine hill the priestess Rhea
brought him forth with secret birth to the light of day—   660
a woman matched with a god—when the Tirynthian victor,
after killing Geryon, reached the Laurentian lands,
and bathed his Spanish cattle in the Tuscan river.
His men are carrying javelins and deadly pikes,
and fight with slender tapering swords and Sabellian darts.   665
He went on foot himself, swinging a lion's skin
with huge and frightening mane and white teeth above his head,
and thus he strode into the royal palace, bristling,
his shoulders covered with the cloak of Hercules.
   Then twin brothers leave together the walls of Tibur,   670
and the people who were named from their brother Tiburtus:
Catillus and keen Coras—they were Argive youths.
They came into the front ranks amid the bristling spears,
as when two Centaurs, born of clouds, come down from a
                                                    mountain,
leaving Homole or snowy Othrys behind,   675

in their rapid course; the mighty forest yields
to them as they go and bushes noisily give way.

The founder of Praeneste's town was also there:
Caeculus, the king who, as people have always thought,
was born to Vulcan in the fields and found on the hearth.   680
A rustic band of straggling men follow their king,
all those who live in steep Praeneste, and the fields
of Gabine Juno, the frigid Anio, and Hernican crags
with dewy streams; those nourished by the rich Anagnia,
and Father Amasenus. Not all of them have armor   685
or shields or chariots: most of them carry slingshots
with leaden pellets; some of them are wielding darts;
instead of helmets they wear hats of tawny wolfskins.
Their left feet, as they plant their footprints, are all naked;
a boot of untanned leather covers the other foot.   690

But Messapus, tamer of horses, offspring of Neptune,
the man whom none can ever kill with fire and sword,
calls to arms his people long unaccustomed to war,
all of a sudden, and seizes again his trusty sword.
These are from Fescennium and Aequi Falisci,   695
those from Socrate's heights and the Flavinian fields,
Ciminus' lake and mountain, and Capena's groves.
They marched in step and all sang praises of their king.
As often snow-white swans among the liquid clouds
return from feeding, uttering from their long necks   700
melodious song; the river echoes from afar,
and Asia's plains resound . . .
One would never think that heavy-armed foot soldiers
were marching by, but rather that, high aloft, a cloud
of raucous birds was heading shoreward from the deep.   705

There is Clausus of the ancient Sabine blood,
leading a mighty army, and like an army himself,
from whom the Claudian tribe and family now has come
all through Latium, since Rome was shared with the Sabines.
With him the cohorts of Amiternum and Quirites,   710
and all Eretum's band, and olive-bearing Mutusca;
and those who live in Nomentum's town and the Rosean country;

by Lake Velinus and Tetrica's crags, and Mount Severus;
Casperia and Foruli, and Himella's river;
the drinkers of Tiber and Fabaris; and those sent 715
by chilly Nursia, the Ortine troops, and Latin peoples;
and those whom ill-starred Allia separates with its stream;
as many as the waves that roll on Libya's sea,
when harsh Orion hides beneath the wintry waves,
as thick-set as the ears of grain which the early sun 720
scorches on Hermus' plain or Lycia's yellow cornfields.
The shields ring out, the whole earth trembles beneath their feet.

Next, Agamemnon's man, Halaesus,[2] foe to the name
of Troy, yokes his steeds to the chariot, and leads
a thousand savage tribes for Turnus, who turn with the hoe 725
Massic soil, rich in wine; and those whom Auruncan elders
sent from the lofty hills and nearby Sidicine plains,
and those who leave Cales, and those who dwell by the shallow
stream
of Volturnus, the hardy Saticulan, and the bands
of Oscans. They are carrying shapely javelins, 730
but their custom is to fit them with a leather thong;
a shield on their left hand and curved sabers for hand-to-hand
combat.

You, too, Oebalus, shall have honor in our songs—
whom, so they say, the nymph Sebethis bore to Telon,
when he held the kingdom of Teleboan Capreae; 735
now he is old; but not content with his father's land,
even then the son ruled over Sarrastian tribes
—a land stretching far and wide, and the plains that Sarnus waters,
and dwellers in Rufrae, Batulum, and Celemna's fields,
and those that apple-bearing Abella's walls look down on; 740
in Teutonic fashion they hurled their barbèd spears,
and their helmets were made of bark torn from the cork tree;
their shields and swords glittered alike with shining bronze.

You also, Ufens, mountainous Nersae sent to war,
noble in reputation, fortunate in arms, 745

---

[2]or possibly, "Agamemnon's son".

whose rugged tribe came from the harsh Aequiculan soil—
a savage people, used to hunting in the forest.
They all wear weapons while farming, and their chief delight
is to carry off fresh booty and to live by plunder.
There was, moreover, a priest of the Marruvian race,   750
with a crown of olive leaves adorning his helmet,
sent by King Archippus: Umbro, a man most valiant.
With incantations and touch he was able to put to sleep
the viper-race and water-snakes of venomous breath,
mollifying their anger, and healing their bites with his art.   755
But his art was of no avail against the Dardan spears;
all his somniferous charms and herbs from Marsian hills
were no aid to him in curing his own wounds.
Angitia's grove wept for him, and the glassy waters
of Fucinus, and the limpid pools . . .   760
    Hippolytus' son also went forth to battle:
the comely Virbius, whom his mother Aricia sent.
He was raised in Egerian groves around the marshy shores,
where Diana's rich and placable altar stands.
For men tell how Hippolytus, after he had died   765
by stepmother's wiles, fulfilling his father's vengeance with
                                                              blood,
and torn to pieces by his frenzied steeds—he came
back to behold the stars and Heaven's upper air,
recalled by Apollo's herbs and by Diana's love;
then the Almighty Father, angry that a mortal   770
should rise from the Underworld back to the light of life,
with his own thunderbolt hurled down to the Stygian waves
the son of Apollo,[3] inventor of the healing art.
But kindly Diana hid Hippolytus secretly
and gave him to the nymph Egeria and her grove,   775
where all alone in Italian woods he lived his life
without renown, changing his name to Virbius.
And that is why horn-footed horses are not allowed
in Trivia's temple and sacred groves: for horses, frightened

---

[3]Aesculapius.

by sea-monsters, spilled the youth and chariot on the shore.   780
Nevertheless the son was driving fiery horses
and chariot across the level plain, to war.

   And in the foremost ranks, the mighty Turnus himself
moves, sword in hand, a full head taller than the rest.
His lofty helmet is crowned with triple plumes, and bears   785
a Chimaera breathing Etna's fire from its jaws;
the fiercer the battle waxes and the more blood is spilled,
the more Chimaera rages with her dreadful flames.
And on his polished shield was Io, wrought in gold,
with upraised horns and bristles—already she was a heifer,   790
a terrible device! and Argus, the maiden's keeper,
and Father Inachus pouring his stream from a carvèd urn.
A cloud of soldiers follows, and columns with their shields
fill the entire plain. The youth of Argos is there,
Auruncan bands, Rutulians, and Sicanians,   795
Sacranian lines, Labicians with painted shields,
and those who plow the Tiber's glades and Numicius' shore,
and likewise those whose plowshares turn Rutulian hills
and Circe's ridge, and over whose farmlands Jupiter
of Anxur reigns, and Feronia rejoicing in her forests;   800
and those from Satura's marshes where the chilly Ufens
runs through gloomy valleys and hides himself in the sea.

   Finally comes Camilla, a maid of Volscian race,
leading squadrons of cavalry all shining with bronze,
a warrior-maid,who never trained her woman's hands   805
to Minerva's distaff and wool-basket, but to war—
to endure the burden of battle and outrun the wind.
She could have flown above the tops of uncut wheatfields
without even bruising the tender stalks as she ran;
or run across the middle of the swelling sea   810
without once wetting the soles of her swift feet in the water.
The young men and their mothers stream from fields and houses
and gaze at her in admiration as she goes by,
with mouths agape to see the splendor of royal purple
clothing her smooth shoulders, and golden clasp in her hair,   815
and how she bears a Lycian quiver in her hand,
and carries a shepherd's myrtle staff tipped with a spearhead.

BOOK VIII

THE EMBASSY TO EVANDER

When Turnus raised the battle-flag from the citadel
of Laurentum, and the trumpets blared their raucous tones,
and when he spurred his mettlesome steeds and clashed his
weapons,
straightway the people were dismayed, and all of Latium
join in the uprising; the savage youth runs berserk.   5
The leaders, Messapus and Ufens, and Mezentius
who scorned the gods, muster their troops from every side,
until the fields are stripped of all their laborers.
Venulus is sent to the city of Diomedes,
to ask for aid and bring the news that the Teucrians   10
have come to Latium; and Aeneas with his fleet
and conquered gods, claiming that he is the fated king;
that many tribes are allying themselves to the Trojan hero;
and that his name is spreading far and wide in Latium.
What end there would be to this, what outcome of the fight   15
(if Fortune were with him), Diomedes himself could judge
better than King Turnus or King Latinus. This is how
things stood in Latium. The hero of Laomedon's line,
seeing the whole affair, is tossed on a sea of troubles:
he turns his mind this way and that, and now one plan   20
seems best for him to follow, but soon he thinks of another;
as when in brazen vessels a flickering tongue of light,
reflection of the shining rays of sun or moon,
plays to and fro over everything, now in the air,
now on the fretted ceiling of the lofty roof.   25

It was night, and weary creatures all throughout the earth,
animals and birds, enjoyed a peaceful slumber;
Father Aeneas stretched his limbs on the river bank

beneath the chilly sky, and fell asleep at last,
for he was deeply troubled by the dismal war.   30
To him appeared the god of the place, the pleasant Tiber,
raising his aged head among the poplar branches.
He was draped in a covering of thin gray linen,
his hair was covered with a wreath of shadowy reeds.
He spoke and with his words removed Aeneas' cares: 35
"O offspring of the gods who bring us back our Troy,
our eternal citadel, preserved from the foeman's hands,
Aeneas, long-awaited by the Latin fields
and Laurentian soil, here your home is assured, and here
your gods are safe; do not be frightened by threats of war,   40
for Heaven's anger has abated . . .
And now, lest you think my words are but an empty dream,
you shall find a sow beneath the oaks by the river's bank,
newly delivered of a litter of thirty offspring,
and both the mother and the suckling young are white—   45
[this is the site of your city: here you may rest from your
                                                        labors.][1]
This means that after thirty years have come and gone,
Ascanius shall found a city, glorious Alba.
I know whereof I speak: and now, in a few words
I shall tell how you may escape from your present troubles.   50
Arcadians live nearby, sprung from the race of Pallas,
companions of King Evander, who followed his name and
                                                        banner;
they have chosen a site: their city is on the hills,
and it is called Pallanteum from their ancestor Pallas.
These men are always waging war with the Latin people: 55
take them into your camp and make of them your allies.
I myself shall guide you up the river banks,
so that your oars may overcome the adverse current.
Up then, son of a goddess, and as the stars are setting,
offer prayers to Juno to mollify her anger   60
and put an end to her threats. You shall pay me my due

---

[1]Cf. III, 390 ff. Some MSS. omit line 46.

when you are victorious. I am the river Tiber
whom you see flowing between my banks among rich fields:
my blue waters are most belovèd of the gods.
Here is my home, my fountain-head amid mighty cities."   65

So the Tiber spoke, then plunged into his deep waters,
seeking the lowest depths; both night and sleep left Aeneas.
He wakes and turns to the rising sun's celestial beams
and lifting water from the river in his hands,
as was the custom, prays to Heaven with these words: 70
"Nymphs, Laurentian Nymphs, from whom the rivers flow,
and you, O Father Tiber, with your sacred stream,
receive Aeneas, and safeguard him at last from dangers.
Whatever springs contain you, who pity our afflictions,
from whatever soil you issue in your beauty,   75
you shall always be graced by me with gifts and honors,
horn-bearing stream, and ruler of Hesperia's waters.
Only be at my side, confirming your will by your presence."
He speaks and he selects two warships from the fleet,
mans them with oarsmen and equips his friends with arms.   80
And lo! a sudden omen, miraculous to behold:
shining white in the forest, and of the selfsame color
as her suckling brood, a sow stretched out on the verdant bank.
The good Aeneas offers her to you, great Juno,
in sacrifice, and puts her with her young at your altar.   85
The Tiber calmed his current for them all night long,
and flowing gently backwards, kept his surface silent,
like the waters of a stagnant pool or lake, he smoothed
his stream, so that their oars would have no need to struggle.
The men urge on the moving ships with encouraging shouts,   90
the well-caulked fir glides through the waters; the waves are
                                                  astonished;
the groves are not used to the sight of a ship, and are amazed
to see from afar the shining shields and painted hulls.
Day and night the men keep rowing unceasingly,
passing the long curves under the varied foliage,   95
and cutting through the woods reflected in the water.

The burning sun had climbed to the midpoint of the sky
when they beheld, from a distance, walls and a citadel,
and scattered roofs of houses—now Rome has exalted them
to the heavens, but then, Evander ruled a meager state.   100
They swiftly turn the prows to the shore and approach the city.

   On that day, by chance, the Arcadian king was performing
accustomed rites for the great son of Amphitryon[2]
and other gods, in a grove near the town. His son Pallas
was there with the people's leaders and the modest Senate,   105
offering incense, and warm blood steamed at the altars.
When they saw the tall ships between the shady branches
gliding up the river with their silent oars,
they all were frightened at the sight and rose from the tables.
But the fearless Pallas forbids them to stop the rites   110
and seizing up a spear, he goes to meet the strangers,
and stands on a far-off hill, saying: "You men, what reason
drives you to explore these unknown paths? Where are you
                       going?
Who are you? Where do you come from? Do you bring peace
                       or war?"

Father Aeneas answers him from the lofty stern,   115
holding in his hand a peaceful spray of olive:
"You see men of Troy, and arms hostile to Latins
who have sent us into flight with arrogant war.
We seek Evander: tell him that captains of Dardania
have come to him in search of a military alliance."   120
Pallas was astonished at that mighty name.
"Whoever you may be," he says, "disembark from your ship.
Come into my house as a guest, and speak to my father in
                       person."
He welcomed Aeneas with a warm and friendly handshake.
The Trojans advance and enter the grove and leave the river.   125
Aeneas then speaks to the king with friendly words:
"Best of the sons of Greece, you to whom Fortune wishes me

---

[2]Hercules: see Glossary.

to pray with suppliant branches wreathed with woolen fillets,
I did not fear you, a Danaan chief and Arcadian
related by ties of blood to the twin sons of Atreus;   130
my own merit and sacred oracles of the gods,
the kinship of our fathers and your world-wide fame
have brought me here to you, glad to follow the Fates.
For Dardanus, the first father and founder of Troy,
was born, so the Greeks relate, of Electra the Atlantid,   135
and came to Troy. Electra was the daughter of Atlas
who on his mighty shoulders holds the spheres of Heaven.
Your father is Mercury, whom the fair Maia conceived
and bore upon the summit of frigid Cyllene,
but Maia, if we can believe these tales, is the daughter   140
of that same Atlas who holds up the starry sky.
So our two families are descended from common blood.
Secure in this, I used no envoys or crafty approaches;
instead of these, I came myself, in my own person,
appearing as a suppliant upon your threshold.   145
The same Daunian race harasses both us and you
with savage war. If they drive us out, nothing will stop them,
they think, from putting all Hesperia beneath
the yoke, and holding the seas that wash her above and below.[3]
Receive and return our friendship. Our hearts are valiant in war,   150
our spirits high, our manhood has proved itself in action."

     Aeneas finished. As he spoke, Evander was gazing
long and earnestly at his face and eyes and figure.
Then he answered briefly: "Bravest of all the Trojans,
how willingly do I receive and recognize you!   155
How well I remember your father Anchises' voice and words!
For I recall how Priam, son of Laomedon,
going to Salamis to see his sister Hesione,
continued his journey to Arcadia's chilly borders.
In those days my cheeks were in the earliest bloom of youth: 160
I marvelled at the Trojan chiefs, and at the son

---

[3] i.e. the Adriatic and Tyrrhenian Seas.

of Laomedon, but Anchises towered above the others.
My youthful heart was burning with a fierce desire
to speak to the Trojan prince and clasp his hand in mine.
I approached and eagerly conducted him to Pheneus' city,   165
and when he left he gave me a beautiful quiver, with arrows
from Lycia, and a cloak all interwoven with gold,
and a pair of golden bits that now belongs to Pallas.
Therefore the hand of friendship which you seek is yours,
and when tomorrow's Dawn restores her light to earth,   170
I shall give you an escort and supplies to cheer you.
Meanwhile, since it is as friends that you have come,
help us to keep our annual rite, which we may not postpone,
and make yourselves at home at the tables of your allies."
He orders all the food and drink, which have been removed,   175
to be replaced, and sets the guests on grassy seats
with his own hand; Aeneas has the place of honor:
a lion's shaggy hide upon a chair of maple.
Chosen youths and the priest of the altar vie with each other
in bringing roasted meat of bulls, and heaping the baskets   180
high with the gifts of Ceres, and pouring the wine of Bacchus.
Aeneas and the other Trojans eat their fill—
the long chine of an ox and the sacrificial entrails.

After hunger was banished and no more food was desired,
King Evander spoke: "These solemn rites of ours,   185
these accustomed banquets and altars to a mighty god,
no idle superstition or ignorant belief
impose them on us; but because we have been saved
from terrible dangers, Trojan Guest, therefore these rites.
Now look first at that craggy overhanging cliff,   190
with rocks strewn all about the deserted mountain dwelling,
desolate, with scattered boulders all around.
Once there was a cavern here, of tremendous depth,
where sunlight never entered. Here there lived a monster,
Cacus, half-human in shape. The ground was always reeking   195
with freshly spilled blood, and nailed to the haughty doorposts
the faces of men hung pale and rotting—a ghastly sight.
The monster's father was Vulcan, hence the pitchy fire

he belched from his awful mouth as he moved his giant frame.
Time brought to us at last the answer to our prayers: 200
the aid and arrival of a god. For the Great Avenger,
Alcides, proud of the death and spoils of triple Geryon,
travelled this way, driving enormous bulls he had won;
the oxen filled the entire valley and river-side.
But Cacus, in a frenzy lest he overlook   205
or leave any crime or fraud unattempted or undared,
stole away from their stables four magnificent bulls
and as many heifers of surpassing beauty,
and to prevent their leaving any telltale tracks,
he dragged them backwards by the tail into his cave;   210
their footprints reversed, he hid them in the rocky gloom,
so that no clues could lead a searcher to his cavern.
Meanwhile, as Amphitryon's son moved his well-fed herd
out of the stalls in preparation for the departure,
the oxen lowed as they moved away, and filled the grove   215
and all the hills around with bellows as they went.
One heifer returned an answering bellow, deep in the cave,
and cheated the hopes of Cacus from her dreary prison.
Then the anger of Hercules blazed furiously
with venomous black bile; seizing in hand his weapons   220
and heavy knotted cudgel, he speeds to the craggy mountain.
That was the first time we ever saw Cacus afraid:
panic was in his eyes; and swifter than the wind
he flees back to his cave: fear lends wings to his feet.
Just as he shut himself in his cave, by breaking the chain   225
and letting fall a giant rock (which his father's skill
suspended from the iron) so that it blocked the doorway,
lo! the Tirynthian came, furious in his anger,
scanning every possible entrance, gnashing his teeth,
looking this way and that. Three times, boiling with rage,   230
he circles the Aventine Hill; three times he tries in vain
the rocky door; three times, fatigued, he sinks down in the valley.
There was a pointed flinty crag—a pinnacle
cut sheer around above the cave—of tremendous height;
a suitable nesting-place for loathsome birds of prey.   235

This pinnacle, as it leaned on the left side towards the river,
he pushed from the right, shaking it and wrenching it loose
from its lowest roots, and thrust it suddenly aside.
The whole vast sky resounds with thunder at that thrust.
The river-banks leap apart, the river flows backward in terror.   240
The monstrous den and castle of Cacus stood revealed:
the dark and gloomy cavern deep below lay open,
as if a sudden earthquake made the ground gape wide
and deep below unlocked the infernal dwelling-places,
disclosing the pallid kingdom, hated by the gods,   245
till the whole abyss is seen, and ghosts tremble at the light.
The monster, caught by the sudden unexpected glare,
bellows with rage as he is trapped in his rocky cave.
Hercules throws rocks and tree-trunks down upon him,
using every available weapon in his rage.   250
But Cacus, who now had no escape from impending doom,
belches forth from his monstrous throat (wonder of wonders!)
thick black smoke, filling the cave with blinding darkness,
blotting it from the eyes, amassing a smoky night
mingled with fire in the depths of the murky cavern.   255
Hercules in his rage leaped headlong through the fire,
and where the smoke was thickest he jumped into the cave,
right through the inky fog that rolled in surging billows,
and there in the dark, as Cacus belches fire in vain,
he seizes him by the neck, as in a mighty knot,   260
and chokes him till his eyes pop out and his throat is bloodless.
Then he breaks down the doors, revealing the gloomy den;
the stolen cattle—plunder disavowed—are there,
laid bare for all to see. He drags the shapeless corpse
out by the feet. The people cannot get their fill   265
of gazing at the terrible eyes and face and chest,
monstrous, bristling, shaggy, the throat with extinguished fires.

   Hence we celebrate these rites; the younger folk
gladly keep the day. Potitius was the first,
of the Pinarian house, Guardian of Hercules' rites—   270
he set this altar in the grove: we call it the 'Greatest'
and forever as the 'Greatest' it shall be honored.

So come, young men, in honor of these glorious deeds,
wreathe your hair with leaves, hold the cups in your hands,
call our common god, and gladly pour the wine."   275
     He finished. His hair was veiled with the poplar of Hercules,
so that the two-colored leaves hung down and intertwined.
He held the sacred cup in his hands, and speedily
they pour libation on the table, invoking the gods.

     Meanwhile the Evening Star descends from Heaven's slope   280
and now the priests come forth, Potitius at their head,
girt with skins, according to custom, carrying torches.
The banquet is renewed: a second meal begins,
they pile the altars high with heavy-laden platters.
Then the Salii come to sing at the kindled altars,   285
their temples crowned with poplar branches: one band of youths,
the other of old men, and they extol with their songs
the deeds of Hercules; they tell how, with his own hands,
he strangled the snakes, twin monsters of his stepmother,[4]
and how in war he destroyed two great and mighty cities,   290
Troy and Oechalia; how he suffered a thousand labors
under King Eurystheus, because of cruel Juno:[4]
"You, the Invincible, who slew with mighty hand
the double cloudborn creatures, Hylaeus and Pholus,
and the Cretan Bull, and the great Nemean Lion,   295
at your approach the Stygian Lakes were all a-tremble;
Hell's Watchdog, lying on half-gnawed bones in his bloody
                                                          cave,
trembled; no monster frightened you, not even Typhoeus,
towering in his arms. Your wits did not even fail you
when the Lernaean snake surrounded you with thronging heads.   300
Hail, true offspring of Jove, increaser of gods' glory!
Graciously come to us and your rites with propitious feet!"
     Such are the songs they sing. And to crown the hymns
they tell of Cacus' cave and the fire-breathing monster.

---

[4]Juno, in her jealousy, sent two serpents to kill Hercules in his cradle;
and forced him to serve Eurystheus for twelve years.

The groves ring out with the clamor and the hills resound.   305
When the rites are finished they all return to the city.
The king, advanced in years, walked slowly; at his side
Aeneas and Pallas, his own son, went as companions,
and as they walked they lightened the journey with
                                    conversation.
Aeneas marvels, quickly turning his eyes about,   310
delighted with the place; and eagerly he asks
and learns about the stories of the former heroes.
Then King Evander, founder of Rome's citadel, says:
"Native Fauns and Nymphs once lived in these forests,
and a race of men sprung from the trunks of sturdy oaks,   315
who had no rules or customs, could neither yoke the ox
nor lay up supplies, nor save what they had gained.
But boughs of trees and the rough fare of hunters fed them.
First came Saturn from the heights of Mount Olympus,
fleeing the arms of Jove and exiled from his kingdom.   320
He collected the rude people dispersed through the mountains,
and gave them laws and called the land by the name of Latium
since he had found a safe asylum in these shores.[5]
Men have called the reign of this king the Golden Age,
because he ruled the nations in peace and harmony,   325
but little by little the gold was tarnished; a meaner race
came into being, mad for war, enamored of gain.
Then came the Ausonian band and Sicanian peoples,
and the land of Saturn frequently changed its name.
Then kings arose—rough Thybris of gigantic body;   330
because of him Italians call this river Tiber—
its original name of Albula has now been lost.
I myself was an exile, wandering over the seas,
but almighty Fortune and inexorable Fate
sent me to this land, as did the awful warnings   335
of my mother the nymph Carmentis, and Apollo's commands."

   When he had finished speaking, he pointed out the altar

---

[5]"lateo" in Latin means "to lie hidden"—a fanciful etymology, found in
Varro.

and the gate the Romans call the Carmental,
which was an ancient tribute to the nymph Carmentis,
the prophetess who first foretold the future fame   340
of Aeneas' race, and the glory of Pallanteum.
Here was a great forest where Romulus proclaimed
the Asylum, and the Lupercal below chilly cliffs,
named in Arcadian fashion after Lycaean Pan.
He shows the Trojans the sacred grove of Argiletum,   345
calling the place to witness, telling of Argus' death.[6]
He leads them to the Tarpeian House and Capitol,
golden now, but once a-bristle with woody thickets.
Even then the place's holiness awed the peasants;
even then they trembled at the rock and forest.   350
"This grove," he says, "this hill with its crown of foliage,
some God lives here—we do not know which one—my people
think that they have seen Almighty Jove himself
shaking his dark aegis and gathering the storm-clouds.
And in these two towns with their crumbling walls, you see   355
the relics and memorials of ancient heroes.
This fort was built by Father Janus, this one by Saturn,
This was called Janiculum, and that Saturnia."
Talking in such fashion they approached the home
of the poor Evander; they saw cattle here and there,   360
bellowing in the Roman Forum and bright Carinae.
When they reached the house he said: "Victorious Alcides
once passed through these doors: my palace sheltered him.
Dare, my guest, to despise riches and make yourself
worthy of a god; do not scorn poverty."   365
He spoke, and led the great Aeneas beneath the roof
of his humble dwelling-place, and showed him to his bed,
a bed that was made of leaves and the skin of a Libyan bear.
Night falls, enveloping the earth in her dusky wings.

But Venus' maternal heart was alarmed, and not in vain,   370
by all the threats and uprisings of the Laurentes.

---

[6]Actually, the name of the town does not come from Argus, but probably
from "argilla," a white clay.

She speaks to Vulcan in the golden bridal chamber,
breathing the passion of a god into her words:
"While Argive kings were sacking Troy with cruel war,
her citadel destined to fall a prey to hostile flames,   375
I asked no help from you for my afflicted people,
no arms or art did I seek from you, my dearest husband:
I did not wish to cause unnecessary trouble
however heavy the debt I owed to Priam's sons,
however many the tears I wept for my poor Aeneas.   380
But now by Jove's decrees he is in Italy,
and so, a suppliant to your power, I plead for armor;
a mother praying for her son. The daughter of Nereus
could sway you with her tears, likewise the wife of Tithonus.[7]
Look and see what peoples gather behind closed gates   385
to whet the sword of destruction against me and my Trojans!"
    She finished speaking, and as he hesitates, she throws
her snow-white arms about him in a soft caress;
he quickly caught the familiar flame, which ran through his bones
and marrow, and permeated his trembling body;   390
as when sometimes a lightning flash in a burst of thunder
races through the storm-clouds with its fiery glow.
She is pleased that her wiles have succeeded, aware of her beauty.
Then Father Vulcan spoke, enchained by undying passion:
"Why such far-fetched pleas? What has become, O goddess,   395
of your trust in me? If your anxiety was so great,
even then I could rightfully have armed the Trojans,
for neither was Almighty Jove nor Fate unwilling
that Troy and Priam should survive for ten more years.
And now, if war is what your heart and soul desire,   400
whatever skill and craft I have at my command,
whatever can be made of iron or molten electrum,
or from the strength of fire and air—cease to entreat me
as if you doubted your own powers!" Speaking these words,
he gave his wife the desired embrace and sinking down   405

---

[7]Thetis, daughter of Nereus, had asked Hephaestus (Il. xviii) to make arms
for her son Achilles; Aurora for Memnon, her son.

upon her bosom, courted sleep in every limb.

But when repose had banished sleep in the midcourse
of the waning night, the hour when a housewife
who ekes out slender livelihood by means of the distaff
and Minerva's toil, awakes the embers and sleeping fires,   410
adding night to her working hours, and keeping her servants
working late by lamplight, so that she may preserve
the purity of her home and rear her little sons:
even so, and as diligent at that hour, the Fire-God
rises from his pleasant couch and goes to the smithy.   415
Near Sicily's coast and the Aeolian Lipare
there is an island, steep and sheer with smoking cliffs.
Below it is a cave hollowed by Cyclopes' forges;
the vaults of Aetna groan with the ringing blows of anvils;
the hissing of Chalybean steel is also heard,   420
together with the panting of fire in the furnace.
This is the home of Vulcan—the place is called Vulcania.
To this place the God of Fire came down from Heaven.
In the huge cave the Cyclopes were forging steel,
Brontes and Steropes and bare-armed Pyracmon,[8]   425
they had a thunderbolt—part was already polished,
part was still unfinished—of the sort that Jove
hurls down from the heavens to earth in great numbers.
They had added three coils of hail and three of rainclouds,
another three of glowing fire and wingèd South Winds.   430
They were blending frightening flashes and sound and fear
and anger with pursuing fires mixed all together.
Elsewhere they hastened to complete a task for Mars:
a chariot with flying wheels to stir up men and cities;
and the terrifying Aegis to arm the angry Pallas   435
was being polished with its golden serpent-scales,
and Gorgon herself on the goddess' breast, with writhing snakes—
although the head was severed, the eyes were rolling still.
"Put all this away!" he said, "stop what you are doing,

---

[8]i.e. Thunder, Lightning, and Fire-Anvil.

Cyclopes of Aetna, and listen to what I say: 440
arms must be made for a hero: now you will need your strength,
now your swift-moving hands, and now your master-skill:
do not delay!" That was all he said, but they, with speed,
all bent to the task, allotting equal labors.
Bronze and golden ore are flowing in molten rivers,   445
and deadly steel is melted in the mighty furnace.
They make a massive shield, one fit to stand alone
against all Latium's missiles, welded in seven circles.
Some of them work the panting bellows to and fro,
while others dip the hissing brass in troughs of water.   450
The whole cavern resounds and groans to the clang of anvils.
The giants raise their mighty arms in rhythmic cadence
and turn the massive metal with their grasping tongs.

    While the Lemnian god works on Aeolian shores,
the kindly light and early birds below the eaves   455
awaken old Evander in his humble house.
The aged king arises and puts his tunic on,
and laces his Etruscan sandals on his feet.
He fastens his Tegean sword to side and shoulder,
throwing back a panther's hide that hangs to the left.   460
Two watchdogs go with him, from the lofty doorstep,
and trot behind their master as he walks ahead.
To the separate lodging of his guest the hero went,
remembering his promised service and his words.
And no less early was Aeneas up and stirring.   465
with one walked Pallas his son; Achates with the other.
When the two men met they clasped each others' hands
and sat together in the space between the houses.
The king began to speak:
Greatest captain of the Trojans, for while you live,   470
I never shall admit that Troy is completely conquered,
our strength in battle is not in proportion to our name;
on this side the Tuscan river hems us in,
on that the Rutulians clamor round our walls in arms.
But I will join great peoples to you, and a camp rich   475

in kingdoms, and safety revealed by unexpected chance.
Surely it is by Fate's command that you have come.
Not far from here the city of Agylla lies,
built of ancient stone, where once the Lydian race,
famous in war, settled on the Etruscan hills.   480
For many years they prospered, till King Mezentius
held the sway with haughty rule and cruel warfare.
Why should I tell of the cruel tyrant's hideous murders
and his wicked deeds? May the gods reserve such things for him!
Why, he would even attach the living to the dead,   485
fitting them hand to hand and face to face (what torture!)
and in the slimy gore and poison of that embrace,
kill the poor wretches with a long and dreadful death.
At last the wearied citizens were up in arms,
and they besieged the raving monster in his palace,   490
and killed the tyrant's henchmen and set the place on fire.
Amid the slaughter he fled to Rutulia for safety,
finding asylum with the arms of Turnus his host.
Now Etruria has risen in righteous indignation
demanding the king for punishment with threats of war.   495
I will make you the leader of these thousands, Aeneas;
their clamoring ships are crowded all along the shore,
bidding the standards advance, but the old seer holds them back
with these words: 'Chosen warriors of Maeonia,
flower and pride of an ancient race, whom righteous anger   500
sends against the foe, and Mezentius kindles with wrath,
no Italian may ever lead a race so proud:
choose strangers for your leaders.' Then the Etruscan lines
settled on this plain, frightened by Heaven's warning.
Tarchon himself has sent me envoys, who brought to me   505
the royal crown and scepter of command, asking
that I should join his force and mount the Tuscan throne;
but old age with the sluggish chill of many years
and strength too slow for valor denies me the command.
I would urge my son, were it not that from his mother   510
he has inherited a mingled Sabine blood.
You, who are favored by Fate in years and race, and demanded

by Heaven, lead the Trojans and Italians alike.
Moreover, I shall give you Pallas, my only hope
and solace: under your leadership let Pallas learn   515
to suffer warfare and the tasks of Mars: let him see
your glorious deeds and admire you from his earliest years.
I give him two hundred Arcadian horsemen—flower of our youth,
and Pallas in his own name gives you as many more."
Scarcely had he spoken: Aeneas and Anchises   520
and trusty Achates kept their eyes fixed on the ground
and would have thought on many woes in their sad hearts,
had not Cytherea given them a sign from Heaven:
for suddenly there is a mighty crash of thunder,
and lightning flashes making all things shake and reel,   525
and Etruscan trumpets blared forth from the sky.
They looked up: again and again the deafening thunder rumbled.
In the serene sky they see weapons among the clouds
glowing red in the clear air and clashing in thunder.
The others were astonished, but the Trojan hero   530
recognized the promise and sound of his goddess-mother.
Then he said: "Do not ask, my friend, do not seek to know
what these omens mean: it is I whom Heaven demands.
This is the sign my divine mother promised to send me
if war was at hand: Heaven-sent weapons, made by Vulcan   535
would come to my aid through the air . . .
Alas! What slaughter awaits the wretched Laurentians!
What penalties you will pay me, Turnus! How many shields
and helmets and bodies of heroes shall you engulf, O Tiber,
beneath your waves! Let war be declared and treaties broken!"   540
Having said these words he arose from his lofty seat
and kindled the sleeping altars with fire for Hercules,
approaching the Lar worshipped yesterday and lowly Penates
with gladness. Evander and the Trojan youth alike
slaughter two-year sheep chosen according to custom.   545
Then he returns to his ships and sees his friends again.
From them he chooses men to follow him into battle,
men of outstanding valor; the others meanwhile glide
gently down the river with its friendly current,

to bring Ascanius the news of his father's fortunes.   550
Horses are given the Trojans seeking Tuscan fields;
for Aeneas a chosen steed is led forth, bedecked in the skin
of a tawny lion, gleaming with its golden claws.
Suddenly a rumor flies through the little town
that horsemen are speeding to the gates of the Tyrrhene king.   555
Mothers, frightened, redouble their vows, and terror follows
closely on danger's heels. War's image looms ever larger.
Evander clasps the hand of his departing son
clinging to him with endless tears and speaks as follows:
"If only Jupiter could restore the years that are gone,   560
and make me as I was when, under Praeneste's walls,
I cut down the foremost ranks and burned the heaped-up shields,
victorious, and with this hand sent down to Tartarus
King Erulus, to whom at his birth his mother Feronia
had given (horrible tale!) three lives and three sets of armor   565
to wear; he had to be killed three times, but nonetheless
I stripped him of all three lives and of his armor as well—
then I would never be torn away from your dear embrace,
my son, and never would Mezentius, scorning his neighbor,
have caused so many cruel deaths with insolent sword,   570
nor widowed the city of so many of her sons.
But you, O heavenly powers, and Jupiter, King of the Gods,
have compassion, I pray, on the Arcadian king,
and hear a father's prayers: if it is your will
to keep my Pallas safe—if this is what is fated,   575
if I may live to see him and to meet him again,
I pray for life, and I shall patiently endure
all tribulations. But if Fortune threatens me
with unspeakable disaster, now, O now let me die
and break off cruel life, while fear is doubtful, and hope   580
uncertain, while I hold you, my dearest son, in my arms,
my late and only joy, and may no sadder message
wound my ear!" These parting words the father poured forth
and then he fainted. His servants carried him within.

And now the horsemen had come forth from the opened gates.   585

Aeneas was at their head, together with trusty Achates
and other Trojan princes, Pallas himself in mid-column,
conspicuous in his cloak and gaily-colored armor,
just as when the Morning Star, whom Venus loves
beyond all other starry fires, bathed in the Ocean,   590
lifts his sacred head to the sky and melts the darkness.
Trembling mothers stand on the wall, and follow with their eyes
the dusty cloud and squadrons flashing in their bronze.
They go through the bushes, where the pathway is the shortest,
in their armor; a shout arises, the column forms.   595
the hoofbeats shake the dusty plain with galloping thunder.
Near the cold stream of Caere there is an enormous grove
held in traditional awe, and curving hills surround it
on all sides, and gird the grove with dark fir trees.
The story goes that the ancient Pelasgians, who first   600
in former days held the Latin borders, consecrated
the grove and day to Silvanus, god of fields and cattle.
Not far from there was the camp of Tarchon and the Etruscans
in a sheltered spot; and one could see their camp
from a lofty hill; their tents were pitched across the plain.   605
Father Aeneas and the warriors chosen for battle
came to this place and rested their horses and weary bodies.
Venus, the beautiful goddess, approached, bringing gifts
amid the heavenly clouds; when she saw from afar
her son alone in a sheltered valley near a cool stream,   610
the goddess appeared to him and spoke the following words:
"See! The gifts perfected by Vulcan's promised skill.
So you need not shrink, my son, from challenging
the haughty Laurentes or fierce Turnus in battle."
So spoke Cytherea, embracing her son, and placed   615
the shining armor near him beneath an oak. Aeneas,
rejoicing in the splendor of the divine gift,
cannot have his fill of gazing at each piece,
admiring and turning over in his hands and arms
the helmet, terrifying with plumes and spouting flames;   620
the deadly sword, and corselet, huge and stiff with bronze,
blood-red in color, just as when a dark blue cloud

is set afire by the sun's rays and gleams from afar;
the polished greaves of electrum and refined gold,
the spear, and the shield of indescribable design.   625
   There the Fire-God had fashioned Italy's story
and Rome's triumphs, since he was versed in prophecy
and knew of the things to come. There was each generation,
the whole line of Ascanius, and the battles in order.
He had shown the Mother-Wolf in Mars' green cave   630
lying outstretched; around her teats the twin boys hung
playing, and suckling their foster-mother fearlessly,
while she with graceful neck bent back was caressing them
in turn, and licking their bodies into shape with her tongue.
Nearby was represented Rome, and the Sabine Women   635
carried off illegally from the Games in the Circus
amid the seated crowd; and the outbreak of war between
Romulus' men and old Tatius and the stern Cures.
Then the same kings, having made peace, stood in arms
before the altar of Jove, with goblets in their hands   640
and made a pact with each other over slaughtered swine.
Not far away, four-horse chariots, driven apart,
had torn Mettus to pieces (but you should have kept your word,
O Alban!); Tullus dragged through the woods the liar's limbs,
until the leaves and branches dripped with bloody dew.   645
Porsenna, too, was there, commanding them to receive
the exiled Tarquin, surrounding the city with mighty siege.
Aeneas' descendants rushed on the sword for liberty's sake.
And you could see Porsenna angry and threatening,
because Horatius Cocles dared to break down the bridge,   650
and Cloelia broke her chains and swam across the river.
At the top was Manlius, guard of the Tarpeian Fort,
standing before the temple, holding the Capitol;
the palace was crude, with the thatched roof of Romulus.
A silver goose flew through the golden colonnades   655
cackling that the Gauls were on the very threshold.[9]

---

[9]Rome was besieged by the Gauls in 390 B.C. Manlius, awakened by the
cackling of geese, defended the citadel against the attack.

And the Gauls were in the bushes, grasping the citadel
under cover of the darkness of the night.
Golden is their hair and golden are their garments—
they gleam in stripèd coats, their necks are white as milk,   66
with golden necklaces. Each has two Alpine spears
shining in his hand; long shields protect their bodies.
The dancing Salii and naked Luperci,
their caps crested with wool, and the shields fallen from Heaven,
were hammered out; the chaste mothers in cushioned cars   66
moved through the city in sacred throng. At a distance from them
he fashioned Tartarus' realm and the lofty gates of Dis,
the punishment for crimes, and you, O Catiline,
hanging from a cliff and trembling at the Furies.
Far apart the good are given laws by Cato.   67
Between them, a broad band depicted the swelling sea,
its blue waters and white billows wrought in gold.
Dolphins swam around, brightly shining in silver,
sweeping the water with their tails as they cleft the surface.

   In the middle the brazen ships and battle of Actium   67
could be seen, and all Leucate was afire
with the array of war; the water shimmered with gold.
Here Augustus Caesar leading Italians to war,
with elders and people and the great gods of the Penates,
stands on the lofty stern, twin flames on his happy brows,   68
and above his head his father's star appears.
Elsewhere, Agrippa with auspicious winds and gods
leads his column, towering, his temples shining
with the prow-girt Naval Crown—a great distinction in war.
And Antony, with barbaric wealth and varied weapons,   68
a victor from the Orient and Red Sea's shores,
brings Egypt with him and Eastern forces from utmost Bactra,
with his disgraceful Egyptian consort[10] following him.
They all rush forward at once; the sea is churned to foam,
swept by the oars and triple-pointed beaks of ships.   69
They seek the deep; one would think the Cyclades, uprooted,
floated on the sea, or mountains clashed with mountains,
so mighty were the warships with their towering sterns.

Blazing tow and wingèd steel flies from their hands;
Neptune's fields are reddened with the recent carnage. 695
The queen[10] in the midst marshals her hosts with brazen rattle,
not yet looking behind her at the twin serpents.[11]
Monstrous Egyptian gods of all sorts, and barking Anubis
brandish arms against Neptune, Venus, and Minerva.
In the midst of the destruction Mars is raging, 700
engraved in iron, with dreadful Furies in the air,
and Discord with torn garments strides in exultation,
attended by Bellona with her bloody scourge.
Actian Apollo was looking on, and bent his bow
from on high, so that all the Egyptians and the Indians 705
and all the Arabs and Sabaeans turned in flight.
The queen herself seemed to be calling on the winds:
she spread the sails and even now she loosened the ropes.
Amid the slaughter, the Fire-God had made her pale
with impending death, borne by the waves and the Northeast Wind. 710
Opposite was the mighty bulk of the mourning Nile-God,
opening wide the folds of his garments, calling the conquered
into the dark blue bosom of his hidden streams.
But Caesar was borne within Rome's walls in triple triumph,[12]
dedicating to Italy's gods an immortal offering: 715
three hundred mighty temples all throughout the city.
The streets of Rome were ringing with joy and games and applause.
In all the temples were bands of matrons, in all were altars,
with slaughtered bullocks before the altars on the ground.
Augustus himself was seated on the snowy threshold 720
of shining Phoebus, reviewing gifts from all the nations,
hanging them on proud doorposts. The conquered peoples
walked by,
in long lines, as varied in dress and arms as in tongue.

---

[10]Cleopatra.

[11]The twin snakes are either a general symbol of doom (Cf. Laocoön's death, II, 203, and Allecto, VII, 450), or else a specific reference to the manner of Cleopatra's own death.

[12]In 29 B.C. Augustus celebrated a triple triumph for his victories of Dalmatia, Alexandria, and Actium.

Vulcan had fashioned the Nomad race, and ungirt Africans,
Leleges, Carians, and arrow-bearing Gelonians;   725
the Euphrates, flowed with smoother and more humble waves,
the Morini, remotest of men, the Rhine with his two horns,[13]
the untamed Dahae and Araxes, resenting the bridge.[14]
    All these he admires on Vulcan's shield, the gift of his mother;
though ignorant of the events, he rejoices in their portrayal,   730
and lifts on his shoulders the fame and fate of his descendants.

End of Book VIII

---

[13]River gods were frequently represented with horns. Cf. above, line 77.

[14]Augustus had rebuilt the bridge over the Araxes River. A flood had
destroyed the original bridge built by Alexander the Great.

BOOK IX

THE SIEGE OF THE TROJAN CAMP

And while in a distant part these things were happening,
Saturn's daughter Juno sent Iris down from Heaven
to gallant Turnus, who, as it chanced, was seated within
his ancestor Pilumnus' sacred grove and valley.
The daughter of Thaumas addressed him with her rosy lips: 5
"Turnus, what no god would have dared to promise you
if you had prayed, the circling day unasked has brought:
for Aeneas has left his comrades, town and ships,
seeking the Palatine power and the home of Evander.
Not only that, but he has reached the remote cities   10
of Corythus, to muster troops of Lydian peasants.
Why do you wait? Now is the time to call for horses
and chariots. End all delay! Take the camp by surprise!"
She spoke, and poised herself on her wings, and flew away
cutting the enormous rainbow beneath the clouds.   15
He recognized her, and raising both his hands to Heaven
the youth pursued the flying goddess with these words:
"Iris, glory of Heaven, who has sent you to me,
wafted by the clouds to earth? Whence this sudden brilliance?
For I see the misty heavens split asunder   20
and the starry firmament. I follow this great omen,
whoever you are that call me to arms!" And with these words
he went to the stream, and took up a handful of swirling water,
praying long to the gods and troubling Heaven with vows.

    And now the army advanced across the open plain,   25
rich in horses, rich in embroidered cloaks and gold,
Messapus in the forefront, Tyrrhus' sons in the rear,
while the general Turnus, in the column's center,
[moves sword in hand, a full head taller than the rest:]¹

---

¹This line is not found in some MSS. It is taken from VII 784.

like the deep Ganges rising with seven placid streams,   30
silently, or like the rich flood of the River Nile,
ebbing from the fields, and now sunk in its channel.
The Trojans see a sudden somber cloud of dust
gathering, and darkness arising over the plain.
Caïcus is the first to shout from the foremost ramparts: 35
    "What is this cloud of inky black, my countrymen?
Quickly, to arms! Seize your weapons! Man the battlements!
See, the enemy is upon us!" With mighty shouts
the Trojans pour in through the gates and climb the walls.
For, as he left, Aeneas, their great leader, had told them   40
that in case of an attack while he was absent
they should not form their battle-lines or trust to the field,
but guard the camp and walls, protected by the ramparts.
And so, though shame and anger urge them to join battle,
nonetheless they bar the gates and follow orders,   45
awaiting the foe in arms, shielded by the towers.
Turnus, riding ahead of the slowly-moving column,
accompanied by twenty chosen youths on horseback,
is suddenly at the city; he rides a Thracian horse
spotted with white, and wears a red-plumed golden helmet.   50
"Which of you men will be first with me against the foe—
look!" he cries, and hurls a javelin through the air
beginning the battle, riding proudly across the plain.
His men shout back and follow him with dreadful clamor.
They marvel at the Trojans' lack of fighting spirit: 55
they will not trust themselves to the field; they will not face
the foe in arms, but cling to the camp. Hither and thither
he rides round the walls, seeking an entrance that is not there.
As when a wolf, lying in wait at the crowded fold,
howls round the pens, enduring midnight winds and rains,   60
while the lambs are bleating safely under their mothers—
he rages fierce and furious against the prey
he cannot reach, exhausted by the madness of hunger
which he has known so long; his bloodless jaws are dry:
so the Rutulian's anger rages, as he looks   65
at camp and walls; his iron bones burn with resentment.

How can he force an entrance? How can he drive out
the imprisoned Trojans from their walls onto the plain?

   The fleet was lying at anchor near the side of the camp,
fenced about with mounds of earth and the flowing river.   70
He attacks it, calling his triumphant men for fire;
eagerly he takes a blazing torch in his hand.
Then the others fall to the task, inspired by Turnus.
They arm themselves with smoking torches, plundering hearths.
The smoky firebrands give off a pitchy glare   75
and clouds of glowing ash are wafted to the stars.
   Tell me, Muses, what god averted the savage flames
from the Trojans? Which one drove the fire from the ships?
Credence in the tale is old, but its fame is immortal.
When Aeneas began to build his fleet on Phrygian Ida,   80
and he prepared to venture forth upon the deep,
the Berecyntian Mother of the Gods, it is said,
spoke these words to Jove: "Grant this prayer, my son,
for your dear mother who asks it, since you are lord of Olympus:
I had a forest of pine trees, beloved for many years,   85
on top of a mountain ridge, where offerings were brought me;
it was dark with pitchy pines and maple trees.
Willingly I gave it to the Trojan youth
when he needed a fleet, but now sharp fears distress me.
Banish these fears, and let a mother's prayer avail   90
that they may never be shattered by force of wind and wave:
let them have this reward for growing on my mountains."
   Her son who rules the starry heavens answered: "Mother,
what are you asking the Fates? What do you seek for your people?
Shall ships that were built by mortal hands have immortal
                                   rights?   95
And shall Aeneas safely come through unsafe perils?
To which of the gods has such great power been allowed?
However, one day, when they have done their task, and lie
safe in Italian harbors—whichever escape the waves
and carry the Trojan chief to the Laurentian fields—   100
I shall take their mortal shape away, and transform them

into sea-goddesses, such as the Nereid Doto
and Galatea, who cleave with their breasts the foaming waves."
    So Jupiter spoke, and by his Stygian brother's river,
and by the banks all swirling with their pitch-black whirlpools,   105
he nodded confirmation, and all Olympus trembled.

    The promised day was now at hand: the Fates had fulfilled
the allotted time, when Turnus' attack reminded the Mother
to drive away the torches from the sacred ships.
A strange new light first flashed before the eyes of men;   110
a huge cloud sped across the sky from the east
with choruses from Ida; a terrifying voice
came through the air to Trojans and Rutulians:
"Do not hasten, Trojans, to defend my ships;
do not take up weapons. For Turnus shall be allowed   115
to burn the sea before he burns my sacred vessels.
Go free! Go, sea-goddesses: your Mother commands it!"
Straightway each ship breaks her cable from the bank,
and like so many dolphins they dip their beaks in the water
only to emerge as maidens (miraculous omen!)—   120
[as many as the brazen prows that had stood on the shore]²
just so many nymphs are swimming in the water.
    The Rutulians were amazed, Messapus himself
was frightened, his horses likewise; the loudly sounding river
stops as Tiber turns his course back from the sea.   125
But the gallant Turnus did not lose his courage;
he cheers his comrades' spirits, chiding them with these words:
"These omens are for the Trojans! Jupiter himself
has taken away their accustomed help. They do not await
Rutulian fire and sword. The sea is closed for the Trojans: 130
they have no hope of flight and half their world is lost.
The land is in our hands, for all of Italy's thousands
are now in arms. I have no fear of oracles—
the fated divine responses that the Phrygians boast of—
Fate and Venus are satisfied that the Trojans have landed   135

---

²This line, not found in many MSS., is taken from X 223.

in Italy's rich fields. I have my destiny, too:
to cut down with the sword this accursed race of people
that stole my bride. The Atreidae are not the only ones
to suffer so; not only Mycenae may take up arms.
'To have perished once is enough!' To have sinned once should
                                        have been   140
enough to make them hate the whole of womankind—
these cowards whose only courage is in their protecting walls
and defensive ditches—such a slight barrier against death!
But have these men not seen the battlements of Troy,
built by the hand of Neptune, sink into the flames?   145
Now which of you chosen men is ready to cut down
their ramparts, and rush with me upon the trembling camp?
I do not need Vulcan's arms, nor a thousand ships to fight them!
Let all Etruria join them as allies; they need not fear
the darkness and cowardly theft of their Palladium   150
nor sentries slaughtered on the topmost citadel,
nor shall we need to hide ourselves in a horse's belly:
in broad daylight we shall surround their walls with fire.
I'll show them that they are not contending with Danaans
and Grecian youth held off by Hector for ten years!   155
    And now, since the better part of this day has passed,
for what remains, refresh yourselves, proud of the deeds
you have performed; await the battle that lies ahead!"
Meanwhile, Messapus is told to block the gates with sentries,
and set a ring of fires around the battlements.   160
Twice seven Rutulian youths are chosen to guard the walls
with soldiers; each of them commands a hundred men
wearing purple plumes and gleaming in their gold.
They run to and fro, take posts in turn, and stretch on the grass,
they drink their fill of wine and empty brazen bowls.   165
The fires glow, and the sentries keep themselves awake
by playing games . . .

    The Trojans, who are on the ramparts under arms,
see all these things; in fearful haste they inspect the gates;
sword in hand, they fasten bridges to the battlements.   170

Mnestheus and keen Serestus direct the task,
instructed by Aeneas, in case of an attack,
to take command of the men and plan the strategy.
On the walls, the whole army, sharing the danger,
keep the watch in turn, guarding their several posts.   175
    Nisus was guarding the gate, the fiercest of all the Trojans—
the son of Hyrtacus, he was sent by the huntress Ida
with Aeneas—swift with javelin and light arrows.
With him was Euryalus: no fairer youth
ever followed Aeneas or bore the Trojan arms.   180
His unshaven cheeks were in the first bloom of youth.
A mutual love was theirs: they always fought together,
and now took their turn together as sentries at the gate.
Nisus said: "Do the gods put this fire into our souls,
Euryalus, or does each man's desire become a god?   185
My heart has long desired battle or some great exploit—
this quiet inactivity is hard for me to bear.
You see how overconfident the Rutulians are:
their fires are few, they are relaxed in drunken slumber.
Their whole camp is silent. Listen to my plan   190
and learn what purpose now arises in my mind:
the people and the Senate all agree that Aeneas
must be summoned: men are needed to bring the news.
If they promise what I ask for you (for myself
the glory of the deed is enough) I think I can find   195
a path at the foot of the hill to the walls of Pallanteum."
Euryalus was amazed and dazzled by love of honor,
and he spoke these words at once to his eager friend:
"Nisus, do you hesitate to take me with you
on this adventure? Shall I let you go alone   200
into such danger? It was not thus the warrior Opheltes
raised me amid the Argive terrors and Trojan woes;
it is not thus that I have borne myself at your side
following great Aeneas and his utmost fates.
Here is a soul that despises the light of life, and thinks it   205
a small price to pay for the glory you desire."
    Nisus answered; "I had no such fears of you—

it would be wrong; so may Jupiter, or whatever god
looks auspiciously on this deed, bring me back in triumph.
But if, as often happens on these perilous missions,   210
some god or some mischance should sweep me into disaster,
I want you to live: your age is more worthy of life.
Let someone survive to bury my corpse, if it is brought back
or ransomed; and if Fortune forbids, as is her wont,
at least to render the last rites to an empty tomb.   215
I could not cause such suffering to your poor mother
who, alone of all the mothers, has followed her son,
never caring for the walls of great Acestes."
    But the other said: "These excuses are all in vain:
I have not changed my mind nor weakened my resolve.   220
Let us make haste!" He rouses the guards at once to relieve them.
They come and take their posts; Euryalus goes off
with Nisus at his side as they go to seek the prince.

All other living things throughout the earth were resting,
soothing their cares with sleep, forgetful of their sorrows.   225
The Trojan leaders, a chosen band, were holding council
on matters of gravest importance to all: what should be done
and who should bring the news to Aeneas. They stand there,
                                                          leaning
on their long spears and holding their shields, in the middle space
of the camp, when Nisus and Euryalus, together,   230
come in eager haste and beg for an audience:
important business, they say, and worth the delay.
Iülus received the excited pair and asked Nisus to speak.
Hyrtacus' son said: "Listen with favorable minds,
men of Aeneas; do not be influenced by our youth.   235
The Rutulians are silent, overcome by sleep
and wine; we have found the spot for a secret attack
where the road forks outside the gate nearest the sea.
The ring of fires is broken there, and only black smoke
rises to Heaven. If you permit us to try our luck   240
and go in search of Aeneas to Pallanteum's walls,
you soon will see us return, all laden down with spoils

of the slaughter we have dealt. We shall not lose our way,
for we have seen the edge of the town from the dark valleys,
and from our constant hunting we know the entire river."   245
    Then the aged Aletes, ripe in wisdom, said:
"Gods of our fathers, who still protect Troy with your power,
you are not planning to destroy us, after all,
since you give our youth such courage and resolution!"
So speaking, he caught them both by the shoulder and shook their
                                                            hands   250
while streams of tears ran down over his face and cheeks.
"What rewards shall I deem fitting for such heroes,
and for such glorious deeds? The gods and your own virtue
shall grant you the first and fairest prizes. As for the rest,
the good Aeneas will promptly repay you, and young Ascanius   255
will never be unmindful of such noble service."
    Ascanius says: "Indeed, Nisus, my only safety
depends upon my father's return, and I swear to you both
by the great Household Gods, and the Lar of Assaracus,
and white-haired Vesta's shrine: all my fortune and trust   260
I give into your care—only bring back my father:
the sight of him will put an end to all my sorrow.
I will give you a pair of engraved silver goblets
taken by my father when Arisba fell,
also a pair of tripods and two great talents of gold,   265
and an antique mixing-bowl that came from Sidonian Dido.
But if it falls to our lot to conquer Italy,
to wield the victor's scepter and distribute spoils,
you have seen Turnus' horse and golden armor:
that horse and shield and red-plumed helmet I set aside   270
even now from all the rest, Nisus, for your reward.
My father will give you besides twelve matrons of wondrous
                                                            beauty,
and captive men, each equipped with his own armor,
and the land that belongs to King Latinus himself.
And you, Euryalus, whose age is so near to mine,   275
I shall take you, noble youth, as my bosom friend,
and make you the companion of my every adventure.

I shall seek no glory on my part without you;
whether in peace or war, my trust will be in you,
in word and deed." Euryalus made answer thus: 280
"I hope the day will never come that proves me unworthy
of such great enterprise, if only Fortune is good
and not adverse. But one thing, apart from all these gifts,
I beg you: I have a mother, of Priam's ancient line,
whom neither the land of Ilium, nor Acestes' walls   285
could keep, poor thing, from following along with me.
I leave her now unaware of the danger, whatever it is,
without a farewell, because—may Night and your right hand
be my witness—I could not bear my mother's tears.
I beg you, comfort the helpless woman, relieve her anguish.   290
Let me leave with this hope in you; I shall go more bravely
into whatever risks may come." The Dardanians
were deeply touched and wept; fair Iülus most of all.
His soul was stirred by the picture of filial devotion
and he spoke as follows: 295
"Be assured that all will be worthy of your great deeds, for she
will be a second mother to me, lacking only
the name of Creusa, and no slight honor is due to her
who brought forth such a son. Whatever chance attend you,
I swear by my own head, as my father used to do,   300
whatever I promised you upon your safe return,
these same things will remain for your mother and family."
So he speaks, weeping, and takes from his shoulder his golden
                                                          sword,
fashioned with consummate skill by Lycaon of Cnossus,
fitted with an ivory sheath for easy use.   305
Mnestheus gives to Nisus a shaggy lion's skin,
and the faithful Aletes changes helmets with him.
Thus armed, they proceed at once, and all the Trojan leaders
go with them as far as the gates, both young and old,
to bid them Godspeed. Moreover, the fair Iülus,   310
with a man's mind and spirit far beyond his years,
gave them messages for his father, but the winds
scattered them all and gave them vainly to the clouds.

They leave and cross the trenches through the gloom of night,
seeking the deadly camp (though they were destined first   315
to bring death to many men). Here and there they see
bodies sprawled in drunken sleep along the grass,
and tilted chariots with men among the wheels and harness,
and weapons and wineskins all around. Nisus spoke first:
"Euryalus, our hands must dare: the occasion demands it.   320
There is the way: be on your guard and look all around
lest some hand be raised against us from behind.
I will lay waste this section and hew a broad path for you."
Having spoken, he checks his speech and attacks with his sword
the haughty Rhamnes, who as it happened, was stretched out   325
on high-piled carpets, drawing the deep breath of sleep.
He was a king himself, and Turnus' favorite augur,
but his auguries could not ward off his own destruction.
Nisus slew three servants lying nearby with their weapons,
and Remus' armor-bearer and the charioteer   330
beside the horses; he cuts their drooping necks with the sword,
then he beheads their master and he leaves the trunk
bubbling and spurting blood—the bed and ground are covered
with warm dark gore. Then he kills Lamyrus and Lamus,
and the young and handsome Serranus, who had played long that
night,   335
and now lay stretched upon the ground, overcome by the god.[3]
How happy he would have been if he had kept on playing
through the whole night, continuing until daybreak!
Thus a starving lion riots through full sheepfolds;
maddened by hunger, he mangles and tears the woolly flock   340
dumb with fear, and rages and roars with bloodstained mouth.
No less is the destruction wrought by Euryalus:
blazing with anger, he falls on many unknown men:
Fadus and Herbesus and Rhoetus and Abaris—
all unaware, except for Rhoetus, who was awake   345
and saw the whole thing and hid in terror behind a huge bowl,
but as he rose, Euryalus plunged his sword to the hilt

---

[3]Bacchus, god of wine, or perhaps the god of Sleep.

into his chest, and drew it forth in a stream of blood.
He vomits dark red life-blood forth, all mixed with wine.
The other eagerly pursues his stealthy labor.   350
Now he approaches Messapus' men; he sees the last fires
flickering, and well-tethered horses cropping the grass;
when Nisus speaks to him briefly (for he saw his friend
carried away by his excessive lust for slaughter):
"Let us stop," he said, "unfriendly day is breaking: 355
enough of vengeance—a path is cut through the enemy's midst."
Many things are left behind: warriors' weapons
mounted in silver, and mixing-bowls, and splendid carpets.
Euryalus takes Rhamnes' trappings and his belt,
studded with gold (a gift to Remulus of Tiber   360
from wealthy Caedicus—a far-off token of friendship,
and on his death he gave them to his grandson to wear;
after his death the Rutulians captured them in battle).
He fits them on his valiant shoulders, but in vain.
Then he takes Messapus' helmet with graceful plumes   365
and puts it on. They leave the camp and head for safety.

In the meantime, riders sent from the Latin city,
while the rest of the army waited on the plain
in full array, came bringing an answer to King Turnus—
three hundred, armed with shields, with Volcens as their leader. 370
Now they approached the camp and were coming under the wall
when, from afar, they see the pair turn on a path
to the left, and in the darkness the helmet betrayed
the thoughtless Euryalus, reflecting rays of light.
It was not seen in vain. Volcens cries from the column: 375
"Halt, strangers! Why this journey? And who are you
that carry arms? Where are you going?" They do not answer
but quickly flee to the woods and trust themselves to the night.
Horsemen bar the way on every side, with guards
covering all the well-known forks to cut them off.   380
The wood stretched wide with bristling thickets and dark ilex;
a heavy growth of brambles covered the whole ground.
Here and there a path could be seen among hidden ways.

Euryalus is hindered by the shadowy branches
and weight of his booty: he is afraid and loses the path.   385
Nisus gets clear. Heedless, he had escaped the foe,
and reached the place later called Alban from Alba's name
(in those days King Latinus had high stables there);
he stopped and looked about in vain for his absent friend.
"Unhappy Euryalus," he said, "where did I leave you?   390
What path shall I follow, unwinding all the twisted ways
of this deceptive forest?" He notes and retraces his footsteps,
wandering here and there among the silent thickets.
He hears the sound of horses and shouts of the pursuers,
and not long afterwards, a cry came to his ears: 395
he sees Euryalus, deceived by the ground and the darkness,
bewildered by the noise. The whole troop had seized him
and now were dragging him away struggling in vain.
    What could he do? By what power or with what arms
could he dare to rescue the lad? Should he rush upon the foe   400
and seek a speedy, glorious death by way of wounds?
Swiftly he draws back his arm and aims his spear,
and looking at the moon on high he says a prayer:
"O Goddess, come and help me in my time of need,
Latonia, glory of all the stars, protector of forests!   405
if ever my father Hyrtacus offered gifts for me
at your altars, if I increased your honors by hunting,
and hung up offerings from your dome and temple roof,
let me scatter this troop, and guide my spear through the air!"
He spoke, and threw the javelin with all his might.   410
The flying weapon whistles as it cleaves the shadows
of night; it strikes the back of Sulmo from behind,
and there it snaps; the broken shaft pierces his heart.
A stream of blood spurts from his breast, he rolls on the ground
in the chill of death, his sides gasping and heaving.   415
They look around in all directions. Nisus, encouraged,
aims another javelin from the tip of his ear.
As they hesitate, it goes through Tagus' temples,
whizzing, and it lodges warm in the transfixed brain.
    Volcens is furious, for he cannot see the man   420

who threw the spear: there is no one on whom to vent his rage.
"But you, meanwhile, with your warm blood, shall give me
                                                        vengeance
for both!" he says, and as he speaks, he rushes with sword
upon Euryalus. Then Nisus is frantic with fear:
he cries aloud, no longer concealing himself in the darkness,   425
no longer able to endure the cruel grief:
"Kill me, me! Here am I, the one who did the deed!
Rutulians, I am the guilty one! He neither dared
nor could have done it! The stars of Heaven, that know the truth
bear witness: he only loved his unlucky friend too well!"   430
But even as he spoke, the sword, fiercely driven,
pierced the ribs and snowy breast of Euryalus.
He rolls in death and blood runs down his lovely limbs,
his neck falls limp and drooping back upon his shoulders,
as when a purple flower, cut down by the plow,   435
languishes in death, or as poppies with weary stems
bow their heads beneath the weight of heavy rain.
    But Nisus rushes into their midst, seeking only Volcens:
Volcens is the only one of whom he thinks.
The enemy crowd around him, closing in on all sides,   440
seeking to hurl him back; he presses on nonetheless,
whirling his blazing sword, until he buries it
in the screaming Rutulian's face, and dying, slays his foe.
Then, pierced through, he fell upon his lifeless friend,
and in the quiet sleep of death found peace at last.   445
    Fortunate pair! If my verse has any power, no day
shall ever erase you from the memory of time,
as long as Aeneas' house rests on the sturdy rock
of the Capitol, and a Roman ruler holds dominion!
    The triumphant Rutulians, laden with loot and spoils,   450
weeping, carried the lifeless Volcens back to their camp.
Nor was the sorrow less in the camp when Rhamnes was found
slain, and so many captains in a single slaughter,
and Serranus and Numa. A milling crowd begins
to press around the dead and dying, and the ground   455
fresh with recent bloodshed, and foaming pools of gore.

They recognize the spoils—Messapus' shining helmet,
and the trappings that were won back with so much sweat.
   And now the Dawn departed from the saffron bed of Tithonus,
arose, and sprinkled early light over all the world;   460
and now the sun poured in, unveiling the world with daylight.
Turnus, armed himself, calls his men to arms,
and each captain marshals his brazen hosts to battle,
whetting their anger to an edge with various rumors.
Indeed, they fix on lifted spears (piteous sight!)   465
and follow with their shouts and clamor, the very heads
of Euryalus and Nisus . . .
   The hardy men of Aeneas, on the left side of the walls
(for the right gave on the river), have set their defenses:
they hold the wide trenches, and stand on the lofty towers,   470
sorrowful, and deeply moved by the transfixed heads
which they know so well, all dark with dripping gore.

   Meanwhile wingèd Rumor flies through the trembling town
with her news, and comes to the ears of Euryalus' mother.
Suddenly all warmth departs from her wretched bones,   475
the shuttle falls from her hands, and all the thread unwinds.
The hapless creature rushes forth with woman's wailing,
rends her hair, and madly seeks the walls and front ranks
without a thought of men or danger or of weapons,
and then she fills the heavens with her plaintive cries: 480
"Is this you that I see, Euryalus? You who were
the last support of my old age? Have you left me alone,
O cruel one? When you were sent into unknown dangers,
could your poor mother not have said one last goodbye?
Alas! You lie in an unknown land, a prey to dogs   485
and birds of Latium! Your mother could not lead you out
—your body, rather—for burial, or close your eyes
or bathe your wounds, or cover you with the robe I worked on
night and day, comforting age's sorrows with weaving!
Where shall I go? What land now holds your poor torn limbs   490
and broken body? Is this what you bring me back of yourself,
my son? Is it for this that I have followed you

over land and sea? Strike me, if you have any pity,
hurl your weapons at me, Rutulians, and kill me!
Or you, great Father of the Gods, have mercy and send   495
this hated life to Tartarus with your thunderbolt,
if in no way else can I break the cruel chains of life!"
They were distressed by her wailing, and a groan of sorrow
went through their midst; their strength is numb and broken for
                                                              battle.
Idaeus and Actor, bidden by Ilioneus and Iülus   500
weeping bitterly, seize her in her burning grief
and, carrying her in their arms, they lay her down in her house.

But now the far-off trumpet sounds its dreadful call
with brazen notes; a shout follows, the heavens echo.
The Volscians attack in even ranks with joined shields,   505
preparing to fill the trenches and tear down the wall.
Some look for an entrance and scale the wall with ladders
where the Trojan lines are thin and the light shines through
the ranks of the defenders. The Trojans hurl down missiles
of every kind, and stave them off with long stout poles,   510
accustomed by long warfare to defend their walls.
They also throw down stones of massive weight, in an effort
to break the shielded ranks. Yet the Rutulians
easily withstand the attack with their tortoise-shields.
But not for long, for where a massed attack is threatening,   515
the Trojans move and roll down an enormous rock
that makes a gaping hole in the enemy's ranks, and breaks
the armored defense. The Rutulians do not wish
to contend with blind attack any longer, but try to drive
the Trojans from the walls with missiles . . .   520
On one side Mezentius (terrible sight!) was brandishing
a torch of Etruscan pine and hurled its smoky flame.
But Messapus, tamer of horses, offspring of Neptune,
tries to break down the walls and calls for scaling ladders.

Calliope and Muses, I pray you, inspire my song   525
as I tell what slaughter, and what death Turnus caused

and what heroes each man sent to the realms of Orcus;
do you unfold with me the mighty scenes of War.
[For you remember, Muses, and you are able to tell.][4]

    There was a tower, high and steep, with lofty gangways,   530
placed in a vantage point: this the Italians tried
with all their might to take by storm, and to overthrow it
with all their skill. The Trojans defended it with stones
and hurled a shower of missiles through the openings.
First Turnus threw a blazing firebrand which clung   535
to the tower's side. The wind began to fan the flames
until they spread, devouring the planks and gateposts.
The men within are terrified and seek in vain
to escape the disaster. While they huddle to the side
not yet attacked by the flames, suddenly the tower   540
came crashing to the ground, making the heavens thunder.
Half-dead, they fall to the earth under the mighty mass,
pierced by their own spears, their breasts impaled by splinters
of rough wood. Only Helenor and Lycus escaped.
Of these, Helenor was a man in his earliest youth   545
whom a Licymnian slave had secretly borne to the king
of Lydia, and sent to Troy with forbidden arms,
with naked sword and a white shield without device.
When he saw himself amid Turnus' thousands,
and the Latin ranks that were standing all around,   550
as a wild animal, fenced about by a hunters' ring,
rages against their weapons, springing to certain death
against the forest of spears and leaping at the foe:
so the young man rushes to death in the enemy's midst
and makes his way to where he sees the weapons are thickest.   555
But Lycus is swifter of foot: through enemy and weapons
he gains the ramparts and tries to clutch the parapet,
striving to gain the outstretched hands of his companions.
Turnus follows him with foot and spear alike,
shouting in triumph: "Madman, did you really think   560
that you could escape my hands?" He seizes him as he hangs

---

[4]This line is not found in most MSS. It is taken from VII 645.

and tears him down along with a large part of the wall,
as when Jove's armor-bearing eagle soars through the air
clutching a hare or snowy swan in his crooked talons,
or as when the wolf of Mars has stolen from the stable   565
a lamb sought by its bleating mother. A shout arises
on all sides. They invade and fill the trenches with earth.
Others are hurling blazing torches on the rooftops.
Ilioneus kills Lucetius with a massive rock
torn off a mountainside, as he comes carrying flames.   570
Liger slays Emathion, Asilas Corynaeus;
one skilled with the spear, the other with far-darting arrows;
Caeneus slays Ortygius, and Turnus Caeneus,
and Itys and Clonius, Dioxippus and Promolus,
and Sagaris and Idas, standing on top of the tower;   575
Capys kills Privernus, whom the light spear of Themillas
had grazed at first: he madly threw away his shield
and reached his hand to the wound. The arrow sped on its way,
pinning his hand to his left side, and buried itself
deep in his body, piercing his lungs with deadly wound.   580
The son of Arcens stood there with his glorious arms,
a cloak embroidered with needlework and Spanish purple—
a noble youth—whom his father Arcens had sent,
reared in the groves of Mars[5] around Symaethus' streams,
where the rich and gracious altar of Palicus stands.   585
Mezentius dropped his spears, and took the whistling sling,
whirling the leather thong three times around his head;
the molten bullet struck him right between the temples,
and stretched him out to his full length in the deep sand.

Then, it is said, Ascanius first aimed a swift arrow   590
in war—until that time, he had only frightened beasts—
and he despatched the brave Numanus with his hand,
whose surname was Remulus, and who had recently
taken the younger sister of Turnus as his bride.
He strode about the battle-line, shouting words   595

---

[5]or, reading *matris* instead of *Martis*, "in the groves of his mother".

fit and unfit to repeat, his heart swollen with pride
in his fresh royalty, and spoke these boastful words:
"Are you not ashamed, you twice-captured Trojans,
again to hide behind walls and fend off death with ramparts?
Look at the men who would take our brides from us by war!   600
What god, what madness drove you men to Italy?
Here are no Atreidae, no deceitful Ulysses!
We are a hardy race, who bring our newborn babies
to the river to toughen them in its icy waters;
as boys they rise early, stalking game and tiring the forests;   605
their sport is taming horses and shooting with the bow.
Our youth, patient of toil, and accustomed to privation,
tame the earth with the hoe or shake great cities in war;
our whole life is spent with iron, as with upturned spear
we goad our cattle's flanks; not even sluggish age   610
can weaken the strength of our hearts and spirits, or change our
                                                            vigor.
We press white hairs beneath the helmet: our chief delight
is to carry off fresh booty and to live by plunder.
But you are dressed in embroidered saffron and shining purple;
indolence is your delight, and luxurious dancing;   615
you wear sleeves on your tunics and ribbons on your caps,
O Phrygian women—not even Phrygian men—go and wander
over Dindyma's heights where the double flute plays your music!
The timbrel calls you, and the Berecyntian boxwood flute
of Ida's mother: leave war to men; give up the sword!"   620

    As he uttered his baneful boasts, Ascanius
could not bear it, but faced the foe and aimed a shaft
with horsehair bowstring, drawing his two arms wide apart,
and paused, invoking Jove with suppliant vows and prayers :
"Almighty Jupiter, favor my brave beginning!   625
I myself shall bring you yearly gifts to your temples
and place before your altar a steer with gilded horns,
shining white, bearing his head as high as his mother;
already he butts with his horns and kicks up sand with his feet."
The Father heard and from the clear sky caused it to thunder   630
on the left; the deadly bow twanged at that instant.

The drawn-back arrow speeds away with a horrid hissing,
and cleaves the head of Remulus and the hollow temples
with its steel tip. "Go, mock courage with boastful words:
thus twice-captured Trojans answer Rutulians!"   635
That was all Ascanius said. The Trojans shout
and cheer the lad with joy, and lift their hearts to Heaven.

  It happened that long-haired Apollo, in the sky,
was looking at the Italian city and the towns
from his seat in the clouds; he spoke to the triumphant Iülus: 640
"A blessing on your courage, boy—this road to the stars,
begotten of gods, begetter of gods that are to be!
All fated wars shall rightly end in peace beneath
the line of Assaracus; Troy cannot contain you."
So speaking, he leaves the sky, and flies through the stirring breeze, 645
seeking Ascanius. He changes the shape of his features
to resemble old Butes, the ancient armor-bearer
of Trojan Anchises, and trusty guardian of his gate;
Aeneas made him Iülus' companion. Apollo went
in every way like that old man—the voice and complexion,   650
the hoary locks on his head, the harshly clanging weapons,
and the god spoke these words to the fiery Iülus:
"Be satisfied, Aeneas' son, that Numanus
has fallen unavenged to your arrow. Great Apollo
gives you the first glory and does not begrudge your skill   655
that equals his own, but in the future, refrain from war."
Thus Apollo began, and vanished from mortal sight
and disappeared from the eyes of men into empty air.
The Trojan leaders recognized the god and his weapons,
and heard the rattle of his arrows in his quiver.   660
And so, at the command and will of Phoebus Apollo
they stopped Ascanius, although he was eager for battle;
then they submit their lives again to the open dangers.
The shout goes from tower to tower all along the rampart;
they bend the eager bows and twist the leather thongs,   665
the ground is strewn with spears; and shields and hollow helmets
ring out as they clash together: fierce battle rages,
great as the storm from the West which under the rainy Haedi[6]

---

[6]i.e. "Kid stars": see Glossary.

lashes the earth, thick as the hailstones that the clouds
hurl on the sea when Jupiter, bristling with South Winds,   67
whirls the watery tempest and bursts the clouds of Heaven.

Pandarus and Bitias, sprung from Idaean Alcanor,
whom the wood-nymph Iaera bore in Jupiter's grove,
youths as tall as their ancestral firs and hills,
open wide the gate entrusted to them by their captain,   67
relying on their arms, and invite the foe to enter.
They within, to the left and right, stand at the towers,
armed with iron, with waving plumes above their heads,
just as, in the air beside the flowing streams,
whether on Padus' banks or near the lovely Athesis,   68
twin oaks rise up to the sky with their unshorn heads
soaring on high, and nodding their majestic crowns.
The Rutulians rush in as they see the open gates.
At once Quercens and handsome Aquiculus, in arms,
and headstrong Tmarus, and Haemon of the race of Mars,   68
are routed and are put to flight with all their columns,
or on the threshold of the gateway give up their life.
Then anger rages fiercely in their fighting spirits,
and the Trojans rally and gather round the place,
battling hand-to-hand and making longer sallies.   69

While elsewhere raging Turnus is throwing the foe in
                                                        confusion,
he hears a report that the enemy, flushed with success
born of recent carnage, has opened wide the gates.
He stops what he is doing and, moved by mighty rage,
rushes on the Trojan gate and the proud brothers.   69
And first Antiphates (for he was the first in line)
—bastard son of great Sarpedon and Theban mother,
is slain by Turnus' spear; the Italian cornel-shaft
goes flying through the gentle air and sticks in his gullet,
deep in the chest; the cavernous wound spurts forth a tide   7
of foaming blood; the steel grows warm in the punctured lung.

Then Meropes and Erymas, then Aphidnus he slays,
then Bitias falls with fiery eyes and raging heart,
not by a javelin (for no javelin had killed him)—
but hissing loudly, a power-driven pike came flying,   705
driven like a thunderbolt; neither double hides
of bulls, nor a trusty corselet with double scales of gold
could withstand its force; the mighty body wavers and falls,
the earth groans out, the massive shield resounds above him.
Thus sometimes on the Euboic shore of Baiae,   710
a rocky mass falls, built before of giant boulders
and thrown into the sea; falling, it wreaks havoc
as it crashes into the shallows and comes to rest on the bottom;
the sea is all stirred up and piles of dark sand rise;
lofty Prochyta⁷ shakes at the sound, and the rocky bed   715
of Inarime⁷, put by Jove's command above Typhoeus.

And now the warrior Mars gave spirit and strength to the
                                                          Latins,
spurring their hearts to anger with his eager goads,
letting loose upon the Trojans Flight and black Terror.
On all sides they gather, now that they have a chance   720
to fight; the Warrior-god inspires them . . .
When Pandarus sees the prostrate body of his brother,
and how the battle goes, and how Chance and Fortune stand,
with mighty force he swings the gate round on its hinges,
pushing with his broad shoulders, shutting many comrades   725
outside the walls, and leaving them in the cruel battle,
closing others in with him as they rush in retreat.
Madman! who failed to see the Rutulian prince come bursting
through the gates in the crowd, and wantonly shut him up
in the city, like a huge tiger among the helpless flocks.   730
A new light shone at once in Turnus' eyes; his armor
rang with dreadful sound; the blood-red plumes on his helmet
were all a-quiver, lightning rays flashed from his shield.
In sudden dismay the Trojans see and recognize

---

⁷The islands of Procida and Ischia.

the hated face and mighty limbs. Then huge Pandarus   735
leaps forth, blazing with anger at his brother's death
and says: "This is not Amata's palace, given in dowry,
nor does Ardea hold Turnus in native walls;
you see the enemy camp: you have no hope of escape!"
And Turnus answers, smiling with unruffled mien: 740
"Begin if you dare: join battle with me, for you shall announce
to Priam that here too an Achilles has been found!"
He finished speaking. The other hurls with all his might
a rough unfinished spear, knotty, with green bark.
But only the winds received it, for Saturnian Juno   745
turned the wound aside; the spear lodged in the gate.
"But you shall not escape the weapon my hand wields:
not such a man is he who sends this wound and weapon!"
So Turnus spoke, and raised his uplifted sword on high;
the steel edge splits the brow in two between the temples,   750
cleaving the Trojan's beardless cheeks with a frightful wound.
A crash is heard: the earth shakes with his massive weight.
Dying, he stretches on the ground his lifeless body
and armor spattered with blood and brains, while in equal halves
his head dangles on this side and that from both his shoulders.   755
The Trojans scatter and they flee in utter terror,
and if at that instant the victor had taken thought
to break the bars of the gates and let his comrades in,
that day would have been the last for the war and the Trojan
                                                    nation.
But rage and insane lust for slaughter drove him on   760
furious against the foe . . .
First he seizes Phaleris and hamstrings Gyges;
he snatches their spears and hurls them at the fleeing Trojans,
for Juno breathes new strength and courage into him.
He sends Halys to join them, and Phegeus with pierced shield,   765
and on the wall, as they raised the war-cry unawares,
Alcander and Halius and Noemon and Prytanis.
As Lynceus comes to meet him, calling on his comrades,
he sweeps his shining sword from the rampart on the right
and cuts his head off with one swift downrushing blow—   770

head and helmet lie far away. Amycus the hunter
of wild animals—no man was ever more skillful
in anointing arrows and arming steel with poison;
and Clytius, Aeolus' son and Cretheus dear to the Muses,
Cretheus, companion of the Muses, who always loved   775
songs and lyres and tuneful notes upon the chords,
who always sang of steeds and arms and heroes and battles.

At last the Trojan captains, Mnestheus and fierce Serestus,
hearing of the slaughter of their men, came together,
and saw their friends in flight, and the foe within the gates.   780
Mnestheus said: "Where, where then are you fleeing, Trojans?
What other walls, what new defenses do you have?
Shall one man, surrounded by your fortifications,
wreak such havoc and slaughter with impunity
throughout the city, and send so many good men to death?   785
You cowards, have you then no pity and no shame
for your poor country, your ancient gods, and great Aeneas?"
They are encouraged by his words, take heart and rally
and close the ranks. Little by little, Turnus retreats,
heading for the stream and the side the river surrounds.   790
The Trojans press more fiercely on, with mighty shouts
and mass together; as when a band of hunting men
attack a savage lion with spears, but he, afraid,
yet fierce and glaring grimly, retreats, for neither do anger
and courage let him turn his back, nor is he able   795
though he desires it, to make his way through men and weapons.
In the same way, the doubtful Turnus retraces his steps
without hastening; his heart is boiling with rage.
Indeed, twice he even charged the enemy ranks,
and twice he drove them in fearful flight along the walls.   800
But reinforcements from the camp come all together
and Saturn's daughter Juno does not dare to help him,
for Jupiter sent Iris flying through the air
from Heaven, bearing no gentle words of command for his sister:
that Turnus must withdraw from the lofty Trojan ramparts.   805
And so, with neither shield nor hand can he hold his ground

but he is overwhelmed by missiles from all sides.
Around his hollow temples the helmet rings and clashes
unceasingly; the solid bronze is battered by stones.
The plumes are torn away, the shield cannot withstand   810
the blows. The Trojans and Mnestheus redouble their attack
with spears, like thunderbolts; the sweat begins to pour
over all his body in a dark stream; he cannot breathe,
and a painful panting shakes his weary limbs.
Then at last he leaps headlong into the river   815
in all his armor. The Tiber with its yellow waters
received him as he came, and washed away the blood
and brought him on gentle waves, rejoicing, to his comrades.

End of Book IX.

BOOK X

THE BATTLE ON THE SHORE

Meanwhile the palace of almighty Olympus is opened.
The Father of Gods and King of men calls a council
to his starry dwelling-place; from there he can look down
upon the earth, the Trojan camp, and the Latin peoples.
They take their seats in the double-doored hall, and Jove begins: 5
    "Great dwellers in the sky, why have you changed your minds,
and why do you contend with such discordant hearts?
I had forbidden Italy to fight with the Trojans;
why this dissension against my commands? What fear has
                                                   provoked
one side or the other to rush to arms and arouse the sword? 10
The proper time for battle will come—do not hasten it—
when cruel Carthage shall open wide the Alps one day
and hurl destruction on the citadels of Rome—
then your strife and hatred, then pillage will be permitted.
Now desist, and gladly arrange the truce I order." 15
    So spoke Jupiter briefly, but golden Venus' answer
was far from brief:
    "O Father, eternal ruler of men and the universe
—for what other power is there to implore? Do you see
how arrogant the Rutulians are, and how Turnus 20
is borne exultant through the midst in his chariot, swollen
with the tide of Mars? The Trojans are no longer protected
by bars and walls: indeed, they fight within their gates
and on the very ramparts; the trenches are swimming with blood.
Aeneas, unwitting, is absent. Will you never allow 25
this siege to be raised? Again an enemy is threatening
the walls of a new-born Troy, yes, and another army;
and once again from Aetolian Arpi a Diomedes
rises against the Trojans. Indeed, I believe my wounds

are still to come: your offspring awaits mortal weapons!
If without your sanction, in spite of your will divine
the Trojans have sought Italy, let them pay for their sins
and do not save them, but if they have followed oracles
of the Powers Above and Below, then why can anyone
now overthrow your commands or build new destinies?
Why should I mention the burning of the fleet at Eryx?
Or the King of the Winds with all his howling tempests
roused from Aeolia, or Iris wafted from the clouds?
And now she stirs the Underworld (this part of Creation
remained untried!) and Allecto, suddenly unleashed,
is raging in the upper air through Italy's cities.
I have no thought of empire—true, I once had hopes
while Fortune was with us—let them win whom you wish to win.
If there is no land for your cruel wife to give
the Trojans, I pray you, by the smoking ruins of Troy,
Father, only let Ascanius go unharmed
from battle, only allow my grandson to survive!
Aeneas may indeed be tossed on unknown waves—
let him follow Fortune wherever she may lead—
but let me take the boy away from savage warfare.
I have Amathus and high Paphus and Cythera,
and Idalium: here let him put his arms away
and live his life in obscurity. Let Carthage press
Ausonia with mighty sway: no hindrance shall come thence
to Tyrian towns. What is the good of having escaped
the plague of war, to have fled through the midst of Argive flames,
and exhausted all the perils of seas and desolate lands
while the Trojans seek Latium and a reborn Troy?
Would it not have been better to settle on the ashes
and ground that once was Troy? Give a Xanthus back, I pray,
and a Simois to a wretched people; let Trojans retrace
again the fates of Troy!" At that the royal Juno
driven by great frenzy, said: "Why do you force me
to break my silence and tell the world my hidden sorrow?
Did any man or god make Aeneas seek this war
and come to King Latinus as an enemy?

30

35

40

45

50

55

60

65

He sought Italy at the Fates' command: so be it—
impelled by the ravings of Cassandra. Did I urge him
to leave the camp, or to entrust his life to the winds,
or commit the conduct of war and the battlements to a child?   70
To stir Etruscan faith and rouse a quiet people?
What god, what cruel power of mine has driven him
to destruction? Where was Juno or 'Iris sent from the clouds'?
It is shameful that Italians surround your new-born Troy
with flames, that Turnus takes his stand on native soil—   75
the grandson of Pilumnus and son of divine Venilia—
but what about the Trojan torches hurled at Latins?
What about yokes on farmlands, and driving off of booty
and choosing a father-in-law, and snatching a bride away?
And offering peace with the hand, while the ships bristle with
                      arms?   80
You can steal Aeneas from the Grecian hands
and instead of a man you give them clouds and empty air;
you can turn their fleet into so many sea-nymphs;
but if I help the Rutulians, is that so dreadful?
'Aeneas, unwitting, is absent.' Let him be unwitting and absent!   85
'You have Paphus and Idalium and Cythera.'
Then why tempt savage hearts and a city teeming with war?
Am I trying to overthrow the Phrygian state
from its foundations? Or is it he[1] who put the Trojans
at the Achaeans' mercy? What was the reason for Europe   90
and Asia to rise in arms and break the peace with treason?
Did I lead the Trojan adulterer to ravage Sparta?
Did I give him weapons and foster war with lust?
Then you should have feared for your people: now, too late
you make your unfair complaints and bandy words in vain!"   95
    Thus Juno pleaded and all the gods murmured assent,
just as when the rising winds caught in the forests
moan and roll about with muffled murmurings,
a warning to the sailors of the coming tempest.
Then the Almighty Father who rules the universe   100

---

[1]She is presumably referring to Paris.

begins, and as he speaks, the house of the gods grows still,
the earth begins to tremble, the heavens all are quiet,
the winds are hushed, and Ocean stills his waves to silence:
  "Listen to my words, and take them to your hearts:
since it cannot be that Trojans and Italians   10
join in alliance, since your discord has no end,
whatever the fortune of each today, whatever the hope
each follows, Rutulian or Trojan, I shall make no distinction;
whether the camp is held in siege by Italy's fate
or by Troy's mistakes and sinister oracles;   11•
I do not absolve the Italians: each one's actions will bring him
evil or good, for Jove is the king of all alike;
the Fates will find their way." By his Stygian brother's rivers,
and by the banks all swirling with their pitch-black whirlpools,
he nodded confirmation, and all Olympus trembled.   11
That was the end of the Council. Jupiter arose
from his golden throne; the gods escort him to the threshold.

  Meanwhile the Rutulians press round every gate
to slay men with the sword and gird the walls with flames.
Aeneas' men are bottled up within the ramparts   12
with no hope of escape. Wretched, they stand on the walls,
and man the battlements in vain with a scanty circle.
Asius son of Imbrasus, Hicetaon's son Thymoetes,
the two Assaraci and Castor and the aged Thymbris
in the front ranks, and the two brothers of Sarpedon,   12
Clarus and Thaemon from high Lycia, are at their side.
One lifts up a giant rock with all his might—
no small part of a mountain—Acmon of Lyrnesus,
as great as his father Clytius and his brother Mnestheus.
Some ward off the foe with javelins, some with stones,   13
or hurling firebrands, or fitting shafts to the bowstrings.
In their midst was Venus' most rightful care,
the Trojan boy himself; his lovely head uncovered,
shining like a jewel inset in yellow gold
upon a crown or necklace, or as ivory gleams,   13
cleverly inlaid in boxwood or terebinth

or Oricum; his neck, as white as milk, receives
the flowing locks clasped in a circlet of soft gold.
You too, Ismarus, your great-hearted people saw
as you were aiming wounds and arming arrows with poison,   140
noble son of a Lydian family, where men till
the rich fields and Pactolus irrigates them with gold.
Mnestheus also was on hand, whom yesterday's glory
—of driving Turnus from the walls—lifts to the stars,
and Capys, from whom the Campanian city takes its name.   145

   Thus both sides met each other in a savage conflict
while Aeneas himself at midnight was on the sea.
For, when he left Evander and entered the Tuscan camp,
he went to the king and told the king his name and country,
and what he sought and offered; of Mezentius' army   150
that was being gathered, and Turnus' furious spirit,
warning him what faith there was in human affairs,
with prayers and entreaties; then, without delay,
Tarchon joined forces and made a pact. So, freed of Fate,
the Lydians embark on orders from the gods,   155
under a foreign leader. Aeneas' ship is first,
with Phrygian lions under her beak, and lofty Ida
above them—a most welcome sight for the Trojan exiles!
Great Aeneas sits there, revolving in his mind
the shifting issues of war, with Pallas at his left   160
asking about the stars, the dark night's course,
and of his many adventures on the land and sea.

   Now, Muses, open the gates of Helicon and sing:
what army comes with Aeneas from the Tuscan shores
meanwhile, arming the ships and riding through the waves.   165
   Massicus cuts the waves at their head, in the brazen "Tiger";
with him a band of a thousand youth, who left the walls
of Clusium and Cosae's town. They are armed with arrows,
light quivers on their shoulders and death-dealing bows.
Fierce Abas is with him—his men are all in shining armor,   170
his ship is decorated with a golden Apollo.

Populonia had given him six hundred sons,
all expert in war, but Ilva gave three hundred
—an island rich in never-failing Chalybean mines.
Third, Asilas, interpreter of gods and men: 175
the entrails of victims obey him, and the stars of Heaven,
the tongues of birds, and the prophetic fires of lightning.
He brings a thousand men to war with bristling spears.
Pisa, Alphean city, but on Etruscan soil,
commanded them to obey him. Next comes handsome Astyr,   180
—Astyr, trusting his steed and many-colored armor.
Three hundred more, all of one mind to follow their leader,
come from the men who live in Caere and Minio's plains
and ancient Pyrgi and the fever-ridden Graviscae.
Let me not pass you by, Cinyras, bravest in war   185
of the Ligurian chiefs, and Cupavo with scanty troop,
from whose crest the plumes of a swan arise (your fault,
Cupid, and your mother's!)—sign of his father's form.
For they say that Cycnus, in grief for beloved Phaëthon,
while he sang and soothed the sorrow of his love   190
amid the poplar leaves that once were Phaëthon's sisters,
drew over himself the soft plumage of white old age
and left the earth, and singing still, followed the stars.
His son, Cupavo, with a band of equal age,
is driving with his oars the monstrous "Centaur"—the vessel   195
towers over the sea, and threatens to hurl a rock
into the waves from above, while her long keel plows the waters.
And there is Ocnus with a band from his native shores,
son of prophetic Manto and the Tuscan river,
who gave you, Mantua, walls, and his mother's name—   200
Mantua, rich in ancestors, though not of one stock,
but three races, and each race has four peoples.
She is the chief, but her strength is of Etruscan blood.
Thence five hundred take arms against Mezentius,
whom Minicius, son of Benacus, crowned with gray reeds,   205
leads down to the sea in ships of sturdy pine.
Aulestes moves heavily, lashing the sea
with strokes of a hundred oars—the sea is white with foam.

He sails in the mighty "Triton," that terrifies the sea
with dark blue conch, his shaggy front swims in the waves   210
like a man down to the waist, but with a fish's belly.
Beneath the monster's breast the waves are churned to foam.
So many chosen leaders sail in thirty ships
to rescue Troy, and plow the salty plains with bronze.

   And now the day had gone from the sky, and gentle Phoebe   215
was driving her night-wandering chariot through the heavens.
Aeneas (for his concern allows no rest to his limbs)
himself sat guiding the tiller and managing the sails,
when lo! in middle-course a band of his companions
meets him: the nymphs whom gracious Cybele had commanded   220
to be goddesses of the sea, and turn from ships to nymphs—
and they came swimming side by side, cleaving the waves,
as many as the brazen prows that had stood on the shore.
They recognize their king from afar and surround him with
                                                         dances.

Cymodocea, who was the most skilled at speaking,   225
grasps the stern with her right hand—her back is out of the water,
and paddles with her left hand over the silent waves.
She accosts the unsuspecting Trojan: "Are you awake,
Aeneas, son of the gods? Awake, and loosen the sheets
from the sails! We are the pines from Ida's sacred ridges,   230
but now sea-nymphs: we are your ships! When treacherous
                                                         Turnus
was driving us in headlong flight with sword and fire,
unwillingly we broke your moorings, and we seek you
over the waters. The Great Mother took pity on us
and changed us into goddesses who live in the waves.   235
But your son Ascanius, within walls and trenches,
is in the midst of weapons and savage Latin soldiers.
Already the Arcadian cavalry, joined with Etruscans,
hold their place; to bar the way with opposing squadrons
lest they approach the camp—that is Turnus' purpose.   240
Come and bestir yourself, and with the rising Dawn
have your men called to arms; do you take up your shield

that the Fire-God gave you, invincible and rimmed with gold.
Tomorrow's Dawn, if you do not think my words are idle,
will see tremendous heaps of slain Rutulians."   245
    She finished, and as she left, she pushed the ship with her right
                                                                      hand,
skillfully; the vessel sped across the waves
faster than a javelin or wind-swift arrow.
The others, too, speed their course. The Trojan son of Anchises
is bewildered and amazed, but his heart is cheered by the omen.   250
He looks up at the arch of Heaven, and briefly prays:
"Dear Cybele, Mother of the Gods, who delight in Dindyma
and tower-bearing cities and lions yoked together,
be now my leader in battle; make these omens come true.
Approach your Phrygians, goddess, with auspicious step."   255
So he spoke; meanwhile the returning light of day
was pouring in, and it had put the night to rout.
First Aeneas bids his comrades to follow his signals,
to tune their hearts for the fray and prepare themselves for
                                                                   combat.

And now, as he stands on the lofty stern, he sees the Trojans   260
and his own camp; he raises high in his left hand
his blazing shield. The Trojans from the walls all shout:
the cry goes up to the stars, as new hope kindles anger.
They hurl their missiles, just as when, amid black clouds,
Strymonian cranes give signal and trail across the sky,   265
noisily fleeing the South Wind with their happy cries.
To the Rutulian king and captains this seemed strange
until they turn around and see the Trojan fleet
steering shoreward: the whole sea is alive with ships.
Aeneas' helmet is ablaze and flames pour out   270
from the crest; the golden boss of his shield is spouting fire,
as when a comet shines blood-red with ominous glow
in the transparent night, or as the fiery Dog-Star,
bringer of thirst and pestilence to wretched mortals,
rises and makes the heavens gloomy with baleful light.   275
But gallant Turnus did not lose his confidence
that he could seize the shore and drive them back from the beach.

[He cheers his comrades' spirits, chiding them with these
                                                    words:][2]
"Your wishes have come to pass—to break their lines with the
                                                    sword!
Comrades, the battle is in your hands: let each man think   280
of his wife and home; recall the great deeds and the glory
of your fathers; let us attack at the water's edge
when they are confused and their feet falter as they land.
Fortune helps those who dare!"
As he speaks, he considers which men to take with him   285
against the foe, and whom to entrust with the siege of the walls.
Meanwhile Aeneas lands his crews from the lofty ships
by means of gangways. Many watch the retreating tide
and boldly leap into the water where it is shallow.
Others slide down the oars. Tarchon looks at the shore,   290
where no shallows heave and no billows are breaking,
but the smooth sea flows in with calm and unchecked flood.
Here suddenly he turns his prows and begs his men:
"Now, my chosen crew, bend to your heavy oars:
lift them, drive us forward! Split the hostile shore   295
with your beaks and let the keels themselves make furrows!
I do not shrink from wrecking the ship at such a landing
if only we can gain the shore!" As soon as Tarchon
has spoken thus, his comrades all rise to their oars,
and drive the foaming ships upon the Latin shore,   300
until the beaks are on dry land and the keels are resting
without any damage. But not your ship, O Tarchon!
She runs aground on a shoal where the bottom is uneven,
hanging in doubtful balance, wearying the waves.
She breaks up and throws all the men amidst the billows,   305
where pieces of oars and floating planks and thwarts impede
                                                    them,
while the undertow sucks at them and makes them lose their
                                                    footing.

---

[2]This line is not found in some MSS. It comes from IX 127.

Turnus does not delay or dally: he fiercely sweeps
the whole army against the Trojans on the shore.
The trumpets blare. Aeneas attacked the rustic troops   31●
first, and laid them low—a favorable omen.
He slays Theron, a mighty warrior, who dared
attack the hero Aeneas: through the bronze armor and tunic
rough with gold, he pierced his side; the sword drank blood.
Next he strikes Lichas, who had been cut from his mother's womb   315
after she was dead, and consecrated to Phoebus
for escaping the knife as an infant. Nearby he kills Cisseus,
a hardy man, and huge Gyas, who were laying low
the ranks with clubs: of no avail were Hercules' arms
nor their strong hands, nor even Melampus, who was their father, 320
friend of Alcides while the earth gave him sore labors.
And lo! as Pharus is flinging forth his boastful words,
a flying javelin strikes him in his screaming mouth.
You too, unlucky Cydon, would have met your doom,
following Clytius, your new delight, whose cheeks were golden   325
with early down, forgetful of all your youthful loves—
you would have perished miserably under Dardan hands
had not your brothers, son of Phorcus, seven in number,
joined ranks in a solid band and hurled their seven spears.
But some glanced off harmlessly from shield and helmet   330
and others only grazed his side, for kindly Venus
deflected them. Aeneas spoke to trusty Achates:
"Bring weapons: not one of those that lodged in Grecian bodies
upon the plains of Troy, shall my hand throw in vain
at the Rutulians!" He seizes a great spear and hurls it.   335
It flies and smashes into the brazen shield of Maeon,
tearing through his breastplate and his breast alike.
His brother Alcanor rushes to his aid, and supports
his falling brother; the flying spear pierced his arm,
still keeping to its bloody course, and sped onward;   340
the arm hung lifeless by the tendons from the shoulder.
Then Numitor plucked the spear out from his brother's body,
and aimed it at Aeneas, but he could not hit him:
instead he only grazed the thigh of great Achates.

Now Clausus of Cures, confident in his youthful body,   345
strikes Dryops underneath his chin with rigid spear
from a distance, piercing his throat as he speaks, and robbing him
of both his voice and life at the same instant. The other
hits the ground with his forehead and vomits forth thick blood.
Three Thracians, too, of Boreas' noble race,   350
and three sent by their father Idas and native Ismarus,
he kills in different ways. Halaesus hastens there
with his Auruncan troops; the son of Neptune too,
Messapus, glorious with his steeds. On every side
they try to drive him back. The battles rages fiercely   355
on Italy's very threshold. As the discordant winds
in the wide expanse of Heaven fight with equal force
and do not yield to each other, nor do clouds nor sea,
but a long and doubtful battle rages as all things struggle,
so the ranks of the Trojans and the ranks of Latium   360
clash—foot against foot and hero against hero.
But in another part, where a torrent had driven rocks
tumbling far and wide, and bushes torn from the banks,
when Pallas saw the Arcadians, who were not accustomed
to fight on foot, give way before the pursuing Latins,   365
(the roughness of the ground had caused them to leave their
                                                          horses)
he did the only thing that remained in such dire straits,
and now with prayers, now with reproaches he fires their spirits:
"Where are you fleeing, comrades? By your brave deeds, I pray
                                                          you,
by King Evander's name, by all the wars you have won,   370
by my own hope of equalling my father's glory,
do not trust to flight! With swords a path must be hewn
through the enemy. Where they are amassed and press the
                                                          thickest,
there your country calls you, with Pallas at your head.
These are not gods that harass us, but mortals fighting mortals—   375
we have just as many lives and hands as they have.
Look! The mighty wall of the sea has cut us off—
no land is left for flight—must we seek the ocean or Troy?"

And as he speaks he charges into the thick of the foe.
Lagus meets him first, drawn by unfriendly Fate,   38
while he was wrenching loose a weighty boulder; the spear
pierced him through the middle, where the spine divided
the ribs; he plucks away the weapon where it clings
to the bones. And Hisbo did not surprise Pallas,
although he hoped to do so—for Pallas, as he charges,   38
reckless and enraged at the cruel death of his friend,
welcomes him and buries the blade in his swelling lungs.
Sthenius he attacks and also Anchemolus
of Rhoetus' line, who dared to defile his stepmother's bed.
You too, the brothers Larides and Thymber, fell   39
on Rutulian plains—identical twins, the sons of Daucus,
whom even their pleased parents could not tell apart—
but now Pallas made a cruel distinction between you:
for your head, Thymber, was cut off by Evander's sword,
and your severed right hand, Larides, sought its owner,   39
the dying fingers twitching and grasping at the sword.

The Arcadians are kindled by his reproaches and deeds,
and mingled sorrow and shame arm them against the foe.
Then Pallas pierces Rhoeteus fleeing in his chariot—
so much respite and reprieve was granted Ilus;   40
for the heavy spear had been aimed at Ilus fom afar,
which Rhoeteus intercepted as he fled from you,
noble Teuthras and Tyres your brother. He rolled from the car,
dead, and struck the Rutulian plain with lifeless heels.
And as a shepherd in summer, when the winds he awaited   40
have arisen, kindles various fires in the woods,
and suddenly the whole mid-space catches on fire,
and Vulcan's bristling flames spread over the wide fields,
and the shepherd, triumphant, gazes at the joyful blaze,
just so, Pallas, do your brave comrades rally round   41
and come to your aid. But Halaesus, the mighty warrior,
advances to meet them, collecting himself behind his armor;
and he kills Ladon and Pheres and Demodocus;
with shining sword he severs the right hand of Strymonius

raised to his throat, and strikes Thoas' face with a rock,   415
scattering the bones all mixed with blood and brains.
Halaesus' father, foreseeing evil doom, had concealed him
in the woods, but when death closed the old man's eyes,
the Fates laid hold of Halaesus and consecrated him
to Evander's weapons. Pallas attacks him with this prayer: 420
"Father Tiber, grant this spear which I hold poised
good fortune and a path through sturdy Halaesus' breast:
these weapons and the hero's armor will hang from your oak."
The god heard him: while Halaesus shielded Imaon,
the Arcadian weapon pierces the wretch's defenceless chest.   425
But Lausus, a great bulwark of war, does not allow
his men to be dismayed by the slaughter; he first kills Abas
who stands opposing him, the support and stay of battle.
Arcadian youth go down before him, Etruscans too
go down, and you, O Trojans, whom the Greeks had spared.   430
The armies clash together, matched in men and might.
The rear pushes the forward lines; so dense is the crowd
that hands and weapons cannot move. Pallas attacks
and Lausus confronts him: the two are nearly alike in age
and outstanding in beauty. But Fortune has denied them both   435
return to their native land. Yet the Lord of great Olympus
does not allow them to meet each other hand-to-hand;
soon each one is to meet his doom from a greater foe.

Meanwhile Turnus' gracious sister warns him to rescue
Lausus, and with his swift car he cleaves right through the lines. 440
He sees his friends and says: "It is time to desist from battle:
I alone shall fight with Pallas, for he is mine!
I only wish his father were here to see the fight!"
He spoke, and his comrades left the field as he had bidden.
As the Rutulians withdraw, the youth is amazed   445
at the haughty command; his eyes dart to and fro at Turnus
and his mighty body; with fierce gaze he surveys the scene
and he speaks these words to meet the words of the king:
"Now I shall win honor, be it for lordly spoils,
or a glorious death. My father is ready for either fate: 450

so cease your threats!" So speaking, he strides into the plain.
In the Arcadians' heart the very blood runs cold.
Turnus leaps from his chariot and prepares for combat
hand-to-hand; like a lion who, from a lofty lookout,
sees a bull standing in the plain and pondering battle,   455
and charges him:—such is the picture of the advancing Turnus.
When Pallas thought that he was within range of a spear-cast,
he advanced first, hoping that Chance would aid one who dared
against overwhelming odds, and cried out to the heavens:
"By my father's hospitality and the tables   460
where you, a stranger, were welcomed, aid me, Hercules!
Let dying Turnus see me strip his bloody armor
and let his expiring eyes behold me as the victor!"
Hercules heard the youth and from deep in his heart
he stifled a heavy sigh, and shed vain and bitter tears.   465
Then the Father[3] spoke to his son with kindly words:
"Each has his appointed day: the span of life for all
is brief and irretrievable. To spread fame by deeds—
this is the task of valor. Beneath the walls of Troy
many sons of gods were slain—yes, even my own son,   470
Sarpedon, perished. Turnus, too, is called by Fate,
and he has reached the goal of his allotted years!"
He finished and looked away from the Rutulian fields.
But Pallas hurls his spear with all his might and main
and whips his flashing sword out of the hollow sheath.   475
The spear flies and strikes where the top of the armor rises
to guard the shoulder, and penetrates the rim of the shield,
finally even grazing the mighty body of Turnus.
Then Turnus, poising his oaken spear tipped with sharp steel,
hurls it straight at Pallas, saying as he throws: 480
"See now if my weapon can penetrate more deeply!"
He spoke: the quivering spear strikes the shield in the center,
through all the plates of iron and all the layers of bronze,
and hides of bulls with overlaying folds, and pierces
the corselet's guard and penetrates the mighty chest.   485

---

[3]Jupiter was the father of Hercules by Alcmena.

In vain he plucks the warm weapon from the wound:
by the same path the blood and life flow out together.
He falls upon the wound; the armor clashes above him,
and dying he strikes the hostile ground with bloody face.
Turnus, standing over him, says: 490
"Listen, Arcadians, and take my words back to Evander:
I send back his Pallas, just as he deserved;
the honor of a tomb and solace of a burial
I freely give; his hospitality to Aeneas
shall cost him dear." So saying he steps with his left foot   495
upon the corpse, tearing away the heavy sword-belt,
with a horrible scene engraved on it: the wedding-night,
the band of youths all slain, the chambers swimming in blood,[4]
which Clonus son of Eurytus had richly wrought in gold.
Turnus exults in the spoil and rejoices in his prize.   500
How blind are men to Fate and coming doom! They know not
to practice moderation in prosperity!
The hour shall come when Turnus will wish to pay a great price
never to have touched Pallas—he will hate the spoils
and the day. With many tears and groans, his comrades   505
throng round Pallas and carry him upon his shield.
O the sorrow and the glory of your return to your father!
The first day gave you to battle; the same day takes you away;
and yet you leave behind great piles of Rutulian dead!

No rumor now of the disaster, but certain news   510
flies to Aeneas: that his men are on the brink
of destruction, that it is time to save the conquered Trojans.
He mows down all the men within his reach with the sword
and furiously hacks a path with the steel, seeking Turnus
arrogant over his recent slaughter. Pallas, Evander,   515
the tables where the stranger was welcomed, the right hands
                                                                    pledged—
all these come to his eyes. Then he seizes four youths
—the sons of Sulmo, and as many sons of Ufens,

---

[4]The murder of the sons of Aegyptus by the daughters of Danaus.

and takes them alive to offer as victims for the dead,
and sprinkle captive blood over the funeral flames.   520
Then he aims a deadly spear from afar at Magus,
who quickly dodges—the quivering spear flies overhead.
He grasps the hero's knees and speaks in supplication:
"By your father's shade and the hope of growing Iülus,
spare my life, I pray you, for my son and father!   525
I have a lofty house and talents of chased silver
are buried there, and treasure of gold, wrought and unwrought.
The victory of Troy does not depend on me—
my one life will not make such a difference."
So he spoke, and Aeneas said these words in answer: 530
"These many talents of gold and silver that you speak of—
save them for your son. Turnus has done away
with all the amenities of war by slaying Pallas:
so says my father Anchises' shade, and so Iülus!"
He speaks, and grasps the helmet with his left hand,   535
bends back the suppliant's neck and drives the blade to the hilt.
Nearby was Haemon's son, priest of Phoebus and Trivia;[5]
the fillet wreathed his temples with a sacred band
—all shining in his robe and his resplendent armor.
Aeneas drives him over the plain, and standing above him,   540
slays him, wrapping him in great darkness; and Serestus
takes the armor on his shoulders—a trophy for Mars.
Caeculus of Vulcan's race, and Umbro, who came
from the Marsian hills, rally the line of battle.
The Trojan rages against them. He severed the left hand   545
of Anxur, along with the whole circle of his shield
(for he had spoken boastfully, and thought his strength
would match his words; perhaps he lifted his soul to Heaven
promising himself a long life and a ripe old age).
Then Tarquitus, exulting in his shining armor   550
(whom the nymph Dryope had borne to silvan Faunus)
crossed Aeneas' blazing path; he drew back his spear
and pinned the corselet and the heavy shield together,

---

[5]i.e. Apollo and Diana.

and as the youth prayed in vain and tried to speak,
dashed his head to the ground, and kicked the warm body,   555
speaking from above him with a merciless heart:
"Lie there, O terrible warrior! No loving mother
shall lay you in the earth in your ancestral tomb!
The birds of prey will feast on you, or the rolling waves
engulf you and the hungry fish will lick your wounds!"   560

Then he pursues Antaeus and Lucas, the foremost ranks
of Turnus, and brave Numa, and blond Camers, the son
of greathearted Volcens, the richest in land of all the Italians,
who once reigned over the silent Amyclae. Just as Aegaeon
who, they say, had a hundred arms and a hundred hands,   565
and blazed forth fire from fifty mouths and fifty chests
while he clashed as many matching shields against
the thunderbolts of Jove, and drew as many swords:
so Aeneas raged victorious over the plain
when once his sword grew warm. Indeed, he even turns   570
on the opposing chests of Niphaeus' four-yoked horses.
When they catch sight of his long strides and deadly rage
they turn around in sudden terror and gallop away,
throw out the driver, and whirl the chariot to the shore.
Meanwhile, the brothers Lucagus and Liger, with two white horses   575
drive into the midst of the fray; Liger holds the reins
while fierce Lucagus brandishes his naked sword.
Aeneas could not bear their frenzied fury; he rushed
upon them, looming with mighty frame and threatening spear.
Liger said to him: 580
"These are not Diomedes' horses that you see,
nor Achilles' chariot, nor Phrygian plains. Here and now
this war and your life will end together!" Such are the words
of the mad Liger. Aeneas does not reply in words:
instead he throws his javelin against the foe;   585
Lucagus was leaning to urge his steeds with the flat of his sword
—his left foot was thrust forward and prepared for battle—
the spear goes through the lower rim of his gleaming shield
and then it pierces his left groin; he is thrown out

of the chariot, and rolls in death upon the ground.   590
The good Aeneas speaks to him with bitter words:
"Lucagus, no craven flight of horses has betrayed
your chariot; no empty shadow turned them away;
but you yourself leaped from the wheels and deserted the horses!"
with this, he caught the steeds; the wretched brother also   595
had fallen from the car, and raised his helpless hands:
"Trojan hero, by your own self, and by the parents
who begot you, spare this life: have pity on my prayer!"
Aeneas cut his pleading short: "That is not how you spoke
before: now die, and let not brother forsake his brother!"   600
And with the sword he pierced his breast, life's hiding-place.
Such destruction the Dardanian leader dealt
across the plains, raging like a torrent of water
or a black tornado; at last the boy Ascanius
and the soldiers besieged in vain burst forth and leave the camp.   605

   Meanwile Jupiter spoke of his own accord to Juno:
"My sister and most beloved wife, it is Venus,
just as you had thought—your judgment did not deceive you—
who is sustaining the Trojan power, not their strength
or valor in war, or proud spirits, patient of peril."   610
And Juno meekly answered, "Why, my fairest lord,
do you trouble a sick heart that dreads your dismal words?
If my love still had the force that once it had
and should have even now, you would not deny me permission
to rescue Turnus from the fight, Almighty one,   615
preserving him in safety for his father Daunus.
But now let him die and with guiltless blood atone to the Trojans,
even though he is of our lineage, for Pilumnus
was his father's great grandfather; he has often given
many gifts with generous hands upon your altars."   620
The lord of heavenly Olympus briefly answered:
"If all you ask is a delay of present death—
a short reprieve—if you understand that such is my will,
then take your Turnus away from his immediate doom:
thus much may I indulge you. But if any deeper favor   625

lurks hidden in your prayer, if you think the whole war
can be disturbed or changed, you cherish idle hopes."
Juno said, weeping: "What if your mind should allow what your
voice
refuses, and Turnus were permitted to live? But now
grave doom awaits a guiltless man—if I am not mistaken.   630
Would that I rather were deceived by groundless fears
and you, who can, would change your purposes for the better."
When she had said these words, straightway she flew from
Heaven,
driving her chariot, girt with storm-clouds, through the air,
and sought the Trojan lines and the Laurentian camp.   635
Then out of hollow mist she makes a powerless phantom,
a likeness of Aeneas—sight marvellous to behold!
fits it with Trojan arms, simulating the shield
and plumes on his godlike head, and gives it empty words,
a voice without a mind, and the steps of a walking man;   640
like phantom forms that flit about, they say, when death
is past, or like dreams that delude the sleeping senses.
The happy phantom exults in the front line of battle,
provoking the hero with flying weapons and taunting words.
Turnus attacks it from afar with a whistling spear;   645
the image turns its steps around, as if to flee.
Then indeed Turnus believed that Aeneas was yielding,
and his confused mind fed on empty hopes, and he said:
"Where are you fleeing, Aeneas? Do not desert your bride!
My right hand will give you the land you seek beyond the seas!" 650
Shouting these words he pursues, whirling his naked sword,
and does not see the winds carry away his triumph.

A ship happened to be moored to the edge of a rock;
the ladders were in position and the gangplank ready;
King Osinius had sailed on it from Clusium.   655
The restless phantom of Aeneas, fleeing here,
threw itself into the hold; Turnus swiftly follows,
surmounting barriers and leaping up the gangway.
He had scarcely reached the prow, when Juno cut the mooring

and drove the loosened ship across the rolling waves.   660
Aeneas challenges the absent Turnus to battle,
and sends to death many warriors who cross his path.
The airy phantom does not remain in the ship's hold
but flies away and mingles itself with a dark cloud.
Turnus meanwhile is tossed by whirlwinds on the sea,   665
unaware of the truth, ungrateful for his escape.
He looks back and raises both his hands to the stars and prays:
"Almighty Father, am I worthy of such disgrace?
Do you wish me to suffer such punishment for my sins?
Where am I going, Whence did I come? What flight is this?   670
Whom did it save? Shall I see again the Laurentian camp?
What of the band of soldiers who followed me and my arms,
who I have left (O horror!) to a dreadful death!
Now I see them dispersed and hear their groans as they die!
What shall I do? What land can open wide enough   675
to swallow me? Rather, O winds take pity on me
and dash the ship on the rocks and reefs—I, Turnus,
earnestly entreat you—or run her aground on the Syrtes
where no Rutulian, nor Rumor that knows my shame can follow!"
As he speaks, he wavers this way and that in his mind,   680
whether to throw himself for shame upon his sword
and madly drive the naked blade between his ribs,
or hurl himself into the waves, and try to swim
back to the curving shore, again to face the Trojans.
He tried each way three times; and three times mighty Juno   685
restrained him, pitying him in her compassionate heart.
He drifted, cleaving the waves with favorable tides,
and was carried at last to his father Daunus' ancient city.

    Meanwhile, warned by Jove, the fierce Mezentius
entered the fray, attacking the triumphant Trojans.   690
The Etruscan lines rush together and converge on him,
attacking this one man with all their hate and weapons;
just as a cliff that juts out into the vast ocean,
exposed to the furious winds, confronting the raging waves,
endures the threatening forces of the seas and skies   695

while it remains unmoved; he slays Dolichaon's son,
Hebrus, and with him Latagus and fleet-footed Palmus;
Latagus he strikes in the face with a huge boulder
from the mountain, but Palmus he hamstrings, and leaves
writing in agony. He gives his armor to Lausus   700
his son, to wear on his shoulders, and crests to put on his helmet.
He slew the Phrygian Evanthes, and Mimas, comrade of Paris,
and peer in age, whom Theano bore to his father Amycus,
the same night that Hecuba, pregnant with a firebrand,
gave birth to Paris. Paris sleeps in his father's city,   705
and Mimas, a stranger, lies on the Laurentian shore.
As a wild boar, driven by sharp-toothed hounds from the
                                                    mountain top,
sheltered for many years by pineclad Vesulus
and Laurentian marshes, feeding on reedy pastures:
as soon as he has come among the nets, he stops,   710
snorting in his rage and bristling at the shoulders;
no one has the courage or anger to stand against him,
but from a safe distance they hurl their weapons and shouts:—
so, of all who justly hated Mezentius,
no one dared to stand against him with the sword,   715
but from afar they hurl their missiles, and shout at him.
He is not dismayed, but stands his ground against them,
gnashing his teeth, and shaking spears from off his shield.
Acron, a Greek, had come from the ancient land of Corythus,
an exile, he had to leave his marriage unfulfilled—   720
when Mezentius saw him from afar, in the midst of battle,
resplendent in the purple plumes of his plighted bride:—
as a starving lion, driven mad by hunger,
roaming round the high-fenced enclosure, if by chance
he has seen a timid doe or stag with stately antlers,   725
exulting with savage gaping jaws and bristling mane,
he clings to the bloody flesh—his cruel face is bathed
in gruesome blood and gore . . .
so Mezentius leaps lightly into the thick of the foe.
Unlucky Acron is slain and strikes the ground with his heels,   730
and as he dies he stains with his blood the broken spear.

Mezentius did not deign to slay Orodes in flight,
nor lay him low with an unseen thrust of javelin,
but ran to meet him, face to face and man to man,
and conquer him not by treachery, but force of arms.   735
He placed his foot on his foe and pulled at the spear and said:
"Men, here lies the great Orodes, bulwark of war!"
His comrades raised their voices in a shout of triumph.
Dying, Orodes said: "Whoever you are, you shall not
rejoice victorious for long; for a fate like mine   740
awaits you, and you shall soon lie on this same field!"
Mezentius said, smiling, but the smile was mixed with anger:
"Now die; as for me, the Father of Gods and King of men
will see to me!" So saying, he drew his spear from the body;
hard repose and iron sleep press down upon   745
his eyes; his eyelids close in everlasting night.
Caedicus slays Alcathous, Sacrator Hydaspes,
Rapo Parthenius and also Orses of hardy strength;
Messapus kills Clonius and Lycaon's son Ericetes;
one as he lay fallen from his unbridled horse,   750
the other on foot. Lycian Agis had come on foot,
but Valerus, not lacking ancestral courage, slew him.
Salius kills Thronius and Nealces Salius
—Nealces famous with javelin and far-stealing arrows.
Now heavy-handed Mars was dealing out equal woes   755
and equal deaths: alike they killed, alike they died,
conquerors and conquered, and neither thought of flight.
The gods in Jupiter's house pitied the futile wrath
on both sides, sad that mortals should suffer such afflictions.
Venus watches on one side, Saturnian Juno the other;   760
pallid Tisiphone rages amid the warring thousands.

   And now Mezentius brandishes his mighty spear
and, raging, strides across the field, great as Orion
wading through the water in the midst of the ocean,
and towering with his shoulders above the top of the waves,   765
or carrying an ancient ash from the mountain top—
his feet are on the ground, but he hides his head in the clouds—

so did Mezentius stride forth in his massive armor.
Aeneas sees him in the line and goes to meet him.
The other is undaunted and he stands his ground   770
awaiting the noble foe, standing in massive bulk,
measuring with his eye the distance for a spear-cast:
"Now may this right hand—my god—and the spear I throw
come to my aid! I vow that you yourself, Lausus,
will be my trophy, clad in the spoils of the robber Aeneas!"   775
So he spoke and threw from afar the whistling apear.
It flies and glances off Aeneas' shield and pierces
noble Antores nearby, between the side and flank—
Antores, friend of Hercules, who, sent from Argos,
had sided with Evander and settled in Italy.   780
The hapless man falls by a wound meant for another,
looks at the sky and dies, remembering sweet Argos.
Then good Aeneas hurls his spear: it went through the shield—
the triple bronze and linen layers and three bulls' hides
interwoven, and came to rest low in the groin;   785
but its strength was spent. Aeneas rejoices at the sight
of the Etruscan blood and draws his sword from his thigh,
and hotly he attacks the panic-stricken foe.
Lausus groaned and streams of tears rolled down his face
when he saw this, because of his love for his dear father.   790
Your cruel doom, young hero, and your glorious deeds,
if antiquity can win belief for such valor,—
these things and you yourself I shall not leave unsung.

   Mezentius was disabled and impeded now
and he retreated, dragging the hostile spear from his shield,   795
but then the youth dashed forward and plunged into the fray,
and as Aeneas' hand went up to strike a blow,
Lausus caught the point of the blade and parried it.
His comrades gather and follow him with mighty clamor,
until the father, guarded by Lausus' shield, could withdraw;   800
and hurling missiles from afar, kept the foe at a distance.
Aeneas is furious but keeps himself under cover,
just as when the storm-clouds pour down showers of hailstones,
and all the plowmen hastily scatter from the fields,

and all the farmers; the traveller stays under cover   80
by the river's bank, or sheltered by a lofty rock,
during the rain; so that, when the sun comes back again,
they may finish their work; just so, Aeneas, overwhelmed
by missiles on all sides, waits till the war-cloud passes,
reproaching Lausus all the while, and threatening him: 81
"Why do you rush to your death, daring beyond your power?
Your love has lured you into folly!" Yet nonetheless
the lad exults in his frenzy. The anger rises higher
in the Trojan hero's heart; and now the Fates are gathering
the last threads for Lausus; Aeneas drives his sword   81
right through the young man's body and buries it to the hilt.
It penetrated the shield—light arms for one so defiant!
and the tunic his mother had woven him of pliant gold;
his chest was filled with blood, and his life fled through the air,
sorrowing, to the Underworld, and left the body.   82
But when the son of Anchises saw his dying face
—the face so pallid in wondrous wise—he groaned aloud
in pity for the youth, and held his right hand out;
the image of his own filial love came to his mind:
"What now, unlucky boy," he said, "shall good Aeneas   82
give you, for your glory? What is a worthy prize?
Keep your arms that you rejoiced in for yourself;
if this means anything to you, I give you back
to your ancestors' shades and ashes. But this shall console your
                                                              death,
unhappy lad: that the great Aeneas killed you!" He scolds   83
the lagging comrades and lifts their leader from the ground,
where he tainted with his blood his well-trimmed hair.

Meanwhile his father, by the waves of the river Tiber,
stanched his wounds with water and rested his weary body
against the trunk of a tree. Nearby, the brazen helmet   835
hangs from the branches; his heavy armor lies on the grass.
Chosen youths stand around, while he, sick and gasping,
bends his neck; his long beard flows over his chest.
Many times he asks for Lausus and sends men

to recall him and bear the message from his grieving father.   840
The weeping comrades were carrying Lausus on his shield,
lifeless, a mighty man felled by a mighty wound.
His mind, foreboding evil, knew the wail from afar;
he soils his hoary hair with dust, and raises his hands
to Heaven, and clasps the body of his son and says: 845
"My son, was I so much in love with life that I
let you, whom I begot, fall to a hostile sword
instead of me? Am I, your father, saved by your wounds?
Alive by your death? Alas, now, finally I know
the bitterness of exile—now it is driven home!   850
And I myself, my son, have defiled your name with guilt,
driven in loathing from my fathers' throne and scepter!
I owed the penalty of death to the land, and hatred
of my people—I should have forfeited my guilty life
by any kind of death. Now I live and am not yet leaving   855
mankind and daylight—but leave I will!" And with these words
he lifts himself on his wounded leg, though his strength is failing
from the deep wound, and undismayed he calls for his horse,
his pride and solace—on it he had returned victorious
from all his battles. Now he speaks to the sorrowing beast: 860
"Rhoebus, we have lived long, if any time is long
for mortals. Today you shall either bear triumphant
those bloody spoils and Aeneas' head, and avenge with me
the pains of Lausus, or if force cannot find a way,
you shall die with me, for I cannot think, my valiant steed,   865
that you will submit to foreign commands and Trojan masters!"
He spoke and mounted, sitting in his usual fashion,
and holding a pointed javelin in either hand;
his head gleamed with bronze and bristled with horsehair plumes.
So he galloped into the battle. In that one heart   870
a tide of shame wells up, and madness mingled with grief,
[and love spurred on by rage, and consciousness of valor.][6]
    And now in a loud voice he called Aeneas three times.

---

[6]This line, omitted from some MSS. is the same as XII 668. The preceding
1½ lines are also repeated in Book XII.

Aeneas recognized him and made a joyful prayer:
"So may the Father of Gods and great Apollo will it: 87
begin the battle!"
So he spoke and went to meet him with levelled spear.
The other said: "How can you frighten me, O savage foe,
now that my son is dead? That was the only way
to destroy me: I have no fear of death nor respect for gods!   880
Enough, for I have come to die, but first I bring you
these gifts!" He spoke, and hurled a javelin at his foe;
then another and still another he threw, wheeling
in a great circle. But the golden shield withstood them.
Three times he rode around to the left, hurling his missiles;   885
three times the Trojan hero carried around with him
the great forest of spears stuck in his brazen shield.
Then, weary of long delay, and tired of pulling out spears,
and sorely pressed by this unequal kind of conflict,
Aeneas ponders in his mind, and at last he attacks,   890
and hurls a spear between the horse's hollow temples.
The animal rears up and paws the air with its hoofs,
then throws the rider to the ground and falls above him
headlong, entangling him, and dislocating its shoulder.
The Trojans and the Latins fill the sky with shouting.   895
Aeneas flies forward, drawing his sword from its scabbard,
and cries above him: "Where is the fierce Mezentius now,
with all his wild courage?" The Etruscan regained his senses,
looked up at the sky, and drew a breath of air:
"Bitter foe, why taunt me with these threats of death?   900
There is no sin in killing me: not on such terms
did I come to battle; Lausus made no such pact between us.
I ask one favor, if vanquished foes can claim indulgence:
allow my body to be buried: I know the hatred
of my people surrounds me; shield me from their anger,   905
and let me be my son's companion in the grave!"

   He speaks, and deliberately gives his throat to the sword,
and pours his life in streams of blood upon his armor.

End of Book X.

BOOK XI

THE COUNCIL OF THE LATINS

Meanwhile Dawn arose and left her bed in the Ocean.
Aeneas, though impelled by grief to bury his comrades,
although his soul is troubled with the thought of death,
paid the vow of victory to the gods at daybreak.
Stripping off all the branches from a mighty oak tree   5
he plants it on a mound and decks it with gleaming armor
—the spoils of the leader Mezentius—a trophy to you,
great Mars; he fastens the horsehair crests, dripping with blood,
and broken weapons, and the breastplate, battered and pierced
in a dozen places, and on the left he hangs the shield,   10
suspending from the neck the ivory-hilted sword.
Then to his cheering comrades (for a crowd of leaders
was pressing around him) he speaks words of encouragement:
"The greatest deeds have been done, my men! For what remains
put away all fear. These are the spoils and first-fruits   15
of a haughty king: my hands have put Mezentius here.
Now our way is to the king and the Latin walls.
Prepare your arms with courage, anticipate war with hope;
let no delay impede us, so that when the gods above
bid us raise our standards and lead the youth from camp,   20
no faulty purpose can hold us back with slothful fear.
Meanwhile let us commit to earth the unburied corpses
of our comrades—the only honor in Acheron.
Go," he said, "adorn with last rites these noble souls
who have won this fatherland for us with their blood.   25
First let Pallas be sent to the grieving town of Evander
—Pallas, lacking not in courage, whom the dark day
has carried off and plunged into a bitter death."
    So he speaks, weeping, and turns his steps to the doorway
where Pallas' lifeless corpse was laid out, watched by Acoetes,   30

235

the old man who had formerly been the armor-bearer
to Parrhasian Evander, but now, with far less happy omens,
was sent as companion and guardian to his beloved ward.
Attendants stood about, and Trojan men and women,
their hair loosened in mourning according to the custom.
But when Aeneas came into the lofty doorway,
they beat their breasts and raised a mighty moan to the stars.
The royal tent resounded with their lamentation.
When he saw the pillowed head and face of Pallas,
white as snow, with the wound from an Italian spear
gaping in his smooth breast, the tears welled up and he said:
"Was it you, unlucky youth, that happy Fortune
begrudged me, that you might never see my kingdom established.
nor ride back triumphant to your father's house?
Such was not the promise I made to your father Evander
concerning you, when I left him and the old man embraced me
and sent me forth to win a mighty empire, and warned me,
fearing the brave and hardy men we were going to fight.
And now perhaps he, captivated by empty hopes,
is making vows and heaping the altars high with gifts,
while we in sorrow accompany with empty honors
his lifeless son, who now owes nothing to any god.
Unhappy man! you shall see the cruel funeral
of your son! Is this our return and expected triumph?
Was this my promise? Yet, Evander, you shall not see
your son routed with shameful wounds, nor shall the father
pray for a cruel death because his son was spared!
Alas! what a bulwark Italy has lost, and Iülus too!"

When his lament is finished, he orders the piteous corpse
to be raised up, and sends a thousand chosen men
from the whole army to attend the funeral rites,
and share the tears of the father—an inadequate solace
for grief so great, but one due to a father's sorrow.
Others busily weave a bier of wicker frame,
plaiting it from arbutus twigs and oaken branches,
and deck the high-piled couch with a canopy of leaves,
and on the rude litter they lay the noble youth

like a flower plucked by a maiden's hand: a soft violet
or drooping hyacinth, whose loveliness and beauty
have not yet begun to fade, although its mother Earth   70
no longer nourishes it, or sustains its strength.
Then Aeneas brought two robes that were all stiff
with gold and purple, which Sidonian Dido had woven
for him with her own hands, delighting in the toil,
and interweaving the lines of the web with threads of gold.   75
He sadly drapes one around the youth—a final tribute,
covering the hair that the fire soon would claim,
and piles up many spoils of the Laurentian battle,
commanding the booty to be conveyed in a long line.
He adds the horses and weapons taken from the foe;   80
then he had the hands of the victims bound behind
their backs, to send as offerings to the Shades, and sprinkle
their blood on the flames; he bids the leaders carry branches
bedecked with enemy arms, with the names of the foes attached.
The aged and unhappy Acoetes is led along   85
beating his breast with his hands, tearing his face with his nails,
and finally throwing himself prostrate upon the ground.
Chariots spattered with Rutulian blood are brought.
Behind, the war-horse Aethon, his trappings laid aside,
goes weeping, with large teardrops streaming down his face.   90
Others carry the spear and helmet—victorious Turnus
has the rest. A sad procession of Trojans follows,
and Etruscans and Arcadians with their arms reversed.
When the procession had advanced some distance ahead,
Aeneas halted, and sighing deeply, said one word more: 95
"The terrible fate of war calls me to other grief:
hail to you forevermore, O noblest Pallas,
forevermore farewell!" Without speaking further,
he turned to the lofty walls and walked towards the camp.

And now ambassadors arrived from the Latin city,   100
bearing olive branches and asking for a favor,
that he return to them the bodies that were scattered
throughout the fields by the sword, and permit their burial:

for the war was not with the vanquished men who breathed no
                                                      longer;
let him spare those once called hosts and parents-in-law.   10
The good Aeneas is gracious to them and grants their request—
one that is not to be spurned—and adds the following words:
"What cruel fortune, Latins, has entangled you
in such a dreadful war, that makes you shun our friendship?
You ask a truce to bury those slain by battle's chance?   11
Indeed, I would gladly grant it if they were still alive.
I would never have come, had not Fate assigned me a dwelling here.
I have no quarrel with your people: rather, your king
broke the alliance, preferring to trust the arms of Turnus.
It would have been more just for Turnus to face death.   11
If he wants to end the war with arms and drive out the Trojans,
he should have met me in single combat. He would have lived
to whom Heaven or his own right hand had granted life.
Now go, and light fires beneath your unlucky countrymen."
So Aeneas spoke: they remained dumb and silent   12
and turned their eyes and faces toward one another.
Then aged Drances, who always hated the youthful Turnus
with bitterness and recriminations, began to speak:
"O Trojan, great in fame and greater still in battle,
how may I extol you with praises to the sky?   12
Shall I marvel first at your justice or labors in war?
We shall gratefully take your words to our native city,
and if Fortune shows the way, we shall unite you
with King Latinus. Let Turnus make his own alliance!
We shall be glad to build your destined mass of walls   13
and carry on our shoulders the stones of a newborn Troy."
    He finished, and they all with one voice showed agreement.
They made a truce for twice six days; Trojans and Latins
mingling peacefully together, roamed the forests
and mountains. The lofty ash trees ring beneath the blow   13
of double axes. Towering pines come crashing down;
unceasingly they split the oak and fragrant cedar
with wedges, and carry the mountain-ash on creaking wagons.

And now swift Rumor, bearer of woeful tidings, flies
to Evander and Evander's house and walls—Rumor,   140
who only now had told of Pallas' triumph in Latium.
The Arcadians rushed to the gates, seizing funeral torches
according to ancient custom; the road was gleaming with light;
a long pathway of torches separated the fields.
The Trojans come to meet them and join in lamentation.   145
Soon as the mothers saw them drawing near the houses,
they set the mourning town ablaze with their shrieks and wailing.
But no force is sufficient to restrain Evander;
he rushes into the midst, and when the bier is lowered
he throws himself on Pallas and clings to him, weeping and sobbing. 150
Only after a time can the wretched man find words:
"This is not the promise you gave your father, Pallas—
to trust yourself so rashly to the savage Mars!
Well did I know how strong was the first pride in arms,
how very sweet the honor of the first encounter!   155
O sad first-fruits of youth! O what a harsh lesson
in war close at home! O my vows and prayers
that no god heard! O blessed wife, you were fortunate
that you did not survive to know this terrible sorrow!
But I live on, conquering destiny—a father   160
without a son! O, if only I had followed the arms
of Trojan allies and fallen to Rutulian spears!
If only I had died, this funeral would be mine,
not Pallas'—I do not blame you, Trojans,
nor our treaty and pledge of friendship. This is the lot of old age! 165
But if an early death was fated for my son,
at least it is some consolation that he died
leading Trojans to Latium, slaying countless Volscians!
No, Pallas, I could not ask for a more worthy funeral
for you than good Aeneas does and the mighty Phrygians,   170
the Etruscan leaders and the whole Etruscan army.
They bear splendid trophies, to whom your hand dealt death!
You, Turnus, would now be a huge trunk clad in armor
if his age and strength had been the same as yours!
But why do I, poor wretch, delay the Trojans from battle?   175

Go, and remember to take this message to your king:
My only reason for dragging out this hateful life,
with Pallas gone, is your right hand which you see owes
Turnus' death to father and son: this one achievement
is left for your valor and fortune: I do not seek joy in life—　　18
that would be wrong—but to bring joyful news to my son
in Hades!"

　　　　　　Meanwhile Dawn had lifted her kindly light
for weary men, recalling them to work and toil.
Now Father Aeneas and now Tarchon had set up pyres
on the curving shore, according to ancestral custom.　　18
Each brought his kinsmen's bodies, and smoky fires were lit,
veiling the vaults of Heaven in a murky darkness.
Three times in their shining armor they marched around
the burning pyres, and three times they circled on horseback
the mournful fire, uttering cries of lamentation.　　19
The ground and all their armor was sprinkled with their tears.
The cries of men and blare of trumpets rise to Heaven.
Some throw on the fire the spoils from Latin corpses:
helmets and decorated swords and horses' bridles,
and glowing chariot wheels; others, familiar gifts,　　19
their own shields and the unavailing arms of the dead.
Many oxen are sacrificed all around to Death,
and bristling swine and cattle and flocks from all the country
are slaughtered over the flames. Then, along the shore,
they watch their comrades burn and guard the half-burnt pyres,　　20
nor can they tear themselves away till dewy night
comes rolling round the sphere inset with blazing stars.

　　Elsewhere the unhappy Latins likewise build
innumerable pyres. And of their many dead,
some they bury in the ground, others they raise　　20
and carry to the nearby fields or send to the city;
the rest—an undistinguishable heap of corpses—
they burn, uncounted and unhonored; on every side
the fields are aflame with the fierce rivalry of fires.

The third Dawn had taken the chilly shadows from Heaven   210
when sadly they piled high the ashes and mingled bones
from the embers, and heaped a mound of warm earth above them.
Within the walls and in the city of rich Latinus
is the greatest noise and longest lamentation.
The mothers and wretched daughters-in-law, and loving hearts   215
of sisters, and children bereft of their fathers,
all curse the cruel war and Turnus' marriage too.
they say that he alone should decide the issue with arms,
since he claimed Italy's rule for himself, and the highest honors.
And fierce Drances adds weight to their cry and he bears witness   220
that Turnus alone is challenged—alone to single combat.
On the other side, many things are said for Turnus;
the name of the Queen was not without its influence,
and Turnus' reputation and his many trophies.
Amid all the disturbance and confusing tumult,   225
the envoys from Diomedes' great city come
with a gloomy reply: their efforts and expense
have all been in vain: all the gold and all the gifts,
and all the prayers were of no avil. Latinus must seek
other arms, or ask the Trojan king for peace.   230
King Latinus is crushed beneath the weight of sorrow.
Aeneas is called by Fate and the evident will of Heaven—
the angry gods and recent graves are proof of this.
And so he summons by royal command a great council:
the leaders of the people, and gathers them at the palace.   235
They come together, flocking to the royal dwelling,
through crowded streets. In their midst, oldest in years,
and first in royalty, is Latinus, with little gladness
upon his brow. He bids the envoys who have returned
from the Aetolian city to tell what news they bring,   240
asking for full replies in order. Then all were silent,
and Venulus, obeying his word, begins to speak:
"Citizens, we have seen Diomedes and the camp
of Argives. We have gone our way, overcome all dangers,
and touched the hand by which the land of Ilium fell.   245
He was founding the city of Argyripa, named from the race

of his father, on Iapygian Garganus' conquered fields.
When we had entered and received permission to speak,
we offered gifts to him and told him our name and country,
and who had invaded us, and why we had come to Arpi.   25
He listened to us and answered with unruffled mien:
    " 'O fortunate race of people, realm once ruled by Saturn,
ancient Ausonia, what chance is disturbing your peace
and is persuading you to provoke an unknown war?
We who profaned the Trojan field with the sword (I pass over   25
the woes we suffered beneath the lofty walls, and the heroes
engulfed by Simois!)—we, throughout the world, have suffered
unspeakable penalties and tortures for our crimes—
even Priam might pity us! The gloomy star
of Minerva knows, and Euboea's cliffs, and avenging Caphereus.[1]   26
Driven from that warfare to a distant shore,
Menelaus, Atreus' son, is in exile, by the pillars
of Proteus; Ulysses has seen the Cyclopes of Aetna;
shall I tell of Neoptolemus' realm, and the overturned house
of Idomeneus? Or the Locrians who live on Libyan shores?   26
The Mycenean himself—chief of the great Achaeans—
hardly within the threshold was slain by his evil wife:
an adulterer lay in wait for Asia's conqueror![2]
The gods have envied me, and grudged my return to my home—
the altars, the wife I long for, and lovely Calydon.   27
Even now, portents horrible to see pursue me:
my missing comrades fly to the heavens and seek the streams
as winged birds (alas! what a dreadful punishment
for my people!) and fill the cliffs with mournful cries.
This was the fate I had to expect from the very time   27
when I attacked celestial beings with the sword
and violated Venus' hand with impious wound!
No, no, do not urge me into such battles again:
I have had no quarrel with Troy since her destruction,

---

[1]Minerva sent a storm, and the king of Euboea hung out false lights, so
that the fleet was wrecked on the cape of Caphereus.
[2]The reference is to Agamemnon, Clytemnestra, and Aegisthus.

nor do I remember my former ills with joy.   280
These gifts you bring to me from your ancestral shores,
give rather to Aeneas. I faced his savage weapons
and fought him hand to hand. Trust one who knows how high
he towers with his shield, and the whirlwind force of his spear!
If Ida's land had produced two other heroes like him,   285
the Trojans would have stormed the towers of Inachus,
the fates would be reversed, and Greece a land of mourning.
In all our long siege of the walls of stubborn Troy,
it was the mighty strength of Hector and Aeneas
that delayed the victory of the Greeks for ten whole years: 290
both were outstanding in courage, both eminent in arms,
but Aeneas was more righteous. Join your hands in treaty,
whatever the terms may be, but beware of a clash in arms!'
Noble king, you have heard the answer of that king,
and what is his advice concerning this great war."   295
    Scarce had the envoys finished, when a confused murmur
ran among the Ausonians; just as when the rocks
delay a rapid river; the swirling eddies murmur;
the neighboring banks resound to the splashing of the waves.
As soon as they were calmed and the restless tongues were silent,   300
the king invokes the gods and speaks from his lofty throne:
"Truly I wish—and it would have been much better, Latins,
that the country's safety had already been settled,
instead of holding council with the foe at our gates.
We wage a disastrous war, citizens, with a race   305
sprung from the gods, invincible, and never wearied
of battle; even when conquered they cannot give up the sword.
If you had any hope of Aetolian alliance,
abandon it. Any man can hope, but you see how slight
is ours, and for the rest, you see with your eyes, and touch   310
with your hands, the complete and utter ruin of all our fortunes.
I blame no one: what the utmost valor could accomplish
has been done: we have fought with all our country's strength.
Now listen to the judgment of my doubtful mind
as I explain it briefly to you: there is a land   315
—an ancient domain of mine, near the Tuscan river,

stretching far to the west, beyond the Sicanian borders;
Auruncans and Rutulians work the land, and plow
the hills, and feed their flocks upon the barren slopes.
Let all this land, together with the pine-clad mountains,   3:
go to the Trojans in friendship: let us make a fair treaty,
inviting them to share our kingdom as allies.
Let them settle, if such their desire, and build their city.
But if they wish to try their fortunes with other lands
and other peoples; if they are able to leave the country,   3:
let us build them twenty ships of Italian oak
or as many more as they can man. The timber lies
at the water's edge: let them order the number and design
of the ships; let us supply the bronze and labor and docks.
Moreover, I would send, to carry my words, and confirm   3:
the treaty, a hundred Latins of the noblest families,
all carrying peaceful olive branches in their hands
and bearing gifts: talents of gold and ivory,
and the chair and robe of state, the emblems of our power.
Take counsel all, how best to aid our weary state."   3:
    Then the ever-hostile Drances, whom Turnus' glory
goaded with the bitter spurs of secret envy—
a man of great wealth and greater eloquence, but his hand
was cold to war—he was deemed a clever counselor,
skilled in sedition (his mother's nobility had given him   3·
a proud and haughty birth; his paternal descent was obscure)—
he rises now and kindles their anger with these words:
"Good king, the advice you give is clear to every man
and has no need of my eloquence. All confess they know
how our fortunes stand, although they speak in whispers.   3·
Let him grant freedom of speech and stop his blustering
by whose disastrous leadership and evil ways
(I will speak out, though he threaten violence and death!)
we see so many noble leaders have been slain
and the whole city plunged into grief, while he, trusting to flight,   3:
attacks the Trojan camp and terrifies Heaven with arms.
Add one more gift, O best of kings, to those many others
you bid us send and promise to the Dardanians:

and do not allow anyone's violence to deter you,
a father, from giving your daughter to an illustrious son   355
in worthy marriage, and making peace for evermore.
But if we are so panic-stricken in heart and mind,
let us plead with Turnus himself and beg this favor,
that he gives to king and country their proper right.[3]
Why do you send your poor people into such perils,   360
O source and fountainhead of all of Latium's woes?
There is no safety in war: we all are praying for peace,
Turnus—the one inviolable pledge of peace.
Look, I whom you imagine your enemy (I do not care
if I am)—I come as a suppliant. Pity your people!   365
Put away your anger: accept defeat! We have been routed,
and seen enough of death and desolated fields!
Or if glory is your desire, if your heart is so strong,
and if a royal dowry is so dear to you,
then dare to meet Aeneas now in single combat.   370
I suppose, in order for Turnus to get his royal bride,
we worthless souls must be strewn all over the battlefield,
unburied and unwept? No, rather, it is for you
if you have any strength and any ancestral courage,
to face the man who challenges you."   375
    At these words, Turnus blazed forth with violent anger;
he groans aloud, and from the depth of his heart he says:
"Indeed, Drances, you always have a lot to say
when battle calls for action! When the Senate is called
you are the first to appear. But we do not need words   380
—glib speeches, when you are safe—to fill the senate house,
while the walls keep off the foe, and the moats are not yet
                                                    swimming
in blood! Go, rant with your usual eloquence, Drances,
accusing me of cowardice, since you have slain
so many heaps of Trojans, and piled up so many trophies   385
on the battlefield! What living courage can accomplish
you may try for yourself! Indeed, we need not look far

---

[3] or, ironically, "his proper right."

for the enemy—they surround our walls on every side.
Shall we advance to meet them? Why the delay? Will your prowess
always be in that windy tongue of yours, and in   39
those swift feet?
So I have been defeated? You villain, how can anyone
justly say I have been beaten, who has seen the Tiber
swollen with Trojan blood, and Evander's entire line
destroyed, and his Arcadians stripped of their armor?   39
Bitias and great Pandarus did not think I was beaten,
and the thousand men whom I sent down to Tartarus
in a single day, when cooped within the enemy walls!
'There is no safety in war.' Sing those songs, you fool,
to the Trojan prince and your own fortunes. Go on confounding   40
everything with your own great fear, and extolling the strength
of a race twice conquered, and belittling Latin arms!
Now the Myrmidon princes tremble at Trojan weapons,
and Diomedes and Achilles of Larissa—
the Aufidus flows backwards from Adriatic waves.   40
Or when he pretends to be afraid of my reproaches,
the clever villain! Aggravating his slander with terror!
You shall never lose that life of yours to my right hand,
so have no fear! Keep it in your craven breast!
Now, Father, I return to you and your proposals: 41
If you have no more confidence and hope in our arms,
if we are so forlorn, and if with one repulse
our troops are defeated, and Fortune cannot be reversed,
let us pray for peace and hold out helpless hands!
But, oh, if we had any of our accustomed courage!   41
I would count that man blessed above all others,
and of outstanding valor, who to avoid that sight
has fallen in death, and once for all, bitten the dust!
But if we still have resources, a manhood still intact,
and cities and nations of Italy still supporting us,   42
even if the Trojans have won glory with bloodshed
(for they too have their deaths—the storm was equal for all)
why do we fail ignominiously on the very threshold?
Why begin to tremble before we hear the trumpet?

For Time and the varying toils of all the changing years   425
have bettered many ills; and many men, though mocked
by inconstant Fortune, have then regained their footing.
We cannot look for aid to Aetolians and Arpi:
but Messapus is still with us, and lucky Tolumnius,
and all the leaders from many nations—no small glory   430
for the chosen youth of Latium and the Laurentian fields.
We have Camilla, too, of the noble Volscian race,
leading squadrons of cavalry all shining with bronze.
But if I alone am challenged by the Trojans to battle,
if such is your pleasure, if I am thwarting the common weal,   435
Victory has not fled my hands with so much loathing
that I should refuse any risk to gain so great a hope!
I will face him bravely, even though he excel
the great Achilles and don similar armor, made
by Vulcan. To all of you and my father-in-law Latinus,   440
I, Turnus, second to none of olden times in valor,
devote my life. Aeneas calls me alone? Well, let him!
I would not have Drances appease the wrath of Heaven by dying,
nor, if glory is at stake, would I let him win it!"

While they were debating these uncertain issues,   445
Aeneas began to move his camp and battle-line.
Suddenly a messenger rushes into the palace
and fills the great city with terrible alarms:
The Trojans are in battle-formations and the Etruscans
are sweeping down from the River Tiber across the plain.   450
Straightway the peoples' minds are shaken and confused
and their anger is aroused by the sudden shock.
In feverish haste they call for arms, the young men shout,
"To arms!"—the weeping elders sadly moan and mutter.
A discordant clamor rises on all sides to Heaven.   455
just as when flocks of birds alight in a lofty forest,
or when by the river-fisheries of the Padusa,
the raucous swans scream along the echoing pools.
"No, citizens!" says Turnus, seizing the opportunity,
"convene a council! Sit here praising the blessings of peace   460

while they invade the land with arms!" He said no more
but leaped to his feet and rushed out of the lofty palace.
"You, Volusus!" he cries, "Arm the Volscian troops,
and lead the Rutulians. Messapus and his brother Coras,
deploy the cavalry squadrons over the wide plain.   46
Let some of you guard the city gates and man the towers;
the others, under my command, to the attack!"

   At once from all the city, people rush to the walls.
Father Latinus himself, leaving the council, defers
his great proposals, dismayed by the disastrous crisis,   47
many times berating himself for not receiving
Trojan Aeneas freely and taking him as his son
and ally to the city. Some dig trenches at the gates,
and carry stones and stakes. The hoarse trumpet gives
War's bloody signal; a motley ring of mothers and children   47
defend the walls. The final struggle calls them all.
The Queen, surrounded by a great throng of matrons,
rides up to Pallas' temple on the lofty heights,
bearing gifts, the maiden Lavinia at her side—
the cause of all the trouble—her modest eyes cast down.   48
The mothers climb to the temple and fill it with their incense
and from the high threshold utter lamentations:
"Mighty in arms, leader in war, Tritonian goddess,
break with your hand the Phrygian pirate's spear, and cast him
prone upon the ground before the lofty gates!"   48

   Turnus himself, with eager fury, girds himself
for battle, putting on his shining breastplate, bristling
with brazen scales, sheathing his legs in golden greaves,
his head still bare, his sword was fastened at his side.
Gleaming with gold, he runs down from the citadel,   490
exulting in his courage, anticipating the foe;
just as when a horse has broken his tether and fled,
and free at last from the stables, he gallops across the plain,
and either seeks the pastures and the herds of mares,
or, accustomed to bathe in the familiar river,   495
he dashes forth, neighing and rearing his head in the air

proudly, while his mane plays over his neck and shoulders.[4]

    Camilla came to meet him with her Volscian troops,
and at the very gates, the queen leaped down from her horse.
The whole squadron, imitating her, dismounted   500
nimbly to the ground. Camilla spoke as follows:
"Turnus, if the brave may have self-confidence,
I dare and promise to meet the cavalry of Aeneas,
and to ride alone to face the Tuscan horsemen.
Allow my hand to risk the first perils of war,   505
while you remain on foot to defend the walls and ramparts."
Turnus stared at the dreaded maiden, and he said:
"Maiden, pride of Italy, what thanks can I give you?
What gratitude can repay you? But now, since your spirit
rises above all praise, share with me the labor: 510
Aeneas, so the rumor says, and scouts have reported,
has boldly sent his light-armed cavalry ahead
to ravage the plains. He himself has crossed the ridge
and advances on the town by the deserted slopes.
I am preparing an ambush on the forest trail   515
to block the entrance to the gorge with arméd soldiers.
You await them and engage the Etruscan horsemen:
the brave Messapus will be with you, the Latin squadrons,
and Tiburtus' troops; you too shall be a captain."
So he spoke. With similar words he urges Messapus   520
and other leaders to battle, then moves against the foe.

    There is a winding valley, fit for wiles and ambush,
enclosed on either side by a wall of heavy foliage;
a scanty footpath is the only means of access,
a gorge with narrow jaws and difficult approach.   525
Above this valley on the mountain's very top,
there lies a hidden stretch of plain—a safe retreat,
whether you wanted to attack from the right or left,
or stand upon the ridge and roll down heavy stones.
Here the young warrior hastens by a familiar path,   530
seizes the place and settles in the treacherous woods.

---

[4]This simile appears twice in Homer—Il. VI, 506-11; XV, 263-8.

Meanwhile in Heaven's realm, the daughter of Latona
spoke to swift Opis, one of the sacred band of maidens
who are her companions, with these sorrowful words:
"Maiden, Camilla is going forth to the cruel war,   53
and she is girding on her arms, to no avail—
dear to me above all others—for this is not
a new love come to Diana, not a sudden affection.

"When Metabus was driven from his kingdom, through hatred
of his tyranny, and left Privernum's ancient city,   54
fleeing in the midst of battle, he took with him
his infant daughter—companion in exile—and he named her
after her mother Casmilla, slightly changed—Camilla.
Carrying her on his chest, he roamed the woods and mountains
in solitude. Fierce weapons flew on every side;   54
the Volscians encircled him with wide-scattered soldiery.
Suddenly as he fled, the swollen Amasenus
was foaming high in flood, for a cloudburst had filled it
to overflowing. Preparing to swim, he is held back
by his love for the baby, and fear for his precious burden.   550
After considering, he made a sudden decision,
reluctantly: to the great spear of knotted oak
which, as a warrior, he carried in his hand,
he tied the baby encased in bark from a wild cork tree,
and gently bound her to the middle of the shaft.   555
Balancing it in his great hand, he cries to the heavens:
" 'Latona's daughter, gracious forest-dweller, I,
a father, vow this child to your service; she holds your weapon
as through the air, a suppliant, she flees the foe.
Goddess, receive your child, consigned to uncertain breezes!'   560
"He spoke and drew back his arm, and hurled the spinning spear.
The water roared, and over the swiftly rushing river
the poor Camilla flies upon the whistling weapon.
But Metabus, now pursued by a hostile band,
leaps into the river; triumphantly plucks from a bed of grass   565
the infant tied to the spear: Diana's offering.
No cities received him now within their walls and houses,
nor, in his savage nature, would he have submitted;

he spent his days with shepherds in the lonely mountains.
In thickets and in wild beasts' lairs he nursed the baby   570
on milk from the udder of a wild mare from the herds,
squeezing the teats with his hand for the infant's tender lips.
And when her baby feet had taken their first steps,
he armed her with a sharply pointed javelin
and hung a bow and quiver from her tiny shoulder.   575
Instead of gold for her hair, in place of a long robe,
she wore a tiger skin from her head all down her back.
Even then her little hands threw baby darts,
and round her neck she wore a smooth sling of leather,
and brought down Strymonian cranes and snowy swans.   580
Many Etruscan mothers wanted her for a daughter,
but all in vain: content to be with Diana alone,
forever pure, she cherishes her love for weapons
and her virginity. I wish she had not been
swept away by such warfare, trying to fight the Trojans;   585
then she would still be one of my belovèd companions.
But come, since she is doomed to an untimely death,
glide down from Heaven, Nymph, and seek the Latin lands,
where under evil omens they fight the gloomy war.
Take my bow and draw an avenging shaft from the quiver,   590
and with it, let whoever wounds her sacred body
—Trojan or Italian—pay the price with his blood.
Then I will take the unhappy maid in a hollow cloud,
unspoiled, with all her weapons, and bury her in her country."
She spoke, and Opis sped away with clattering weapons   595
through Heaven's gentle breezes, wrapped in a black tornado.

But meanwhile the Trojan army approaches the walls
with the Etruscan leaders and all the cavalry
marshalled in their squadrons. The horses prance and neigh
over the plain, wheeling this way and that, and fighting   600
the tight-held reins. Far and wide, an iron crop
of spears is bristling; the plain is afire with uplifted arms.
Opposite them, Messapus and the swift-footed Latins
and Coras with his brother, and the maid Camilla's troops,

all appear confronting them across the plain,   6
their arms drawn back with levelled spears and quivering lances.
The marching men and neighing horses grow more furious.
And now each army takes its stand, a spear's throw away
from the enemy, and with a sudden shout they charge,
spurring on their horses, hurling showers of missiles   6
as thick as falling snowflakes, veiling the sky in shadow.
Straightway Tyrrhenus and the fierce Aconteus charge
with levelled spears, colliding with a mighty crash.
Their horses dash together, shattering chest on chest.
Aconteus is thrown off like a thunderbolt   61
or like a heavy ball hurled from a catapult.
He flies headlong and scatters his life into the air.
The lines begin to waver; the Latins, put to flight,
sling their shields behind them and make for the city walls.
The Trojans pursue, Asilas at the squadron's head.   62
Now they were approaching the gates; the Latins shout
again, and turn around their horses' supple necks.
The others flee and ride away with loosened reins;
as when the ocean, advancing with alternate swell,
now rushes to the shore and dashes over the cliff   62
with foaming waves and drenches the remotest sands,
now flees in rapid retreat and in the undertow
rolling stones are sucked away from the smooth-drying sand.
Twice the Tuscans drove the Rutulians back to the city;
twice they fled, looking back, with their shields behind them;   63
but when they clashed together in the third encounter,
the lines were interlocked and each man picked his opponent.
Then the groans of the dying rose, and arms and corpses
and lifeless horses' bodies welter deep in blood,
entangled with slain riders: the battle rages fiercely.   63
Orsilochus threw a spear at the horse of Remulus
(he shrank from attacking the rider) and hit him under the ear.
The steed rears furiously at the blow and, chest uplifted,
maddened by the wound, he flings his legs in the air,
throwing the rider to the ground. Catillus strikes down   64
Iollas and Herminius, great in spirit, and great

in body and arms alike; his blond head is bare,
his shoulders unprotected. He has no fear of wounds—
so great a hero faces arms! Through his broad shoulders
the quivering spear pierces, and doubles him up in anguish.   645
Dark blood flows everywhere. They slaughter with the sword
in rivalry, and seek a glorious death by wounds.

In the midst of the slaughter, like an Amazon, there rages
the quiver-bearing Camilla, one breast bared for battle.
Now she hurls a shower of tough javelins,   650
now she tirelessly wields a powerful battle-axe,
the golden bow and arms of Diana clang on her shoulders.
Even when she is beaten back and forced to retreat,
she turns from flight and bends her bow and aims her arrows.
Nearby are her chosen comrades, the maid Larina   655
and Tulla and Tarpeia, shaking a brazen axe,
Italy's daughters, whom godlike Camilla chose for her escort:
good handmaids they were in peace and war alike,
as the Thracian Amazons who make the streams
of Thermodon resound, clad in their painted armor,   660
whether round Hippolyta, or when Penthesilea,
daughter of Mars, returns in her chariot, and with loud shrieks
the warrior-maidens exult in triumph with crescent shields.
Who was the first, fierce maiden, and who was the last
slain by your spear? How many heroes did you lay low?   665
First Euneus, son of Clytius, whose unprotected chest
she pierced with a long spear of fir as he opposed her.
Spurting blood-streams he falls and bites the gory dust,
and as he dies he writhes in pain about the wound.
Then she kills Liris and also Pagasus above him: 670
one as he picks the reins up from his wounded horse,
the other, stretching an unarmed hand to his falling comrade;
headlong, they fall together. To them she adds Amastrus,
son of Hippotas. Leaning forward, she pursues
Tereus and Harpalycus, Demophoön and Chromis—   675
for every spinning spear the maiden threw from her hand,
a Phrygian soldier fell. The hunter Ornytus rides

at a distance, with strange armor, on an Iapygian horse:
his broad shoulders are covered with a bullock's hide,
his mighty head is shielded by the gaping mouth   68[
and savage jaws of a huge wolf with great white fangs;
his hand is armed with a rustic spear. He rides about
in the midst of the ranks, towering a head above the rest.
She caught him (no great task: the cavalry was in flight)—
and ran him through and spoke these words with merciless heart: 68[

   "Etruscan, did you think you were chasing beasts in the forest?
The day has come for a woman's arms to refute your words!
But you shall take to your fathers' shades no slight distinction:
that you have fallen beneath the weapons of Camilla!"

   Then she kills Orsilochus and Butes, two Trojans   69[
with mighty bodies. Butes she pierced with a spear in the back
between breastplate and helmet, where the neck showed white,
as he sat, and where the shield hung from his left arm;
she flees from Orsilochus, chased by him in a sweeping circle,
then, tricking him into an inner circle, pursues the pursuer.   69[
She rises and drives her mighty axe through bone and armor
again and again, although he prays and pleads for mercy;
his face is all bespattered with warm blood and brains.
Now there fell in her path (rooted with fear at the sight!)
the warrior son of Aunus who lived in the Apennines,   70[
not the meanest Ligurian, when Fate allowed him
to deceive[5]—when he sees that he cannot escape the queen
either by speed or by diverting her attack,
then he begins to speak with crafty, guileful words:

   "Where is your glory if you—although you are a woman—   70[
fight on horseback? Away with flight! Dare to fight me
hand-to-hand, and prepare yourself to do battle on foot!"
Then you will know to whom vainglory brings destruction!"
So he spoke and she, burning with bitter rage,
gives her horse to a comrade, and stands with equal arms: 71[
on foot, unafraid, with naked sword and unmarked shield.
Thinking he had won by the trick, the youth now flees

---

[5]The Ligurians were famous liars.

without delay, seizing the reins and rushing off
in headlong flight, goading the horse with iron spurs.
"Silly Ligurian, all puffed up with haughty pride,   715
in vain you try your wiles and slippery native tricks—
your cheating will not bring you unharmed to lying Aunus!"
So the maiden cries and then, with her swift feet,
she crosses the path of the steed and catches it by the reins
and then she takes her vengeance on his hated blood;   720
light as a sacred falcon swooping from a rock,
that overtakes with his swift wings a dove in the clouds,
and holds her in his crooked talons and disembowels her,
while blood and bits of feathers flutter down from the sky.

But the Father of Gods and men, enthroned on high Olympus,   725
is watching all these things with an observant eye.
He rouses the Etruscan Tarchon to fierce battle,
stirring up his anger with no gentle goads.
So, amid the slaughter and the retreating columns
Tarchon rides and exhorts the troops with various shouts,   730
calling his men by name, and rallying the routed:
"What fear, what cowardice, your ever-sluggish Etruscans,
never to be stung to shame, possesses you?
Can a mere woman make you retreat in such disorder?
Why have we swords? Why these idle weapons in our hands?   735
You are not so slack for Venus' nightly battles,
or when the curvèd flute proclaims the Bacchic revels!
Wait for feasts and goblets on the groaning tables—
this is your love and your passion!—till the auspicious seer
announces the rites and fat victims call you to the forest!"   740
So saying, he spurs his horse to the midst, ready to die,
and charges full at Venulus, and, seizing the foe,
pulls him off his horse with his right hand. clasping him
right in front of his chest, and carries him swiftly off.
A shout arises to Heaven and all the Latins turn   745
to watch. Tarchon flies like lightning across the plain,
holding the arms and the man, and breaking the spear-head off,
looks for an unprotected spot where he may strike

a mortal wound. The other keeps on struggling,
keeping the hand from his throat, and parrying force with force.   75
As when a golden eagle, soaring in the sky,
bears a snake it has caught in its tightly-gripping talons,
while the serpent, though it is wounded, writhes with sinuous coils,
and rears its scales, hissing with its sibilant mouth,
towering high; the eagle with its crooked beak   75
attacks the struggling victim, flapping the air with its wings:
in such a way, from the Tiburtine lines, Tarchon carries
his prey, exulting. The Etruscans follow his example
and they attack. Then Arruns, who is doomed to die,
circles round Camilla, anticipating her   76
with spear and craft, always alert for a chance to strike;
wherever the fierce maiden dashed in the battle-line,
there Arruns follows, silently dogging her footsteps.
When she returns victorious, and retreats from the foe,
there the young man stealthily turns his horse's reins.   76
This approach and that he tries, round the whole circle,
the quivering spear intent in his relentless hand.

   It happened that Chloreus, sacred to Cybelus, once a priest,
brightly gleamed a long way off in his Phrygian armor,
spurring his foaming steed caparisoned in bronze   770
arranged in scales like feathers and linked together with gold.
He himself, conspicuous in deep foreign purple,
was shooting Cretan arrows from his Lycian bow,
—the golden bow hung from his shoulders; his seer's helmet was

                                                           gold—
his saffron mantle and its rustling linen folds   775
were gathered up into a knot of yellow gold;
his tunic and foreign hose were embroidered with needlework.
Camilla kept pursuing him blindly like a huntress,
whether to fasten Trojan spoils on a temple door
or array herself in captured gold; she singled him out   780
and recklessly she raged all through the battle-line,
burning with a woman's desire for booty and spoils;
when finally Arruns, seizing the opportunity,
aims his spear from ambush, praying aloud to Heaven:

"Apollo, greatest of gods, warder of holy Soracte,   785
whom we were the first to revere, for whom the pine logs burn,
for whom we worshippers walk upon a bed of embers,
passing through the fire, confident in our faith,
grant, Almighty Father, that our disgrace may be   790
erased by arms. I seek no plunder and no trophy,
no spoils for defeating the maiden—my fame will come to me
from other deeds—if only the dread scourge will fall
beneath my spear, I shall go home without renown."
　　Phoebus heard, and consented to grant part of the prayer,
but the rest he scattered to the flying breezes.   795
He granted the prayer to strike down and slay Camilla,
but the rest, to return to see his native land,
he did not grant; the South Wind carried the voice away.
So when the spear flew from his hand and sped through the air,
all the Volscians turned their eager eyes and minds   800
upon Camilla, but she herself was not aware
of any sound or wind or weapon from the sky
until the spear struck her beneath her naked breast
and lodged there, driven deep, and drank her maiden blood.
Her frightened comrades hurry and catch her as she falls.   805
Arruns himself is frightened, more than all the others,
and flees with mingled joy and fear, no longer daring
to trust his spear, or meet the weapons of the maiden.
As when a wolf has slain a shepherd or a great bullock,
before the hostile weapons can pursue him, straightway   810
begins to flee by trackless ways to the high mountains,
conscious of his reckless deeds, he slackens his tail
and tucks it trembling under his belly and seeks the forest;
even so does Arruns steal from sight in confusion,
and, content with flight, he mingles in the midst of arms.   815
　　The dying Camilla pulls at the spear, but the iron point
clings to the ribs in the deep wound between the bones.
She loses blood and sinks, her eyes sink, cold with death,
the color, once so ruddy, begins to leave her face.
Breathing her last, she addresses Acca, her equal in years,   820
and faithful to her friend Camilla beyond the rest,

with whom she shared her troubles; and she speaks these words:
     "Sister Acca, my strength is failing—the bitter wound
is conquering me, and everything is growing dark.
Run and take this message to Turnus—my last words—   82
to take my place in the fight and keep the Trojans away
from the city. Now farewell!" As she spoke, she dropped the reins
and slipped to the ground unconscious. She grew cold and slowly
released herself from the body and dropped her nerveless neck
and head, overcome by death—her weapons fell; with a groan   83
her spirit fled, resentful, to the Shades below.

     Then a tremendous shout went up to the golden stars;
now that Camilla is dead the battle waxes fiercer.
They rush together with all their forces, the Trojan army,
Etruscan leaders, and Evander's Arcadian troops.   83.
     But Opis, Diana's sentinel, for some time had been seated
on a mountain top, watching the battle undismayed,
and when from afar amid the din of angry youths
she saw Camilla stricken down by a piteous death,
she sighed and from the depth of her heart she said these words: 84C
     "Alas, O maiden, too, too cruel a punishment
that you have paid for trying to harm the Trojans in war!
Nor was it any help to you that you worshipped Diana
in solitary woods and wore our shafts on your shoulder.
But your Queen has not left you dishonored, now that your end   845
has come: your death shall not be unnamed among the nations,
nor shall you bear the reproach of dying unavenged.
Whoever violated your body with a wound
shall pay with his own life!" Beneath the mountain's height
there was a mound of earth, the tomb of King Dercennus,   850
an ancient Laurentian king, screened by a shady holm-oak.
Here the lovely goddess speeds, and takes her stand,
and from the top of the barrow she looks about for Arruns.
When she saw him rejoicing and swollen with his pride,
she said: "Why are you running away? Direct your steps   855
this way! Come here to your death: receive your reward for
                                             Camilla!

Shall you too not die by the weapons of Diana?"
Thus spoke the Thracian nymph and plucked a wingèd arrow
from the golden quiver, stretched the bow and drew it back
until the curving ends came together, and as her hands   860
pulled apart, she touched the arrow with her left hand;
her right hand brought the bowstring hard against her breast.
Straightway, and together, Arruns heard the whizzing weapon
and whistling air, and the shaft was lodged within his chest.
His forgetful comrades leave him there, expiring   865
and groaning in the ignominious dust of the plain.
And Opis flies away to heavenly Olympus.
Camilla's light-armed horse flee first, their mistress lost;
the Rutulians are routed and flee, and valiant Atinas flees.
The dispersed captains and the troops without their leaders   870
make for shelter, and wheeling horses, head for the walls.
None can withstand the attack of the death-dealing Trojans—
nor can they repel them with a fighting stand.
Their unstrung bows are slung behind their drooping shoulders;
the galloping thunder of hoofbeats shakes the dusty plain.   875
An inky cloud of whirling dust rolls up to the walls.
On the rampart tower the mothers beat their breasts
and women's wailing rises to the stars in Heaven.
As they flee in utter rout through the open gates,
a hostile throng mingles with them and falls upon them.   880
They do not escape a miserable death, but right on the threshold
within their native walls and even in their houses
they are run through and breathe their last. Some close the gates
and dare not open them to their friends and let them in
in spite of their prayers. A pitiful slaughter follows, of those   885
defending the gates with arms, and rushing on drawn swords.
Some, shut out before the eyes of their weeping parents,
driven by the rout, roll headlong in the trenches,
some charge blindly on their horses with loosened reins,
and batter at the doors and solidly bolted gates.   890
The mothers themselves on the walls, in keenest emulation
—showing true love of their country—when they saw Camilla,
threw weapons from their trembling hands, and imitate steel

hastily, with stout oak cudgels and charred stakes,
eager to be the first to die in defense of the walls. 8g

Meanwhile, in the forest, Turnus hears the sad news
and Acca brings the youth the tale of terrible tumult—
the Volscian ranks destroyed and routed, Camilla slain,
the enemy advancing fiercely, sweeping the fields
in triumphant battle, and panic now at the very walls. 90
Turnus, raging (for Jove's stern will demands it thus)
deserts his hilly ambush and leaves the rugged woodland.
Scarce was he out of sight and on the level plain
when Father Aeneas enters the unprotected pass,
climbs the ridge and issues from the shady wood. 90
So both march to the walls swiftly, with full forces,
nor are they many paces distant from each other.
At one and the same instant Aeneas saw the plain
smoking with dust from afar, and he saw the Laurentian army,
and Turnus saw the savage Aeneas coming in arms 91
and heard the tramp of feet and snorting of the horses.
And straightway they would have joined in battle, but ruddy
                                                    Phoebus
already was dipping his weary steeds in the Spanish Sea,
and as the day declined, he ushered in the night.
They camp before the city and build walls for defense.

End of Book XI.

BOOK XII

THE DEATH OF TURNUS

When Turnus sees the Latins broken and discouraged
by war's disasters, and his own promise being claimed
and all men's eyes upon him, his spirits begin to rise
with unappeasable anger. As in the Punic fields
a lion gravely wounded in the chest by hunters   5
prepares at last for battle, tossing his shaggy mane
joyously from his neck, and snapping undismayed
at the robber's planted spear, and roaring with bloody mouth:
just so in Turnus' burning soul the passion rises.
He speaks to King Latinus with vehement words: "Turnus   10
will not delay: there is no excuse for the cowardly men
of Aeneas to retract their words or renounce their agreement.
I go to battle: bring sacrifice, Father, and make the truce.
Either my hand will send to Tartarus the Dardanian
—the runaway from Asia—let Latins sit and watch;   15
and I alone with my sword will remove our people's shame,
or let him rule the conquered and wed Lavinia."
    With calm, unruffled mind Latinus answers him:
"O youth of peerless spirit, the more you excel in valor
the more important it is that I take earnest counsel   20
and in my anxiety weigh every possible danger.
You have your father Daunus' lands and many towns
captured by your hands; Latinus has gold and good will.
In Latium and Laurentian fields are other maidens
of no mean birth. Let me now speak frankly, with no pretense,   25
although it may be painful, and take my words to heart.
As gods and men alike foretold, I had no right
to unite my daughter to any one of her former suitors.
But my love for you, and our kinship, and all my wife's sad tears
won me over and made me break all bonds. I snatched   30

261

the girl from her betrothed and waged a wicked war.
From that day, Turnus, you see what calamities
and wars pursue me, what woes you above all have suffered.
Twice conquered in great battles, we can scarce keep in our city
the hopes of Italy. The Tiber's streams are still warm
with our blood; the spreading plain is still white with our bones.
Why do I keep wavering? What madness changes my purpose?
If with Turnus dead I am ready to take them as allies,
why not rather end the fight while he still lives?
What will your Rutulian kin and the rest of Italy
say (may Fortune refute the words!) if I should betray you
to death while you are seeking my daughter's hand in marriage?
Think of the shifting fortunes of war. Pity your father
—an old man grieving far away in his native Ardea."
Turnus' fury is not deflected by these words:
he rages more fiercely—the cure makes his sickness worse.
As soon as he was able to speak, he began and said:
"I beg you, noble sire—the care you have for my sake,
resign it for my sake; let me purchase honor with death.
My hand, too, can shower missiles of strongest steel;
my wounds draw blood just the same as any other's.
His goddess-mother will not be there to cover his flight
with mist (a woman's trick!) and hide in empty shadows!"
, But the Queen was greatly alarmed at this new chance of battle.
She wept and clung to her fiery son-in-law, ready to die:
"Turnus, by my tears, by any regard for Amata
that still can touch your heart—you are my only hope,
the solace of sad old age—in your hands Latinus' honor
and kingdom, our tottering house rests on your support—
one thing I beseech you: do not fight with the Trojans!
Whatever fortune awaits you in that fight of yours
awaits me too; with you I will leave this hateful light;
my captive eyes will never see Aeneas as my son!"

Lavinia heard her mother's words; the tears ran down
her burning cheeks, and a deep blush set her on fire
and quickly spread all over the maiden's glowing face.

And as when someone has stained Indian ivory
with crimson dye, or when white lilies reflect the red
of many blended roses, such colors were in her face.
Turnus, distracted by love, fixes his eyes on the maiden,   70
and burning more fiercely for war, speaks briefly to Amata:
"Mother, do not, I beg you, pursue me with your tears
—such an ill omen—as I go to the cruel fray,
for Turnus has no freedom to delay his death.
Idmon, be my messenger: take these unwelcome words   75
to the Phrygian tyrant: when tomorrow's Dawn, riding
on crimson wheels, makes the heavens blush, let him not lead
the Trojans against the Rutulians: let Trojan weapons
rest, and Rutulians too. With our blood let us settle this war;
on the field of combat let Lavinia be won."   80
    Having spoken thus he quickly returned to the palace.
He calls for his horses and rejoices to see them neighing
—these horses Orithyia herself had given Pilumnus—
they surpassed the snow in whiteness and the wind in speed.
The eager drivers stand around, their hollow palms   85
slap the resounding chests and comb the flowing manes.
Turnus puts on his shoulders a corselet stiff with gold
and pale bronze. At the same time he makes ready and fits
his sword and shield and helmet with its red-crested horns--
the sword the Fire-God himself had made for his father,   90
Daunus, dipping it white-hot in the River Styx.
Then his strong hands seize the mighty spear, which stood
leaning on a great column in the center court,
the spoil of Auruncan Actor—he brandishes and shakes it,
crying aloud: "Now, spear, that never failed my call,   95
now the time has come! The great Actor once carried you,
and now the hand of Turnus wields you. Grant that I may
with my strong hand lay low the body and pierce the armor
of this Phrygian eunuch, and defile with dust his hair
curled with heating-irons and all bedewed with myrrh!"   100
Such is the madness that drives him on. The sparks are flying
from his furious face, his keen eyes flash with fire;
just as a bull before a fight begins to bellow,

trying to concentrate all his anger in his horns,
and charges into a tree-trunk and wounds the winds with blows,   105
and paws the sand and scatters it as prelude to battle.
Meanwhile, no less fierce in the arms his mother gave him,
Aeneas whets his martial spirit and rouses his anger,
rejoicing that the war will be settled by this agreement.
He comforts his companions, and sad Iülus' fear,   110
explaining Destiny, and orders his men to carry
a firm reply to Latinus and fix the terms of peace.

The dawning day was just beginning to sprinkle light
on the mountain tops, and the steeds of the Sun were just arising
from Ocean's depths, and breathing light from uplifted nostrils,   115
when Rutulians and Trojans measured out the ground
for the coming combat beneath the walls of the great city,
with fires and grassy altars to their common gods.
Others were bringing fountain-water and fire, wearing
sacrificial aprons, their temples wreathed with vervain.   120
The Italian army marches out in serried ranks
forth from the crowded gates. All the Trojans and Etruscans
with all their different kinds of armor come hastening,
armed with steel, exactly as if Mars himself
were calling them to battle. In the midst of thousands   125
the captains hurry by, resplendent in gold and purple,
Mnestheus of Assaracus' line, and brave Asilas,
and Messapus tamer of horses and offspring of Neptune.
At a given signal, each side withdraws to its place:
they plant their spears in the ground and lean their shields against
them.   130
The eager mothers and unarmed crowd come streaming forth
out of the houses, with feeble old men, and sit on the towers
and rooftops, while others stand on top of the lofty gates.

But Juno, watching from the summit now called Alban
(in those days it had no name nor honor nor glory)   135
looked at the field and at the double battle-lines
of Laurentines and Trojans, and the city of Latinus.

Suddenly she spoke to Turnus' sister—a goddess
to a goddess—who presided over pools and streams;
such was the honor that Jupiter, Heaven's king, had given her   140
in compensation for her stolen virginity:
"O Nymph, pride of the rivers, dearest to my heart,
you know how I have preferred you to all the Latin maidens
who mounted the ungrateful bed of mighty Jove,
and how I have gladly given you a place in Heaven.   145
Learn of your grief, Juturna, and do not reproach me—
when Fortune permitted, and the Fates allowed Latium
to succeed, I shielded Turnus and your city.
Now I see the youth confront unequal Fates.
The day of doom and hostile power are near at hand.   150
I cannot look upon this battle and this treaty:
if you dare to give your brother more effective aid,
go on, it is fitting: perhaps relief will follow sorrow!"

Scarce had she spoken: Juturna's eyes were filled with tears;
three and four times her hand beat her beautiful breast.   155
"This is no time for tears," Saturnian Juno said.
"Hurry and snatch your brother, if you can, from death,
or stir them to battle and break the truce that they have made:
it is I that tell you to dare!" With this advice, she left her
doubtful and bewildered by the bitter blow.   160

Meanwhile the kings ride out, Latinus in a chariot
huge and massive, drawn by four horses, twelve golden rays
bound around his gleaming temples, a sign of the Sun
his ancestor, and Turnus is drawn by two white horses,
clutching two broad-headed javelins in his hand.   165
On this side, Father Aeneas, source of the Roman race
shining with his starry shield and Heaven-made arms;
nearby Ascanius, second hope of mighty Rome,
comes forth from the camp; a priest in snowy garments
brings the young of a bristling boar and unshorn sheep   170
and puts the animals beside the burning altars.
The leaders turn their eyes toward the rising sun
and sprinkle salted meal from their hands, and mark the foreheads

of the victims with the knife and pour offerings on the altars.
Then good Aeneas, drawing his sword, makes this prayer:　　　175
　　"Now may the Sun witness my vow, likewise the Earth
for whose sake I have been able to endure such labors,
and the Almighty Father, and you, his wife, Saturnia
—now, goddess, in better mood, I pray—and you great Mavors,
who control all warfare, Father, in your mighty dominion,　　　180
and all the Fountains and Streams I call, and the Spirits of Heaven,
and whatever Powers there be in the blue Ocean:
if by chance the victory goes to Ausonian Turnus,
it is agreed the conquered will go to Evander's city;
Iülus will leave the land, and the children of Aeneas　　　185
will never attack again or harass the realm with the sword.
But if Victory grant that the battle goes to us
(as I rather think will happen, and may the gods confirm it!)
I never will make Italians obey the Trojans, nor seek
the land for myself; under equal terms let both peoples　　　190
unconquered enter upon an everlasting agreement.
I will give rites and gods; let my father Latinus keep
the sword and his wonted sway; the Trojans will build my walls,
and Lavinia will give her name to our city."
So Aeneas first, and King Latinus follows,　　　195
lifting his eyes to Heaven and raising his hand to the stars:
　　"I swear by these same powers, Aeneas: Earth, Sea, and Stars,
twin offspring of Latona, and the two-faced Janus,
the might of the gods below and shrines of cruel Dis;
may he hear my words who sanctions pacts with the thunderbolt.　　　200
I touch the altars and call the fires and gods between us:
no day shall break the peace and truce for Italy,
whatsoever things may befall, nor any force
turn aside my will, not though a deluge came
plunging land into water, dissolving Heaven in Hell!　　　205
Just as this scepter (he chanced to have one in his hand)
will never grow with foliage into branch or shade,
now that it has been cut in the woods from the lowest roots,
deprived of its mother, it has shed its leaves and branches:
once it was a tree, but now an artist has clothed it　　　210

in handsome bronze and given it to Latin fathers."
With these words they sealed the agreement between the two,
with the leaders looking on; then duly over the flames
they slaughter hallowed victims and tear out the living entrails
and pile the altars high with heavy-laden platters.   215

But to the Rutulians the fight had long seemed unfair—
their hearts were already torn by great anxiety,
but now even more, as they behold the ill-matched forces.
Turnus increases their turmoil—advancing silently
and humbly adoring the altar with his downcast eyes—   220
by his haggard cheeks and the pallor of his youthful face.
Soon as his sister Juturna saw the whispers spreading
and the hearts of the people wavering in doubt,
into the ranks, in feigned appearance of Camers
(of a noble family, and a glorious father,   225
and he himself a mighty hero and fierce in arms)—
she plunges into the ranks, knowing her business well,
and scatters different rumors, and says such things as these:
    "Are you not ashamed, Rutulians, to risk one life
to save the entire army? Are we not their equals   230
in numbers and in strength? See, this is all of them: Trojans,
Arcadians, doomed Etruscans, enemies of Turnus!
If every other one of us fought, we would hardly find
a foe for each! Turnus shall rise in fame to the gods,
to whose altars he vows his life, and living he shall move   235
upon the lips of men; while we, who now sit listless
upon the fields, shall have to bow to haughty masters!"
With these words the goddess inflames the warriors' spirits
more and more—a murmur steals among the ranks.
Even the Laurentines and the Latins themselves are changed;   240
and they, who only now had hoped for rest from battle
and safety for their fortunes, long for arms and wish
the truce were broken, and pity Turnus' unjust fate.
Juturna adds another and a greater portent
—an omen from the sky, most powerful of all   245
to confuse Italians souls with deceptive augury.

For flying through the rosy sky, the golden eagle,
bird of Jove, was chasing a noisy flock of shore-birds
in a wingèd column, and suddenly swooped down to the sea,
pouncing ruthlessly on a swan with his crooked talons.   250
The Italians watched with excitement, as the whole troop of birds
turned raucously around—a wonderful sight to see!
Darkening the sky with their wings, making a cloud,
they drive the foe through the air, till overcome by their strength
and his heavy booty, he weakened and dropped the prey from his

                                                           claws   255
into the water and fled far away in the clouds.
Then the Rutulians salute the omen with a shout
and free their hands for battle. The seer Tolumnius says:
"This it was, this that I have often been praying for:
I accept the omen and recognize the gods: with me,   260
me as your leader, seize your swords, my hapless friends,
whom a wicked stranger frightens with war, like feeble birds,
and wastes your shores with force. He too will flee and sail
across the seas. Be of one heart; close up your ranks,
and defend with battle the king who has been snatched from you."   265
    He spoke, and rushing forward threw a spear at the foe.
The whizzing cornel-shaft went cutting through the air.
At the same moment a mighty shout goes up, and all
the ranks are in confusion, their hearts aflame with tumult.
The spear flies on its way to where nine stalwart brothers   270
chanced to be standing together; a faithful Etruscan wife
had borne them all to one Gylippus, an Arcadian.
One of them, in the waist, where the stitched belt rubs the belly
and the buckle bites the fastenings of the side,
a youth of outstanding beauty, shining in his armor—   275
is pierced by the spear in the ribs and falls on the yellow sand.
His brothers, a courageous band, are inflamed with grief:
some seize swords in their hands, others snatch up spears,
and blindly they charge upon the foe. The Laurentian lines
rush to the attack, and on the other side   280
Trojans and Agyllines and Arcadians with painted armor,
all are moved by a passion to settle with the sword.

They strip the altars; a cloud of javelins fills the sky—
an iron rain of weapons falls upon the field.
Bowls and braziers are carried off. Latinus himself   285
takes to flight with his outraged gods: the truce is broken.
Others harness cars and leap upon their horses
and rush into the fray, prepared with weapons drawn.
Messapus, eager to break the treaty, spurs his horse
and frightens away Aulestes, an Etruscan king,   290
wearing king's insignia. The other, rushing back,
wretched man, is thrown upon his head and shoulders
right on the altars in his path. Messapus, burning,
flies at him, spear in hand, in spite of his pleading, and strikes him
heavily from above with his mighty shaft, and says: 295
"He has it:[1] a better victim is offered to the great gods!"
The Italians run together and strip the still warm limbs.
Corynaeus seized a firebrand from the altar
and threw it in the face of Ebysus, who was about
to strike a blow at him: his heavy beard caught fire,   300
and gave off a burning smell. Corynaeus followed him;
grabbing his dazed foe by the hair with his left hand
and forcing him to the ground with a thrust of his heavy knee,
he pierced him in the side with a rigid sword. Podalirius
is pursuing with his naked blade the shepherd Alsus,   305
as he rushes amid the flying weapons; raising his axe,
Alsus splits the other's head right down to his chin,
sprinkling all his armor with widely spurting blood.
Hard repose and iron sleep press down upon
his eyes; his eyelids close in everlasting night.   310
But good Aeneas, bare-headed, was stretching out
his unarmed hand and calling loudly to his men:
"Where are you rushing? Why the sudden outburst of strife?
Restrain your anger: the truce already has been made,
the terms are fixed. I alone have the right to do battle!   315
Leave it to me and have no fear: my hand will confirm

---

[1]"hoc habet"—the shout of the crowd when a gladiator was killed.
Cf. our colloquial: "He's had it!"

the treaty: these sacred rites make Turnus already mine!"
   As he is speaking thus and calling on his men,
lo, a strident arrow flew through the air and struck him
—no one ever knew whose was the hand drove it,   320
nor what god or chance brought to the Rutulians
such a distinction. The glory of the deed was kept secret
and no one ever boasted that he had wounded Aeneas.
As soon as Turnus saw Aeneas leaving the ranks,
and the captains all in confusion, he burns with sudden hope,   325
demands his horse and arms, and leaps in his chariot
exultantly, and seizes the horses' reins in his hands.
Many men he sends to death as he speeds along;
many, half-dead, he runs over and crushes with his car,
or, seizing spears, he brings them down as they are fleeing.   330
Just as when swift and bloody Mars, by the icy streams
of Hebrus, rattles his shield and arouses war, and lets loose
his frenzied horses, and they, across the open plain,
outstrip the South and West Winds, and distant parts of Thrace
groan to their hoofbeats; about him, the dark faces of Terror   335
and Anger and Treachery, the retinue of the god:—
so, eagerly, amid the battle, Turnus drives
his horses steaming with sweat, and trampling on the foe
miserably slain. The galloping hoofbeats spatter
a bloody dew and kick up mingled blood and sand.   340
And now he has killed Sthenelus and Thamyrus and Pholus,
the last two hand-to-hand, the first from afar; from afar
the sons of Imbrasus, Glaucus and Lades, whom Imbrasus
himself had raised in Lycia, and given matching armor
to battle hand-to-hand or outstrip the wind on horseback.   345
Elsewhere Eumedes rides into the battle's midst,
offspring of ancient Dolon, illustrious in war,
recalling his grandfather's name, and the hand and heart of his
                                                father
who once, when he approached the Grecian camp as a spy,
dared to demand as his pay the chariot of Achilles,   350
but Diomedes gave him a different reward for his daring,
and never again did he covet the horses of Achilles!

Turnus sees him from afar on the open plain
and follows him with a light javelin through the long space,
then reins in his steeds and leaps from his chariot, 355
comes down on the fallen, dying man, and plants his foot
upon the other's neck and wrests his sword from his hand,
and dyes the blade with blood from his throat, and speaks these
words:

"Look, Trojan, lying here, measure Italy's fields
which you sought in war! This is the reward 360
of those who fight with Turnus; such are the walls they build!"
Then he hurls a spear, and sends Asbytes to join him,
and Chloreus and Sybaris, Dares and Thersilochus,
and Thymoetes, who was thrown from the neck of his horse.
And just as when the blast of the Edonian North Winds 365
howls across the Aegean, and drives the waves to the shore;
wherever the winds pursue, the clouds flee through the sky:—
so wherever Turnus cuts a path the lines give way
and turn in flight—his own momentum carries him on.
The breeze tosses his plumes as the car goes into the wind. 370
Phegeus could not bear his attack and fiery rage;
he threw himself in the chariot's path, and turned aside
the foaming horses' mouths, wrenching with his right hand.
While he was dragged along, clinging to the yoke,
a spear hit his unprotected side and broke the corselet 375
and lightly grazed the surface of the flesh with a wound.
But as he faced the enemy with his shield before him,
trying to defend himself with weapon drawn,
the whirling wheel of the swiftly moving chariot
dashed him to the ground and Turnus, following, 380
cut off his head between the lower rim of the helmet
and the top of the breastplate, leaving his body on the sand.

And as victorious Turnus deals death across the fields,
meanwhile Mnestheus and trusty Achates and Ascanius
together take the bleeding Aeneas back to the camp, 385
leaning every other step on his long spear.
Raging, he tries to pull out the head of the broken arrow

—demanding that they use the quickest way of relief,
and cut the wound with a sword and lay bare the spot
where the arrowhead was lodged, and send him back to battle.   390
And now Iapyx, son of Iasus, dear above all
to Phoebus, was at hand; Apollo, smitten with love,
once had gladly offered to give him all his arts:
his prophecy, the music of the lyre, swift arrows;
but he, to defer the destiny of his dying father,   395
chose rather to learn the powers of herbs and the healing art;
and practice, unknown, the silent art of medicine.
Aeneas, bitterly chafing, stood leaning on his spear,
amid a dense crowd of youth, the sad Iülus among them,
but he was unmoved by their tears. The aged Iapyx   400
with his garment drawn back in the Paeonian fashion,
makes many attempts with his hands and Apollo's healing herbs,
but all in vain—in vain he pulls at the stubborn dart
and with a gripping forceps tugs at the iron point.
No luck attends his efforts: Apollo does not help him.   405
The wild clamor increases more and more on the plain,
and closer comes disaster. Now a cloud of dust
rises in the air, the horsemen come, a shower of darts
falls all around them—a dismal clamor fills the sky
of young men fighting and falling beneath Mars' cruel hand.   410
     Then, deeply stirred by her son's undeserving pain, Venus
his mother plucks from Cretan Ida some dittany—
a plant with downy leaves and a bright purple flower—
it is a herb that is not unknown to the wild goats
when winged arrows have hit them and are lodged in their flanks.   415
This Venus took, her face veiled in an opaque cloud,
and mixed it with her secret skill with river-water
in magnificent vessels, sprinkling it with the juice
of ambrosia and the fragrant panacea.
With this old Iapyx, all unaware, washed out the wound,   420
and suddenly all pain was gone from Aeneas' body,
and all the flow of blood was stanched deep in the wound.
The arrow fell out of its own accord, following the hand
of Iapyx: Aeneas' strength returned to its former state.

"Quickly, bring arms! Why do you stand there?" Iapyx said,   425
the first to fire their spirits now against the foe:
"This was not done by human aid or physician's skill:
it was not my hand, Aeneas, that healed your wound:
a greater god is at work and sends you to greater deeds."

Eager for battle, he sheathes his legs in golden greaves,   430
the right and the left, and shakes his spear, scorning delay.
When the shield is at his side and the cuirass on his back,
he puts his arms round Ascanius in an iron embrace
and lightly kisses his lips through the visor of his helmet
and says: "My boy, learn courage and strenuous toil from me;   435
fortune from others. Today my hand will shield you in war
and it will lead you to where rich rewards can be won.
See that you remember, when you have come of age,
to recall to mind the examples of your kinsmen,
inspired by your father Aeneas and your uncle Hector."   440

When he had spoken, he left the camp, a mighty figure
shaking a massive spear in his hand. In serried column
Antheus and Mnestheus and all the crowd rush out,
leaving the camp deserted. Blinding dust fills the plain;
the shaken earth trembles under the tramping feet.   445
Turnus saw them coming from the opposite rampart,
likewise the Ausonians, and an icy chill
ran through their bones. First before all the Latins
Juturna recognized the sound and fled in terror.
Aeneas flies across the field with his dark column.   450
As when a storm is breaking, a cloud moves toward the land
over the midst of the ocean—the farmers' foreboding hearts
see from afar and tremble at the coming tempest:
trees will be felled, the crops ruined, disaster will spread—
the winds fly on ahead and carry the sound to land: 455
so the Trojan chief moves on against the foe,
leading his column densely packed in phalanx-formation.
Thymbraeus smites the great Osiris with his sword,
Mnestheus slaughters Arcetius, Achates Epulo,
Gyas Ufens; even the seer Tolumnius falls—   460
the one who first threw a spear against the Trojan lines.

A shout goes up to the sky; the routed Rutulians
turn amid clouds of dust and flee across the fields.
Aeneas does not deign to kill the fugitives
nor does he attack the ones he meets on foot   46:
or horseback—Turnus alone he seeks in the murky gloom;
with searching gaze he summons Turnus alone to battle.

   Juturna the warrior-maiden, stricken with great fear,
throws out Metiscus (who was Turnus' charioteer)
from the reins and leaves him fallen from the pole.   470
She herself takes his place and guides the flowing reins,
assuming the voice and form and weapons of Metiscus.
Just as when a black swallow flies through the ample house
of a wealthy lord, winging her way through the stately halls,
searching for her chirping fledglings tiny crumbs   475
and scraps of food, and twittering in the empty house:
even so Juturna is borne through the midst of the foe
and winging her way in the swift chariot, sweeps the field;
showing her exultant brother here and there,
she does not let him fight but keeps flying far away.   480
But still Aeneas threads the twisted maze to find him,
dogging his footsteps amid all the scattered ranks,
calling him loudly. As often as he sees the foe
and tries by running to match the flight of the wingèd steeds,
so often Juturna wheels around the turning car.   485
What could he do? Vainly he tosses on the tide,
and conflicting troubles call his mind this way and that.
Messapus, who chanced to be carrying in his left hand
two tough spears tipped with steel, came advancing lightly;
aiming one of them, he sends it unerringly spinning.   490
Aeneas stopped and gathered himself behind the shield,
dropping to one knee; the swift spear carried off
his helmet-top and dashed from his head the topmost plumes.
Then his anger is aroused by the treachery;
for he sees Turnus' horses and chariot far away;   495
often appealing to Jove by the broken treaty's altars,
at last he invades their midst, borne on the tide of Mars,

and begins to wreak a terrible, indiscriminate slaughter,
throwing to the winds the reins of passion and anger.

What god can tell of the horror, who can sing of the death   500
and fall of innumerable captains, some of them slain by Turnus,
some driven by the Trojan hero across the plain?
Jupiter, was it your will for nations to clash in conflict
so mighty, that thereafter would dwell in eternal peace?
Aeneas, meeting Rutulian Sucro (that battle first   505
brought the Trojan attack to a stand) with little delay
strikes him in the side where death is speediest,
and drives the cruel steel through the ribs that enclose the chest.
Turnus unhorses Amycus and his brother Diores,
attacking them on foot, one with his mighty spear,   510
the other with a sword, and hangs from his chariot
their severed heads, and carries them off dripping with blood.
Aeneas kills Talos and Tanais and brave Cethegus
(three at one attack!) and slays the sad Onites
of Echionian name—his mother was Peridia.   515
Turnus kills the Lycian brothers from Phoebus' fields,
and Menoetes of Arcadia—a youth who hated war
in vain—round fishy Lerna's streams his art had been
and humble dwelling; he did not know the palaces
of the mighty—his father had plowed on hired soil.   520
And like fires driven from the opposite sides
of a dry forest and bushes of crackling laurel,
or as when in swift descent from the mountain's heights,
foaming rivers roar and rush on their way to the sea,
each wasting its own path: with no less fury   525
Aeneas and Turnus sweep through the battle's midst, and now
                                                            anger
rises up within them, their hearts are bursting, they cannot
yield; with all their strength they rush at the enemy's weapons.
As Murranus boasts of his ancestors' ancient fame
—a whole long line traced back through the Italian kings,   530
Aeneas knocks him headlong with a mighty rock
and throws him out of his chariot; under the reins and yoke

the wheels run him over, and thundering hoofs of his own
                                                    horses—
they do not remember their master and trample him to death.
The other, as Hyllus rushes with fury in his heart,   53
meets him head-on and hurls a spear at his gilded temples.
The weapon pierces the helmet and lodges in his brain.
Nor did your right hand, Cretheus, bravest of the Greeks,
save you from Turnus; nor did the gods save their Cupencus
when Aeneas came: he met the weapon with his breast,   54
and the brazen shield was of no avail to the hapless man.
You too, Aeolus, the Laurentian plains saw fall
and stretch your mighty body upon the ground:
you fell, whom neither the Argive phalanx could destroy
nor even Achilles, the conqueror of Priam's kingdom.   54
Here was your goal of death—your home was beneath great Ida,
your stately house at Lyrnesus, but your tomb in Italy.
The entire battle-lines converged here—all the Latins
and all the Trojans, Mnestheus and the valiant Serestus
and Messapus tamer of horses and brave Asilas,
the Etruscan phalanx and Evander's Arcadian troops—   55
every man for himself, with all his might and main,
with no relief or respite in the strain of battle.

   Now Aeneas' beautiful mother gave him the thought
to attack the walls and move his army against the town
swiftly, and confuse the Latins with sudden disaster.   55
As he searched for Turnus through the scattered lines,
turning his gaze this way and that, he saw the city
unharmed by the battle, peaceful and unscathed.
Straightway the vision of a greater battle inflames him;   56
he calls Mnestheus to him and Sergestus and brave Serestus,
his captains, and stands on a mound—the rest of the Trojan army
assemble in closed ranks without laying down their shields
and spears. Standing on the hill in their midst, he speaks :
"Let there be no delay in carrying out my orders: 56
Jupiter is with us. Let no one be reluctant
because of the sudden decision: this city, the cause of war

and seat of Latinus, unless they submit and obey us as victors,
today I destroy and level the smoking roofs to the ground.
Should I perhaps wait until it pleases Turnus,   570
already beaten, to face me, and fight with me again?
Trojans, this is the head and source of the evil war:
fetch firebrands fast; let flames reclaim the broken treaty!"
He finished speaking; they all strive with emulous spirits;
forming a wedge they advance in a dense throng to the walls.   575
Suddenly, scaling ladders and fires are to be seen.
Some rush to the gates and cut down the defenders,
others hurl their weapons and darken the sky with spears.
Aeneas himself in the lead raises his hands to the walls
and in a loud voice reproaches Latinus and calls the gods   580
to witness that he is being forced into war again:
twice the Italians became his foes, two treaties were broken.
Strife arises among the frightened people; some want
to unlock the gates and open the city to the Trojans
and even drag the king himself to the battlements;   585
others bring arms and hasten to defend the walls;
as when a shepherd has tracked bees to a stony crevice
and filled their secret hiding-place with pungent smoke;
they within are frightened and scurry to and fro
throughout the waxen fortress with an angry buzzing;   590
the acrid black smoke rolls through the hive, the rocks resound
with muffled murmur, and smoke escapes to the open air.

The weary Latins now were met by a new misfortune,
one that shook the city with grief to its very foundations.
When from the palace the Queen sees the Trojans approaching,   595
the walls attacked, the firebrands flying to the roofs,
and nowhere the Rutulian ranks, no troops of Turnus;
the wretched woman thinks her champion has been slain
in battle; her mind is distraught by sudden pangs of anguish,
she cries that she is the cause of crime and source of sorrow,   600
and madly, in her frenzy, she pours out cries of grief;
and, resolved to die, she tears her purple garments
and from the lofty beam she ties a noose of death.

When the poor Latin women learn of this disaster,
first her daughter Lavinia tears her flowery tresses   60
and rosy cheeks with her hand, then the other women
go mad with grief; the palace rings with lamentations.
The dreadful news begins to spread throughout the city;
all are in despair, Latinus rends his garments,
dazed at the death of his wife and downfall of the city,   61
he defiles his white hair with showers of filthy dust,
[many times berating himself for not receiving
Trojan Aeneas freely and taking him as his son.]²

  Meanwhile, Turnus is fighting at the edge of the field,
chasing the stragglers, but with a slackening of speed,   61
less and less exultant in his triumphant horses;
the wind brought confused cries and unknown terror
to his pricked-up ears; there came the terrible sounds
and the unhappy murmurs of the stricken city.
"Ah me! he cried, "what is this sorrow shaking the walls?   62
What is this great clamor from the distant city?"
Thus he speaks, and in his frenzy he pulls at the reins.
His sister, who had taken the form of the charioteer
Metiscus, and was driving the horses, reins and car,
spoke these words to him: "This way, Turnus, let us follow   62
the Trojans, where Victory opens up a path for us—
there are plenty of others who can defend their dwellings;
Aeneas drives against the Italians with battle's havoc;
let us too deal out cruel death to the Teucrians.
Neither in count of dead nor glory in war shall you   63
take second place." Turnus said:
"Sister, I recognized you long ago, when you first
broke the truce with your wiles and mingled in the fray.
Now you vainly try to hide your divinity.
But who sent you down from Olympus to suffer such toils?   63
Was it to let you see your brother's cruel death?
What can I do? What chance of safety have I now?
With my own eyes I saw Murranus meet his doom

---

²These two lines, the same as XI, 471-2, are omitted by some MSS.

—no man dearer to me is living—he called my name
as he died; a mighty man felled by a mighty wound.   640
The hapless Ufens has fallen, so as not to behold
our shame; the Trojans have his body and his armor.
Shall I see our homes destroyed (the one thing that is lacking)
and not refute with my right hand the taunts of Drances?
Shall I turn my back? Shall this land see Turnus flee?   645
Is death so very dreadful? Be kind to me, O Shades,
since the gods above have turned away their favor.
I go to you, an innocent soul, untainted by guilt,
and never once unworthy of my great ancestors!"

    Hardly had he spoken when lo! on a foaming steed   650
Saces rides up through the enemy's midst, an arrow-wound
on his face—he gallops up imploring Turnus by name:
"Turnus, you are our last hope: pity your people!
Aeneas thunders in arms and threatens to overthrow
Italy's towers and give them over to utter destruction.   655
Firebrands fly to the roofs: the Latins look to you.
Latinus himself is muttering, uncertain whom to choose
as son-in-law, or which alliance he should adhere to.
Furthermore, the queen who placed her trust in you
has taken her own life and fled from the light in terror.   660
Only Messapus and brave Atinas hold the lines
before the gates, while all around stand serried ranks
and an iron crop of bristling swords drawn from their sheaths—
yet you are driving your chariot over deserted meadows!"
Turnus was aghast and stupefied by the news.   665
He stood there gazing silently. In that one heart
a tide of shame wells up, and madness mingled with grief,
and love spurred on by rage, and consciousness of valor.
As soon as the darkness cleared and light returned to his mind,
he fiercely turned his blazing eyes back to the ramparts,   670
looking back from his chariot to the great city.
Lo! a rolling spiral of flames was billowing
to the heavens, engulfing a tower from floor to floor—
a tower he himself had built of jointed planks
and set on rollers and equipped with lofty gangways.   675

"Now, my sister, Fate prevails! No more delay:
Where God and savage Fortune call, there let us follow!
I am resolved to fight Aeneas, and bear whatever
bitterness death holds. No more shall you see me, sister,
dishonored: allow me this last madness before I die!"   680
     He spoke, and swiftly leaped from his chariot to the field,
and rushing through enemy spears, he leaves his sorrowful sister
and bursts in a rapid course straight through the battle's center.
And just as when a rock comes tumbling down from the
                                                  mountain,
torn away by the blast or by the floods of rain,   685
or loosened from its hold by the theft of passing time,
the reckless mass goes bounding headlong at great speed,
rolling forests, herds and men in its hurtling path,
as it descends:—so Turnus, amid the scattered ranks,
goes rushing to the walls, where the ground is soaked the deepest   690
with bloodshed and the air is strident with whistling spears.
He signals with his hand and calls with a mighty voice:
"Cease fighting, Rutulians! Italians, hold your weapons!
Whatever fortune is left is mine, and I alone
must atone for the truce and resolve the issue with the sword!"   695
And all those in the center moved and made a space.
     But Father Aeneas, when he hears the name of Turnus,
leaves the walls and leaves the lofty battlements,
quickly ending all delay, breaking off his toil.
Joyful and exultant, he thunders in his arms;   700
vast as Athos or Eryx or Father Apennine
himself, roaring with quivering oaks and lifting up
his head, hoary with snow, joyously to the heavens.
All turned their eyes on him, Rutulians and Trojans,
and Italians, those who held the lofty walls,   705
those who beat them from below with battering-rams
—all put their armor down. Latinus himself is amazed
to see these mighty warriors, born in distant lands,
come together to settle the issue with the sword.
And they, as soon as the space was clear on the open plain,   710
dash forward swiftly, hurling javelins from afar,

and charge each other with their shields and ringing bronze.
The earth groans out; they redouble blows with the sword:
chance and courage are mingled together into one.
And as in mighty Sila or on Taburnus' heights   715
when two bulls charge, forehead to forehead, in deadly battle,
the pallid, trembling keepers, terrified, retreat,
the whole herd is mute with fear, the heifers mutter,
pondering who will be lord of the woods, whom they will follow,
while they deal mutual wounds with mighty force and strength,   720
butting with their horns, and bathing necks and shoulders
with flowing blood; the forest resounds with their loud bellows:—
so the Trojan Aeneas and the Daunian hero
clash with their shields; a mighty clamor fills the sky.

Jupiter himself holds up two scales in balance   725
and puts in them the destinies of each, to see
which of them is doomed: whose weight will sink in death.
Turnus springs forth, thinking it safe, with all his height
and rises with uplifted sword and deals a blow.
The Trojans and the trembling Latins cry aloud—   730
both sides are on their feet with excitement. The treacherous
                                                           sword
breaks off in midstroke and it fails its fiery master,
who has no help but flight. Swifter than the East Wind
he flies when he sees an unknown hilt in his unarmed hand.
Rumor says that in his haste to mount his steeds   735
yoked for battle, he left his father's sword behind
and instead he took the blade of the charioteer Metiscus.
It served for a time, when the straggling Trojans were in flight,
but when it met the divine armor forged by Vulcan,
the mortal blade, like brittle ice, flew into pieces,   740
leaving shining splinters on the yellow sand.
So Turnus madly flees here and there on the plain,
now this way and now that he goes in uncertain circles,
for on all sides the Trojans enclosed him in a ring,
here is a swamp, there the ramparts cut him off.   745
Aeneas pursues him none the less, although the wound

from the arrow has made his knees slower than their wont.
He follows the panting foe hotly, foot to foot,
as when a hunting hound has caught a stag penned in
by a stream, or hedged about by fear of the crimson plumes,   750
running and barking around him, the dog pursues him closely;
the stag, afraid of traps and the high river-bank,
flees in a thousand ways, but the lively Umbrian hound
follows with gaping jaws, now biting and now snapping
as though he had bitten, but baffled by his empty jaws.   755
Then indeed the clamor arises, and banks and pools
make answer: the whole sky thunders with the tumult.
Turnus, even as he flees, reproaches his men,
calling them by name, demanding the sword he knew.
Aeneas in his turn threatens instant death and destruction   760
if any approach, and frightens the trembling enemy,
with threats to destroy the town; though wounded, he presses on.
Five times they run around at full speed, and just as often
retrace their steps this way and that; no trifling prize
is now at stake: they strive for the life and blood of Turnus.   765

Here by chance there had stood a bitter-leaved wild olive
sacred to Faunus, formerly worshipped by mariners,
where they were accustomed to fasten gifts to the god of
                                                    Laurentum
when they had been saved from the sea, and hang up votive
                                                    garments.
But the Trojans, with no respect, had cut away   770
the sacred trunk to clear a space where they could fight.
Here the spear of Aeneas stuck, where its impetus
had carried it, holding fast in the tough and stubborn root.
Aeneas bent and tried to wrench away the shaft,
to hurl it at the man he could not overtake on foot.   775

Then indeed Turnus, out of his mind with fear,
cried: "Faunus, have pity, I pray; and you, most gracious Earth:
hold fast the steel, if ever I have kept your worship
which the men of Aeneas have profaned with war."
He spoke, and his prayer to the god was not in vain.   780

For though he struggled long and hard at the stubborn root,
Aeneas was not able with all his strength to loosen
the tough wood's bite; and while he fiercely pulls and strains,
the Daunian goddess,[3] changing again into the shape of Metiscus
the charioteer, runs forward and gives a sword to her brother.   785
But Venus, resentful that the daring nymph was permitted
such freedom, approached and pulled the spear out of the root.
They stood there now, towering, renewed in arms and courage
—one trusting his sword, the other fierce and tall
with his spear. Panting, they face each other, ready for battle.   790

Meanwhile, the King of almighty Olympus speaks to Juno
who is watching the battle from a golden cloud:
"What now will be the end, my wife? What remains for you?
You know, and admit you know, that Aeneas is claimed by Heaven
as a national hero, and Fate exalts him to the stars.   795
With what plans or hope do you stay in these chilly clouds?
Was it right for a god to be profaned by a wound from a mortal?
Or for the sword (for what could Juturna do without you?)
to be given back to Turnus, to swell the strength of the conquered?
Cease now, I beg you: yield at last to my entreaties: 800
let not such grief gnaw you in silence, nor such distress
so often come to trouble me from your sweet lips.
This is the end. You have been able to hound the Trojans
over land and sea, and kindle unspeakable war,
to ruin a home and plunge a wedding into grief.   805
Further attempts I forbid." Thus Jupiter began,
and thus with downcast eyes Saturnian Juno answered:
"Indeed, great Jove, because I knew that this was your will,
reluctantly I left Turnus and the earth; otherwise
you would never see me sitting here alone in the clouds   810
enduring the unendurable, but girt with flames
I'd stand in the front lines, dragging the Trojans to dreadful war.
I admit I persuaded Juturna to help her wretched brother;
to save his life I sanctioned greater deeds of daring,

---

[3]i.e. Juturna.

but not that she should draw a bow or shoot an arrow—   81,
I swear by the inexorable source of Styx,
the one oath held in awe by all the gods of Heaven.
Now for my part I yield, and leave the battle with loathing.
This boon I beg—one which no law of Fate forbids,
for Latium's sake and for the majesty of your kin: 82◉
when they now make peace and a happy marriage (so be it!)
and when they now are joined together in laws and treaties,
do not make the native Latins change their ancient name,
nor become Trojans, nor be known as Teucrians,
nor speak a different language, nor change their way of dress.   82⑤
Let Latium be—let Alban kings exist through the ages,
let the Roman stock be strong, but with Italian valor.
Troy has perished: let her name perish with her!"
   Smiling at her, the Creator of men and the universe said:
"You are truly the sister of Jove, second child of Saturn: 83◉
such great waves of anger surge deep in your breast!
But come now, calm your anger that was begun in vain.
I grant your wish, and freely give you what you ask:
Italy's sons will keep their fathers' speech and customs:
their name shall be unchanged, the Trojans shall disappear,   835
and mingle with the Latin race. Sacred laws and rites
I shall add, and make them all Latins with one language.
From them will come a race of mixed Italian blood
which you shall see surpassing men and gods in piety:
nor shall any nation worship you so devoutly."   840◉
Juno nodded assent and gladly changed her purpose;
meanwhile she left the cloud and departed from the sky.
This done, the Father ponders over another plan,
preparing to detach Juturna from her brother.
Men tell of twin fiends, known by the name of Furies,   845
borne by Dead of Night, along with infernal Megaera
in one and he same birth, wreathed alike with serpent coils
by their mother, and given wings with the speed of the wind.
These attend the throne of Jupiter, and the threshold
of grim Pluto, inciting fear in wretched mortals   850
whenever the King of the Gods plans death and dread diseases

or terrifies the guilty cities with threats of war.
One of these Jupiter swiftly sent from Heaven's height,
commanding her to appear to Juturna as an omen.
She flies, and swoops in a swift tornado to the earth.   855
Just as an arrow shot from a bowstring through a cloud,
poisoned by a Parthian with bitter gall
—a Parthian or Cydonian—a fatal shaft,
whistling and unperceived, speeds through the swift shadows:—
so the child of Night went speeding to the earth.   860
    When she saw the Trojan ranks and Turnus' troops,
she quickly shrank into the form of a tiny bird
which perches in the night on tombs or deserted rooftops,
singing its late and ominous song amid the shadows.
In this shape the fiend flies screeching to and fro   865
in front of Turnus' face, and beats his shield with her wings.
His limbs are paralyzed with a strange, numbing terror;
his hair stood up on end, his voice stuck in his throat.
But when unhappy Juturna recognized from afar
the Fury's whizzing wings, she tears her loosened hair,   870
and mars her face with her fingernails and beats her breast
and says: "How can your sister help you now, Turnus?
What is left for me, who have endured so much?
How can I prolong your life? How oppose such a monster?
Now I leave the field. Obscene birds, do not frighten me   875
who already am afraid! I know your beating wings
and their fatal sound: I recognize the haughty commands
of noble Jove. Is it thus he requites my maidenhood?
Why did he make me immortal? Why did he take away
the common lot of death? Now I could surely end   880
my sorrow and go with my poor brother to the Shadows.
I am immortal? What pleasure can there be in life
without you, my brother? Would that the earth would open wide
and send me, though I am a goddess, to the Shades!"
So she spoke, and covered her head with a gray mantle   885
and with many a moan she plunged into the deep river.

    Aeneas presses against the foe, brandishing

a huge, tree-like spear, and speaks from his angry heart:
"Now, what more delay? Why do you draw back, Turnus?
This is not a race, but a hand-to-hand fight with deadly weapons!　890
Change into any shape you will; muster your forces
of strength or art or guile: fly to the stars above,
or hide yourself in the depths of the earth!" Then Turnus said,
shaking his head: "Your fiery words do not dismay me,
savage! The gods dismay me, and Jupiter my foe!"　895
He says no more, but glancing around, he sees a rock—
a huge and ancient stone, which chanced to lie in the field,
set up as a boundary, to divide disputed lands.
Scarce twelve chosen men could lift it to their shoulders
—men with such bodies as the earth produces today—　900
but the hero, with trembling hands, seized and hurled the rock,
rising to his full height and quickening his speed.
But he does not recognize himself, as he walks and runs,
or raises up his hands or hurls the mighty stone.
His knees give way, his blood freezes in his veins.　905
The stone he threw went whirling through the empty space
but did not traverse the distance, and did not strike the mark.
And as in dreams, when languid Sleep presses our eyelids
at night, we seem to want desperately to run—
but all in vain: we sink down helpless in mid-course,　910
our tongue is powerless, our wonted strength of body
fails, and neither words nor voice can we bring forth:—
so with Turnus, however he might try with valor,
the dreaded goddess frustrates him: his senses whirl
with shifting images; he sees the Rutulians　915
and city; he hesitates, he trembles at the spear,
he sees no way to escape, and no means of attack;
nor his chariot, nor his sister the charioteer.

　As he wavers, Aeneas poises the fatal spear,
looks for an opening, and hurls it with all his might.　920
Never did a stone shot from a catapult
crash with such a roar, never a thunderbolt
burst with such a peal. The spear flew like a whirlwind,
bringing destruction, opening the corselet's rim,

piercing the outer circle of the sevenfold shield;   925
whizzing, it passes through the thigh. Under the blow,
Turnus sank to the ground, his leg doubled beneath him.
The Rutulian forces all jump up with a mighty groan,
the hills re-echo and all the wooded slopes resound.
Turnus humbly lifts his eyes in supplication,   930
raises his hand and says: "I deserve it: I ask no pity.
Use your good fortune. If any thought of parent's grief
can touch your heart, I beg you (you had such a father
in Anchises)—pity Daunus' old age, and return me
or my dead body, if you prefer, to my own people.   935
You have won the victory: the Italians have seen
my hands stretched forth in defeat. Lavinia is your wife.
Do not press your hatred further!" Aeneas stood fiercely
in arms, rolling his eyes, and lowered his right hand;
more and more he was moved by Turnus' pleading words,   940
when suddenly he saw high on the other's shoulder
the fatal sword-belt, shining with familiar studs—
the belt of young Pallas, whom Turnus had overcome
and slain; now he wore on his shoulder the hostile emblem.
When Aeneas saw this relic of his cruel grief,   945
and drank in the reminder, his burning rage was tremendous.
He cried: "Shall you, clad in the spoils of my dear friend,
escape me? It is Pallas, yes, Pallas who with this blow
sacrifices you, and takes vengeance on guilty blood!"
So saying, he buried the sword in his breast with blazing anger.   950
The limbs of Turnus grew relaxed in the chill of death;
his spirit fled, resentful, to the Shades below.

End of Book XII.

GLOSSARY OF NAMES

This is by no means a listing of all the names that occur in the *Aeneid*, but only of some of the more frequent and important ones. Vergil often uses different names for the same person (e.g., Ascanius and Iülus) or god (e.g., Minerva and Pallas). All these variants are included. Places of significance with their modern equivalents, Roman gods with their Greek counterparts, relevant items from mythology—these are usually given. Omitted are: insignificant or unknown warriors, unimportant or unidentified places. In general, those items are included which make the story or references more clear, and which facilitate the reader's identification of some of the names which appear most frequently in the *Aeneid*.

ACESTES– A king of Sicily. The name Acesta (also called Egesta and Segesta) is presumably derived from his name.

ACHAEMENIDES– A companion of Ulysses, deserted by him and rescued from the Cyclops by Aeneas.

ACHATES– The trusty companion and squire of Aeneas.

ACHAEANS– General term for the Greeks.

ACHERON– A river of the Underworld, or the Underworld itself.

ACHILLES– The hero of the *Iliad*.

ACRAGAS– A town in Sicily, now Agrigento.

ACTIUM– Site of the battle where Octavian defeated Antony in 31 B.C.

AEACUS– Father of Peleus and Telamon. The patronymic Aeacides is applied to any of his descendants, e.g., Achilles, Ajax, etc.

AEGAEON– A giant who fought against the gods.

AENEAS– Legendary ancestor of the Roman people. Son of Anchises and the goddess Venus. In Homer he is a captain of the Trojans, and it is prophesied that he will survive and that he and his descendants will rule the Trojans. Ascanius, or Iülus, is his son by Creusa, his first wife. At the end of the *Aeneid*, he founds the city of Lavinium, named after Lavinia, Latinus' daughter, whom he marries.

AEOLIA– Now Lipari: an island or group of islands off the coast of Sicily.

AEOLUS– God of the winds.

AETNA– (Etna) The famous volcano in Sicily.

AGAMEMNON– King of Mycenae, leader of the Greek forces at Troy.

AGATHYRSES– A Thracian tribe.

AGRIPPA– An admiral of Augustus, commander of the fleet at Actium.

AGYLLA– An Italian town, also called Caere. Now Cerveteri.

AJAX– 1. "The Greater"–son of Telamon, a hero in the Trojan War. 2. "The Lesser"–son of Oileus; he dragged Cassandra from Pallas' temple the night Troy fell, and as a result he was killed and his ships destroyed.

ALBA or ALBA LONGA– A city in Latium, built by Ascanius: the mother-city of Rome.

ALCIDES– A descendant of Alcaeus, chiefly Hercules.

ALLECTO (or ALECTO)– one of the Furies.

ALPHEUS– A river of the Peloponnesus, near Olympia. The god Alpheus was in love with the nymph Arethusa, who fled from him and was transformed into a fountain in Sicily. Alpheus flowed under the sea, emerged in Sicily, and mingled his waters with Arethusa's.

AMATA– Wife of King Latinus.

AMAZON– A legendary tribe of warrior-maids. The story that

their right breasts were cut off (a-mazos) to facilitate shooting the bow is an obvious piece of popular etymology with nothing in art or legend to justify it.

AMOR– Cupid, the god of love.

AMPHITRYON– Husband of Alcmena, the mother of Hercules.

ANCHISES– Father of Aeneas.

ANDROGEOS– 1. A Greek warrior. 2. A son of King Minos, killed by the Athenians.

ANDROMACHE– The widow of Hector.

ANNA– Sister of Dido.

ANTENOR– A Trojan who founded Patavium (now Padua).

ANTONIUS– Mark Antony the triumvir.

ANUBIS– A dog-headed Egyptian god.

APOLLO– Son of Jupiter and Latona, brother of Diana, also called Phoebus. The god of medicine, prophecy, archery, poetry, etc. Sometimes confused with Helios the Sun-God.

AQUILO– The North Wind.

ARCADIA– A region in the central Peloponnesus.

ARDEA– Capital of the Rutulians, birthplace of Turnus, now Terracina.

ARETHUSA– A nymph, also a fountain in Syracuse. See Alpheus.

ARGILETUM– A street in Rome. The name was fancifully derived from "Death of Argus" (see Argus 2).

ARGUS– 1. The monster who guarded Io. 2. A treacherous guest of Evander. 3. A region in Greece: hence the Greeks are called Argives.

ARIADNE– Daughter of King Minos, who helped Theseus escape from the Labyrinth.

ARPI– Apulian city founded by Diomedes; also called Argyripa.

ASCANIUS– Son of Aeneas and Creusa. Also called Iülus.

ASIA– Asia Minor.

ASSARACUS– Son of Tros, father of Capys and grandfather of Anchises.

ASTYANAX– Infant son of Hector, killed by the Greeks.

ASYLUM– A depression between two peaks of the Capitoline Hill in Rome, made a refuge by Romulus.

ATLAS– A king of Mauretania or giant who supported the heavens on his shoulders. Also the mountain range in northwest Africa.

ATREIDES– A son of Atreus: Agamemnon or Menelaus. The plural is Atreidae.

AUGUSTUS– The imperial title of Octavian, whose minister Maecenas was the patron of Vergil.

AULIS– A town of Boeotia where the Greeks left for Troy, and where Iphigenia was sacrificed.

AURORA– Goddess of the Dawn, wife of Tithonus, mother of Memnon.

AURUNCANS– Early inhabitants of Italy.

AUSONIA– Italy.

AUSTER– The South Wind.

AVERNUS– A lake in Campania, thought to be the entrance to the Underworld. Popular etymology derives the name from "a-ornos" (birdless).

BACCHUS– Son of Jupiter and Semele, god of wine and vegetation, also called Liber, Lyaeus, and Dionysus.

BACTRA or BACTRIA– Part of the Persian Empire, now part of Afghanistan.

BAIAE– A Roman seaside resort near Naples, now Baia.

BEBRYCIA– A region of Asia Minor.

BELLONA– Roman goddess of War, sister of Mars.

BELUS– 1. The father of Dido. 2. An ancestor of Dido.

BERECYNTUS– A mountain in Asia Minor sacred to Cybele, who is called "Berecyntia" or the "Berecyntian Mother."

BOREAS– The North Wind.

BRIAREUS– A giant, also called Aegaeon.

BYRSA– The citadel of Carthage.

CACUS– A monster, son of Vulcan, slain by Hercules.

CAENEUS– 1. A girl changed into a man by Neptune, later restored to her former sex. 2. Also an Italian warrior.

CAERE– A city in Etruria, the modern Cerveteri.

CAIETA– The Nurse of Aeneas, also a town in Latium named after her, now Gaeta.

CALCHAS– The soothsayer of the Greeks at Troy.

CALLIOPE– One of the Muses.

CALYDON– A city of northwestern Greece, scene of the famous boar hunt.

CAMILLA– A Volscian warrior-maiden.

CARTHAGE– The city of Dido in northern Africa. The bitter enemy of Rome, destroyed in 146 B.C.

CASSANDRA– Daughter of Priam and Hecuba. She received the gift of prophecy from Apollo, who loved her, but when she spurned his love, he brought it about that no one would believe her prophecies. She foretold the fall of Troy. Afterwards, Agamemnon took her to Mycenae, where Clytemnestra killed them both.

CATILINE– A conspirator whose plot to overthrow Rome was foiled by Cicero in 63 B.C.

CATO– 1. "The Censor"—a stern moralist and implacable foe of Carthage. 2. "Cato of Utica"—a descendant of the former.

CELAENO– One of the Harpies.

CENTAURS– Monsters, half horse, half human, who lived in Thessaly.

CERBERUS– Watchdog of the Lower World. In Vergil he has three heads; elsewhere the number is fifty or a hundred.

CERES– Goddess of grain; by metonymy, bread, flour, etc. The Greek Demeter.

CHARON– Ferryman of the River Styx. Son of Erebus and Night.

CHARYBDIS– A whirlpool in the Straits of Messina. See Scylla.

CHIMAERA– A monster, part lion, part goat, part dragon. Also the name of a ship.

CIRCE– Daughter of the sun, a sorceress who changed men into animals. In Homer, she lived on an island; Vergil locates her on the Italian coast between Naples and Rome.

CLOANTHUS– One of the Trojan leaders.

CLOELIA– A Roman heroine who escaped from the Etruscan Porsenna and swam across the Tiber.

COCLES– The famous Horatius who held the bridge.

COCYTUS– A river of the Lower World.

CORYBANTES– Priests of Cybele (q.v.).

CORYTHUS– A city in Italy, whence Dardanus migrated to Troy.

CREUSA– Daughter of Priam, wife of Aeneas. Her name, which occurs elsewhere in mythology, means "female ruler."

CUMAE– An ancient town near Naples, home of the Cumaean Sibyl.

CUPID– Son of Venus, the god of Love. Identified with Eros.

CURES– A Sabine town, home of Numa, an early king of Rome.

CURETES– Cretan priests of Jupiter.

CYBELE– A Phrygian goddess, the Roman Magna Mater. Also known as Dindymene, the Idaean Mother, the Berecyntian Mother; identified with Rhea, the Greek Mother-goddess.

CYCLADES– A group of islands "encircling" Delos in the Aegean Sea.

CYCLOPS– One of the Cyclopes, a race of one-eyed giants who worked in Vulcan's forges in Sicily.

CYLLENE– A mountain in Arcadia, birthplace of Mercury, who is called "Cyllenian."

CYNTHUS– A mountain or hill in Delos, birthplace of Apollo. He and Diana are known as "Cynthus" and "Cynthia" respectively.

CYPRIAN– Epithet of Venus, who had shrines in Cyprus.

CYTHERA– An island south of Greece, sacred to Venus, who is called "Cytherea."

DAEDALUS– A legendary artist and craftsman, builder of the Labyrinth, inventor of wings, etc.

DAHAE– A Scythian tribe, east of the Caspian Sea.

DANAANS– Greeks: from Danaus, and Egyptian king who settled in Argos.

DANAË– Daughter of Acrisius, mother of Perseus.

DARDANIA– Troy (Dardans, Dardanians = Trojans), from Dardanus, son of Zeus and Electra, and founder of Troy. Aeneas is called Dardanides.

DAUNUS– Father of Turnus.

DEIPHOBUS– Son of Priam, married to Helen after the death of Paris.

DELOS– Island in the Aegean Sea, birthplace of Apollo and Diana.

DIANA– Sister of Apollo, goddess of the moon and the hunt, identified with Artemis. She is also known as Phoebe, Hecate, Luna, Cynthia, Trivia, etc.

DICTE– A mountain in Crete, where Jupiter was raised.

DIDO– Founder and queen of Carthage, also called Elissa.

DINDYMA– A mountain in Asia Minor, sacred to Cybele.

DIOMEDES– A greek hero in the Trojan War, founder of Arpi or Argyripa.

DIRA, DIRAE– Fury, Furies.

DIS– Pluto or Hades, the god of the Lower World.

DODONA– An oracle of Jupiter in Epirus (northwestern Greece).

DOLON– A Trojan spy in the *Iliad* who undertook to explore the Greek camp, but was captured and slain.

DOLOPES– A people of Thessaly, who took part in the Trojan War.

DRANCES– A Latin, enemy of Turnus.

DREPANUM– A town on the west coast of Sicily, now Trapani.

EGERIA– An Italian nymph, wife of Numa.

ELISSA– Another name for Dido.

ELYSIUM– The dwelling of the Blessed in the Lower World.

ENCELADUS– A giant killed by Jupiter for trying to overthrow the gods. He was imprisoned beneath Mount Etna.

ERATO– Muse of love poetry and the lyre.

EREBUS– Darkness, sometimes personified; the Underworld.

ERIDANUS– The River Po.

ERINYES– The Furies.

ERIPHYLE– Wife of Amphiaraus, killed by her son Alcmaeon.

ERYX– King of Sicily, son of Venus. A famous boxer, killed by Hercules. Also the name of a mountain in Sicily (now Erice), a shrine of Venus.

ETRURIA– The land of the Etruscans, an ancient people, thought to have come from Lydia in Asia Minor. Now Tuscany.

EUANDER or EVANDER– King of Pallanteum, ally of Aeneas.

EUMENIDES– "The Kindly Goddesses"—a euphemistic name for the Furies.

EUROTAS– The river of Sparta.

EURUS– The Southeast Wind.

EURYALUS– A Trojan youth, friend of Nisus.

EURYSTHEUS– A king of Tiryns, who imposed the "Twelve Labors" on Hercules.

FABII– An important Roman family. Fabius Maximus saved the Roman army from Hannibal.

FABRICIUS– A Roman general who conquered Pyrrhus.

FAUNUS– Son of Picus, father of Latinus. Identified with the god Pan.

FURIES– Goddesses of vengeance: Allecto, Tisiphone, and Megaera.

GAETULI– A people of northern Africa, probably in what is now Morocco.

GANYMEDE– Son of Laomedon or Tros, carried to Heaven by Jupiter's eagle, to become the cupbearer of that god.

GARAMANTES– A people of Lybia.

GAULS– A Celtic people who invaded Rome in 390 B.C.

GERYON– A triple-bodied monster whose oxen Hercules took after slaying him.

GETAE– A Thracian tribe on the Danube.

GLAUCUS– 1. A sea-deity. 2. A Trojan warrior. 3. Another Trojan warrior, in Hades.

GORGO, GORGON– Daughter of Phorcus, especially Medusa, who had the power of turning to stone anyone who looked at her head.

GRADIVUS– An epithet of Mars.

HADES– Pluto, king of the Underworld. Also the Lower World itself.

HAEDI– See Kid-Stars.

HALAESUS– A son or follower of Agamemnon.

HAMMON or AMMON– An African god identified with Jupiter.

HARPIES– Monsters with the heads of women and the bodies of birds. The name comes from Greek "harpazein"–to snatch.

HEBRUS– A river in Thrace, the modern Maritza.

HECATE– A goddess of the Underworld, sorcery, witchcraft, etc. Identified with Diana and Luna, the Moon.

HECTOR– Son of Priam and Hecuba, the chief hero of Troy, slain by Achilles.

HECUBA– Wife of Priam.

HELEN– Wife of Menelaus, whose abduction by Paris was the cause of the Trojan War.

HELENUS– Son of Priam; a soothsayer or prophet. Married to Andromache.

HELICON– A mountain in Greece, home of Apollo and the Muses.

HERCULES– Son of Jupiter and Alcmena (but also called the son of Amphitryon); a hero of great strength, who was compelled to undergo a series of "impossible" tasks.

HERMIONE– Daughter of Menelaus and Helen, married to Orestes.

HESPERIA– Italy (the "Western" or "Evening" land).

HESPERIDES– Daughters of Hesperus, the Evening Star, guardians of the fabled Golden Apples.

HIPPOLYTA or HIPPOLYTE– An Amazon queen, married to Theseus.

HIPPOLYTUS– Son of the above. Beloved by his stepmother Phaedra, he spurned her love; she committed suicide, falsely accusing him. He was cursed by his father Theseus and slain by a bull sent by Neptune. Brought back to life by Aesculapius, he was hidden by Diana in the Grove of Aricia, under the name Virbius (from vir + bis: Twice-man).

HORATIUS– The hero who defended the bridge. Also known as Cocles (One-Eye).

HYDRA– A fifty-headed monster killed by Hercules.

Hyrcani– A people who lived near the Caspian Sea.

Iapyx– 1. Iapygian or Apulian. 2. A wind. 3. A physician.

Iarbas– An African king, suitor of Dido.

Icarus– Son of Daedalus. When flying through the air with his father, he flew too high, the wax on his wings melted, he fell into the (Icarian) sea, and was drowned.

Ida– 1. A mountain of Crete. 2. A mountain of Asia Minor. 3. The mother of Nisus.

Idalium or Idalion– A city of Cyprus, shrine of Venus.

Idomeneus– A Cretan hero with the Greeks at Troy.

Ilia– Also called Rhea Silvia, the mother of Romulus and Remus.

Ilium– Troy.

Ilus– 1. A king of Troy. 2. A Rutulian. 3. Earlier name of Iülus.

Ilva– An island off the Etrurian coast; now Elba.

Inachus– King of Argos, father of Io.

Inarime– An island in the Tyrrhenian Sea, now Ischia.

Io– Daughter of Inachus, loved by Jupiter, changed into a heifer. Argus, a hundred-eyed monster, was sent to watch her. Mercury slew Argus. After being driven all over the world by a gadfly, Io settled in Egypt.

Iris– Personification of the rainbow, messenger of the gods.

Ithaca– An island off the west coast of Greece; home of Ulysses.

Iülus– Another name for Ascanius, suggesting kinship with Julius Caesar and his adoptive son Augustus; thus, by implication, the latter's descent from Aeneas and ultimately from Jupiter.

Ixion– A Lapith who attempted to violate Juno and was bound to a wheel in punishment.

Janus– Two-faced Roman god. The doors of his temple were opened in time of war.

Jove– Jupiter.

JUNO– Queen of the gods, sister and wife of Jupiter. Daughter of Saturn, hence her epithet Saturnia. Her implacable hostility to the Trojans is explained by the Judgment of Paris, the substitution of Ganymede for Hebe, and other causes. She is identified with the Greek Hera.

JUPITER– King of the gods, son of Saturn; identified with Zeus.

JUTURNA– Sister of Turnus, a nymph of streams and lakes, ravished by Jupiter and given immortality in compensation.

KID– STARS (Haedi) Part of the constellation Auriga, associated with the rainy season.

LABYRINTH– A building or maze in Cnossus in Crete, where the Minotaur was kept.

LACEDAEMON– Sparta.

LAERTES– Father of Ulysses.

LAOCOÖN– Priest of Neptune at Troy.

LAOMEDON– Father of Priam, king of Troy.

LAPITHS– A people of Thessaly, famous for their battle with the Centaurs.

LAR– A Roman household god.

LATINUS– King of Latium; his people are called Latins.

LATIUM– The plain between the Tiber and Campania.

LATONA– The mother of Diana and Apollo.

LAURENTES, LAURENTIANS, LAURENTINES– The people of Laurentum, the city of King Latinus.

LAUSUS– Son of Mezentius, slain by Aeneas.

LAVINIA– Daughter of Latinus, later the wife of Aeneas.

LAVINIUM– Town in Italy founded by Aeneas.

LEDA– Mother of Helen, Clytemnestra, Castor and Pollux. Visited by Jupiter in the shape of a swan. Wife of Tyndareus, hence Helen is called Tyndarid.

LETHE– The river of Forgetfulness in the Lower World.

LIBER– Another name for Bacchus.

LIBYA– A country of North Africa.

LIGURIA– A region of Italy, around the modern Genoa, famous for its liars.

LIPARE– One of the Aeolian Islands, now Lipari.

LUPERCAL– A cave in Rome, sacred to Lupercus of Lycaean Pan. The priests who presided over the festival of the Lupercalia were called Luperci.

LYAEUS– Another name for Bacchus.

LYCIA– A country in southwestern Asia Minor.

LYDIA– A country in Asia Minor, whence the Etruscans were thought to have come; hence the name Lydians, used of the Etruscans.

MAEONIAN– Lydian, or Etruscan.

MAIA– Daughter of Atlas, mother of Mercury.

MANES– Spirits of the dead; also the Lower World.

MANTO– A prophetess.

MANTUA– A city of northern Italy, near Vergil's birthplace.

MARCELLUS– 1. A Roman general who defeated the Gauls in 222 B.C. 2. The nephew and designated successor of Augustus, who died in 23 B.C. at the age of 20.

MARS or MAVORS– Roman god of war, identified with Ares. Also, war in general.

MARSI– A people of Italy.

MASSYLIAN– of the Massyli, an African tribe.

MAXIMUS– Q. Fabius Maximus, a general in the war against Hannibal (Second Punic War), called "Cunctator" (The Delayer) because of his guerrilla tactics.

MEMNON– Son of Tithonus and Aurora. King of the Ethiopians, slain by Achilles.

MENELAUS– Son of Atreus, king of Sparta, brother of Agamemnon.

MERCURY– Messenger of the gods and guide of the dead. Identified with Hermes.

MESSAPUS– One of the Italian leaders. Eponymous hero of Messapia or Iapygia.

MEZENTIUS– An Etruscan king, exiled for his tyranny.

MINERVA– Goddess of wisdom, handicrafts, etc. Identified with Pallas Athena.

MINOS– A king of Crete who became a judge of the Lower World after his death. He caused Daedalus to build the Labyrinth for the Minotaur. The Athenians were compelled to pay him an annual tribute of seven youths and seven maidens, to be eaten by the Minotaur. Theseus of Athens killed the monster with the help of Ariadne, Minos' daughter, whom he later abandoned on the island of Naxos.

MINOTAUR– A monster: offspring of Pasiphaë, wife of Minos; part man, part bull.

MISENUS– The trumpeter who gave his name to Cape Misenum (now Miseno).

MNESTHEUS– One of the Trojan leaders.

MUSES– Goddesses of poetry and poetic inspiration, song, etc.

MYCENAE– Agamemnon's city; hence, Greece in general.

MYRMIDONS– A Thessalian tribe that fought at Troy under Achilles.

NEMEA– A town in the Peloponnesus, where Hercules killed the famous lion.

NEOPTOLEMUS– The son of Achilles, also called Pyrrhus.

NEPTUNE– God of the sea, identified with Poseidon.

NEREUS– A lesser sea-god, father of the Nereids.

NISUS– A Trojan youth, friend of Euryalus.

NOTUS– The South Wind.

NUMA– The second king of Rome. Also, the name of two different Italian warriors.

NUMICIUS or NUMICUS– A sacred stream in Latium.

NYMPHS– Minor deities of the sea, rivers, trees, mountains, etc., respectively called Nereids, Naiads, Dryads or Hamadryads, and Oreads.

OCEAN– The stream running around the edge of the earth.

OENOTRIA– Southern Italy, or Italy in general.

OLYMPUS– The highest mountain of Greece, home of the gods (perhaps because its summit is almost constantly shrouded in mist and clouds).

ORCUS– Death; the god of the Underworld; Pluto; the Lower World itself.

ORESTES– Son of Agamemnon. Pursued by Furies for killing his mother Clytemnestra.

ORION– A hunter beloved by Diana, later a constellation.

ORPHEUS– A fabulous bard, whose music charmed the spirits of the Lower World and won back his wife Eurydice from the dead. In another tradition, he was torn to pieces by Thracian women.

ORTYGIA– 1. Delos. 2. An island in the harbor of Syracuse.

PACHYNUS– A cape in southern Sicily.

PADUSA– One of the mouths of the Po.

PALAMEDES– A Greek hero, killed on a false charge of treason.

PALATINE– One of the Seven Hills of Rome.

PALINURUS– The pilot of Aeneas.

PALLADIUM– A statue of Athena (Pallas), stolen from Troy by Ulysses and Diomedes.

PALLANTEUM– The city of Evander; on the site that later became Rome.

PALLAS– 1. Athena or Minerva. 2. Ancestor of Evander. 3. Son of Evander.

PAN– God of woods and shepherds. Faunus is identified with him.

PANDARUS– The name of two Trojans. One violated the truce in the *Iliad*; the other was slain by Turnus.

PAPHUS or PAPHOS– A town of Cyprus, sacred to Venus.

PARIS– Son of Priam and Hecuba. He judged Venus the most beautiful of the goddesses ("Judgment of Paris"), and thereby won Helen, caused the Trojan War, and incurred the undying animosity of Juno for himself and all the Trojans.

PAROS– An island of the Cyclades, famous for its pure white marble.

PARTHENOPE– The ancient name for Naples.

PARTHIANS– A warlike people near the Caspian Sea.

PASIPHAË– Wife of King Minos, mother of the Minotaur.

PENTHESILEA– Queen of the Amazons at Troy.

PELIDES– Son of Peleus, i.e. Achilles, or one of his descendants.

PENATES– The household or state gods of the Romans.

PENTHEUS– King of Thebes who scoffed at Bacchus, and was torn to pieces by his mother Agave and her Bacchantes.

PERGAMUM– The citadel of Troy, therefore Troy itself. Also the name of the ciy Aeneas tried to found in Crete.

PERSEPHONE– See Proserpina.

PHAEDRA– Stepmother of Hippolytus (q.v.).

PHAETHON– Son of Helios, the Sun-God, who drove his father's chariot, but when he lost control, was slain by a thunderbolt from Jupiter.

PHLEGETHON– A fiery river of the Underworld.

PHOEBE, PHOEBUS– Epithets of Diana and Apollo (the name means "Shining").

PHORCUS– A sea-god.

PHRYGIA– A region in Asia Minor. "Phrygians" means Trojans, often in an uncomplimentary sense.

PILUMNUS– An ancestor of Turnus.

PIRITHOUS– Son of Ixion, king of the Lapiths. Companion of Theseus, with whom he tried to abduct Proserpina.

PISA– 1. A city in the Peloponnesus. 2. A city in Etruria.

PLUTO– Brother of Jupiter, king of the Lower World.

POLYPHEMUS– A Cyclops blinded by Ulysses.

PORSENNA– An Etruscan king who tried to restore Tarquinius in 510 B.C.

PRAENESTE– A city of Latium, now Palestrina.

PRIAM– Son of Laomedon; the last king of Troy.

PROCHYTA– An island off the Campanian coast, now Procida.

PROSERPINA– (Greek Persephone) Daughter of Ceres and wife of Pluto, who abducted her. She was obliged to spend half the year on earth, the other half below the earth. This myth explained the change of the seasons.

PROTEUS– A sea-god. The Pillars of Proteus are near Egypt.

PYGMALION– Dido's brother, who killed her husband Sychaeus.

PYRRHUS– The son of Achilles, also called Neoptolemus.

QUIRINUS– The name of the deified Romulus.

QUIRITES– Roman citizens.

REMUS– Brother of Romulus.

RHEA– 1. Greek goddess identified with Cybele. 2. Rhea Silvia or Ilia, mother of Romulus and Remus.

RHESUS– A Thracian king whose horses were captured by Diomedes and Ulysses.

ROMULUS– The mythical eponymous founder of Rome, together

with his brother Remus, whom he later killed. Worshipped under the name of Quirinus.

RUTULIANS– A tribe of Latium, the men of Turnus.

SABELLIAN– A generic term including Italian tribes such as the Volscians, Samnites, Frentani, etc.

SABINE– An Italian tribe of central Italy. The well-known story of the Rape of the Sabine Women is probably an etiological explanation of the old wedding-cry "Talassio!"

SALII– The twelve dancing priests of Mars, who had the task of guarding the sacred shields that fell from Heaven.

SARPEDON– A son of Jupiter and king of Lycia, killed by Patroclus at Troy.

SATURN– A deified king of Latium, identified with Kronos, father of Zeus and Hera. The latter is called "Saturnia."

SCYLLA– A monster who lived on one side of the Straits of Messina, opposite Charybdis. Also the name of one of Aeneas' ships.

SCYTHIA– The land north of the Black Sea.

SERRANUS– 1. A Roman summoned from the plow to take over the government. 2. An Italian warrior.

SIBYL– A prophetess, especially the Cumaean Sibyl.

SICANIAN– A race of Sicilians; also, Sicilians in general.

SIDON– A city of Phoenicia. "Sidonian" refers to Dido.

SIGEUM– A promontory near Troy.

SILA– A forest in Bruttium, in the "toe" of Italy.

SIMOIS– A river near Troy.

SINON– The Greek spy who induced the Trojans to take the Wooden Horse into their city.

SIRENS– Fabulous monsters whose songs lured sailors to their death on the Campanian coast.

SORACTE– A mountain near Rome.

STROPHADES– Two islands near Messenia in the Peloponnesus.

STRYMON– A river in Macedonia, now Struma, famous for its cranes.

STYGIAN– referring to the Styx.

STYX– A river of the Lower World. The one oath held sacred by the gods was an oath sworn by the River Styx.

SYCHAEUS– The husband of Dido, treacherously slain by her brother Pygmalion.

SYRTES– Two shallow bays or gulfs on the northern coast of Africa, very dangerous to sailors.

TANAIS– A river of Thrace (now the Don); also a Rutulian.

TARCHON– An Etruscan king—the name suggests Tarquin.

TARPEIAN– The rock of the Capitol in Rome.

TARQUINIUS– The name of two Etruscan kings of Rome; the second was expelled in 510 B.C.

TARTARUS– The dwelling place of the wicked in Hades; the ancient Hell.

TATIUS– A Sabine king who first fought against the Romans, then ruled jointly with Romulus, after making peace.

TEUCER– 1. The first king of Troy. 2. A greek archer, half-brother of Ajax 1.

TEUCRIANS– The Trojans, from Teucer 1.

THALIA– 1. The Muse of Comedy. 2. A sea-nymph.

THAUMAS– The father of Iris.

THEBES– The capital of Boeotia in central Greece.

THERSILOCHUS– The name of two different Trojans.

THESEUS– King of Athens, son of Aegeus, slayer of the Minotaur. Attempted to carry off Proserpina, for which his punishment was to sit forever on a rock.

THETIS– Sea-nymph, mother of Achilles.

THYBRIS– An Etruscan king. Also the river Tiber.

TIBER– The river that flows through Rome; also the god of that river.

TIRYNS– A city in Peloponnesus, where Hercules was raised, hence his epithet "Tirynthian."

TISIPHONE– One of the Furies.

TITHONUS– Son of Laomedon, husband of Aurora. He was granted the gift of eternal life, but not of eternal youth.

TITYUS– Son of Jupiter, a giant killed by Apollo and Diana for trying to do violence to their mother Latona.

TOLUMNIUS– A Rutulian augur.

TORQUATUS– T. Manlius Torquatus, who wore the collar of the Gaul he had slain in single combat. He put his own son to death for disobeying orders.

TRINACRIA– Sicily, so-called from its triangular shape.

TRITON– A sea-god, son of Neptune.

TRITONIAN– An epithet of Pallas or Minerva, probably because of her birth near Lake Triton in Africa.

TRIVIA– An epithet of Diana or Hecate, whose statues were placed at the crossroads.

TROY– The city of Ilium, destroyed by the Greeks; also a city in Epirus; also a game played by the Roman boys.

TURNUS– Son of Daunus, the king of the Rutulians. The name is possibly a contraction of "Tyrrhenus" or Etruscan.

TYDEUS– Father of Diomedes.

TYNDAREUS– Husband of Leda, mother of Helen.

TYPHOEUS– Son of Earth and Tartarus. He had a hundred heads and breathed fire; was slain by lightning and buried under Etna or Ischia.

TYRE– Chief city of Phoenicia, famous for the "Tyrian purple," a rich dye made from local shellfish. The Carthaginians are called "Tyrians."

TYRRHENIAN, TYRRHENE= Etruscan.

TYRRHUS– A herdsman of King Latinus.

UFENS– 1. A river of Latium. 2. A Rutulian warrior.

ULYSSES– Odysseus, hero of the Odyssey.

UMBRIA– A district of north central Italy, famous for its hunting dogs.

VENUS– Goddess of love and beauty; mother of Aeneas; identified with Aphrodite.

VESTA– Goddess of the hearth, whose fire was always kept burning.

VIRBIUS– See Hippolytus. Apparently, also the name of the son of Hippolytus.

VOLSCIANS– An Italian tribe.

VULCAN– The god of fire—by metonymy, fire itself. The Greek Hephaestus.

XANTHUS– A river of the Troad, also a river in Epirus, also one in Lydia.

ZEPHYRUS– God of the West wind; also the wind itself.